T0293981

SPURS' CULT HEROES

MICHAEL LACQUIERE

Series Editor: Simon Lowe

www.knowthescorebooks.com

First published in the United Kingdom by Know The Score Books Limited, 2010
Copyright © Michael Lacquiere, 2010

This book is copyright under the Berne convention.

No part of this book may be reproduced, sold or utilised in any form or transmitted in any form or by any means, electronic or mechanical, including photocopying, recording or by any information storage and retrieval system, without prior permission in writing from the Publisher.

© and ® Know The Score Books Limited. All rights reserved

The right of Michael Lacquiere to be identified as the author of this work has been asserted by him in accordance with sections 77 and 78 of the Copyright, Designs and Patents Act, 1988.

Know The Score Books Limited
118 Alcester Road
Studley
Warwickshire
B80 7NT
Tel: 01527 454482   Fax: 01527 452183

www.knowthescorebooks.com

A CIP catalogue record is available for this book from the British Library
ISBN 978-1-84818-108-3

Jacket and book design by Graham Hales

Printed and bound in Great Britain by Cromwell Press Group, Wiltshire.

Contents

Author's Acknowledgements

The irony is not lost on me that the first people to whom I offer my thanks on having written Spurs' Cult Heroes are Arsenal fans, but without the help of Michael Hawthorne and Carly Madden, as well as Greg Brennan (die-hard Celtic) this tome would probably still be a twinkle in the eye.

Having spent years asking me when I would grow out of football, Mum and Dad have gone out of their way to assist wherever possible, while the support of siblings and spouses – Rich, Lind and Peter, Dave and Char – has also been hugely appreciated. One hopes that nephews Isaac and Ethan, and niece Eleanor, will in time be suitably taken by their uncle's efforts and themselves become Spurs fans...

Others to whom I have reason to doff my cap include regular fellow attendees of Spurs games, Ian Bristo, Paul Jobber, Pat Jobber, Lisa Kennedy and Mark Hanson; as well as Phil Brooks, Alan Hawkins, David Hawthorne, Marc Cohen, Gus Selassie, Nigel Lloyd, Adam Breen, Matt Hall, Emi Murata, Sarah Lowth, Rod James, James Allison, Rob McTiernan, Dragana Ignjatovic, Gaelle Marinoni and Lubica Cechova; while established writers Martin Cloake, Paolo Hewitt, Lee Weeks, Chas Newkey-Burden and Norman Giller have generously lent their time and imparted their wisdom to a novice. I am also grateful to the staff of the National Newspaper Archive Library in Colindale for their assistance, and everyone from Johnny Cash to Dizzee Rascal for helping keep me sane while I typed.

Much of the momentum for Spurs' Cult Heroes has been generated via the internet, and to all who have supported my Spurs blog – www.allactionnoplot.com – I raise a glass. It may not meet many search engine requirements, but having watched for years as the sublime and ridiculous have merrily gamboled hand-in-hand across the turf of White Hart Lane, "All action, no plot" regularly seemed the most appropriate conclusion to draw, with a weary shake of the head, on trudging down the High Road after the final whistle.

Memories of the players featured in Spurs' Cult Heroes have been offered by Geoff Howe, Alan Granville, Julian Clarke, Richard Early, Geoff Harrow, Chris Paterson, Jill Lewis, Gary Wright, Matt Fletcher, Darren Southcott, Ian Stokes, John Craig, Dick Carpenter, Marlon Green, Alan Fisher, David Durbridge, Justin Bendon, Dan Stratford, Terry Dignan, Steve Smith, John Craig, Michael Grayeff, Doug Nash, Ian Stokes, John Peddubriwny, Alan Beer, Bill Clark – these contributions, and those of countless others, have been immensely helpful.

Fellow bloggers have also offered assistance, and as such I'm grateful to the writers of the blogs:
www.dearmrlevy.com; www.oleole.com/blogs/harryhotspur; tottenhamonmymind.wordpress.com; www.oleole.com/blogs/who-framed-ruel-fox; and ibleedhotspur.com.

Keith Burkinshaw, Gary Mabbutt, Ricky Villa and Steve Perryman were each charming and generous in responding to my requests (although I will be forever piqued at Mr Burkinshaw for taking one look at me and likening me to a certain Arsenal striker). I am particularly grateful to Nev Addison, and all at the Hop Poles pub for their assistance in organising these interviews. Critical assistance has been provided by John Fennelly, Jon Raynor and the legendary Andy Porter at Spurs, while of course I am massively grateful to Simon Lowe at Know The Score Books, for the opportunity.

Last but by no means least, countless friends, family members and colleagues have offered enthusiasm, assistance and good humour for which I am hugely appreciative. Much obliged, one and all.

Michael Lacquiere
January 2010

Introduction

WE Tottenham folk have been spoilt. Admittedly it does not always seem that way, as we look on aghast at our heroes so regularly ensuring that ignominy is snatched from the jaws of glory; or when that rarest of beasts – a settled management structure – is slaughtered, seemingly on a whim, and we have to start again from scratch. However, when dipping nib into ink in order to write *Spurs' Cult Heroes* – and even when simply compiling the list of 20 players to be featured – I realised that we have, over the years, boasted riches of which other sets of fans can only dream. With good reason does Tottenham Hotspur have a tradition for 'glory glory football', for when one considers the array of talent that has purred around the White Hart Lane turf, it would have been plain lunacy to have adopted any other approach than that of devilish, breath-taking entertainment.

So how to select from the rich band of swashbucklers, goalscorers and servants so loyal that directly beneath the cockerel on their shirt one suspects they also had that same cockerel tattooed on their chest?

It was a glorious conundrum – so, inevitably, I initially went down the Ossie Ardiles route, and tried to include the whole ruddy lot, every player who has ever had the regulars at the Lane gawping in awe-struck wonder. Just as Ossie discovered, however, it quickly became evident that this 'Tottingham' line-up just would not accommodate quite so many big names. In a moment of realisation that has no doubt struck countless Spurs managers over the years, I reluctantly concluded that for all the wonderful talent available, some semblance of order would be necessary in order to set the wheels in motion.

For a start, all those featured had to rank amongst the very best White Hart Lane has seen; no room for those players whose glaring inadequacies we gloss over just because we love them and they love us. A stringent criterion perhaps, but after over 125 years of trophies, goals, loyalty and downright mind-boggling flair, it seemed a legitimate parameter. (As a crucial addendum, such greatness must have been achieved in a Spurs shirt, rather than, say, from the halfway line whilst adorned in the colours of a Spanish outfit – even if the victims were that 'orrible lot from down the road.)

Nor was this just to be a list of the 20 best players – they also had to be the sort who, to this day, will make the most foul-mouthed South Stand die-hards suddenly go misty-eyed, and profess their undying love. Popularity counted, a criterion which ought to answer any queries from the Campbell and Berbatov households.

A difficult balancing act? Those of a certain vintage have argued that the task straightforwardly involves selecting the entire Double-winning team of 1961, and throwing in Greaves, Hoddle and Gazza. One appreciates the sentiment, but one vital requirement of the *Cult Heroes* collection was to capture the long tradition and very essence of the club. Tottenham Hotspur were formed in 1882; won the FA Cup in 1901; became the first English side to win the Double in 1961; the first British side to win a European trophy, two years later; and won the centenary FA Cup Final in 1981. In the words of the White Hart Lane faithful every matchday:

"And if you know your history, it's enough to make your heart go woo-ooo-oooah..."

An effort has therefore been made to convey this glorious, if allegedly ineffable, history of the club, those elements which make Spurs one of the proudest and most famous teams in the country. I pre-emptively hold up my hands and offer a *mea culpa* straight away, for the absences of any players from the 1921 FA Cup-winning side (Jimmy Dimmock and Arthur Grimsdell having been popularly supported). Similarly, star names from our first ever League Title-winning team of 1951 (Ted Ditchburn, captain Eddie Baily and Len 'The Duke' Duquemin sprang to many minds) are glaring omissions. Naturally, in gauging popular opinion, much of the focus fell upon those from the latter half of the 20th century, and the content of *Spurs' Cult Heroes* reflects this. However, the chapter on Sandy Brown, whose extraordinary goalscoring feats helped bring the FA Cup to White Hart Lane in 1901, is aimed at conveying the sense of the club in its nascent years, as well as paying tribute to an individual Cult Hero. Likewise, the late, great Bill Nicholson, whose association with the club spanned over 60 years, was a member of the 1951 League Championship winners, and deference is duly shown to this team in the relevant chapter.

Of those not included in *Spurs' Cult Heroes*, few players had their credentials promoted quite as vigorously as John White. An attacking midfielder, White was crucial in driving Spurs to the Double in 1961 and European Cup Winners' Cup in 1963, but was tragically killed on 21 July 1964, when struck by lightning whilst sheltering under a tree at a golf course. That he is not included amongst the final 20 is due primarily to the quality and popularity of so many of his peers. The list already includes Blanchflower and Mackay, as well as Cliff Jones and the manager of that glorious team, Bill Nicholson, not to mention Jimmy Greaves, signed in the winter of 1961. While White's case for inclusion was strong, it was felt that another member of the team from that era would skew the balance of the final list; but such an opinion is by no means definitive.

Others conspicuous by their absence include Lineker, Sheringham, Coates, Crooks and Archibald, while wide-eyed rants of fury were also directed this way for the omissions of Cameron, Ditchburn, Ramsey, Smith, England, Peters, Neighbour, Conn, Thorstvedt and Freund, to name but a handful. The compilation of the final list of 20 was rather unscientific at times, but a huge number of opinions were sought and reminiscences collected.

Disagreements about the personnel may be inevitable, but it is to be hoped that *Spurs' Cult Heroes* does at least capture much of that tradition of the club – not just the silverware, but all those other factors unique to Spurs. Football played 'the Tottenham way'. Glorious European nights at the Lane. Gleaming white shirts. Years ending in '1'. Magic Wembley moments. *Audere est Facere*. Questionable musical offerings. Big-name signings. Exotic foreign arrivals. Flair players; club servants; the occasional hardmen; and goalscorers so prolific you almost wanted to offer a consoling pat on the shoulder of the hapless goalkeeper who would soon be left wondering what had hit him.

Tottenham Hotspur's history is packed with heroes. If the White Hart Lane turf could speak – well, I would like to think it would pretty much read from these pages.

Michael Lacquiere
January 2010

SANDY BROWN

'SANDY'

1900-1901

SPURS CAREER

Games	28
Goals	25
Caps	1

MAGIC MOMENT

Scoring in Spurs' 1901 FA Cup Final triumph

IN the beginning was Sandy Brown. The history of Tottenham Hotspur FC stands proudly and compares with the very best, like some aged veteran of battle, bedecked in medals and eyes a-gleaming with lavish tales of glory. Within this illustrious history, spanning well over a century, the first in the long line of major honours was collected in 1901, with victory in the FA Cup. In winning the trophy the contribution of one man leaps from the yellowed pages of the archives – for one Alexander Brown Esquire scored 15 goals for Spurs in that season's competition, in just 8 games played against 5 different opponents, from First Round to final. Goalscorers *par excellence* have always featured heavily in the memories and on the lips of the club's followers, and where Greaves, Chivers, Allen and Lineker were later to follow, first Sandy Brown trod. Without his contribution, who knows quite how the history of the club would have transpired.

The FA Cup is as much a part of the history of Spurs as the cockerel in the club emblem. Over a period of 90 years the oldest club competition in world football was won 8 times by Tottenham, birthing legends and creating unforgettable moments – some ingrained in the mind's eye as black and white images, such as completion of the first Double of the 20th century by the 'Super Spurs' of Bill Nicholson and Danny Blanchflower; while others are captured in glorious technicolour motion, like the greatest Cup final goal of all time, by Ricky Villa in the Centenary final. This famous association of Tottenham with the FA Cup was first framed in sepia, back in 1901. It was to be the first of 8 years ending in '1' in which Spurs claimed silverware – another quirk of the club's long and illustrious history – and the triumph was all the more impressive for being the only occasion in history in which the FA Cup has been won by a non-league side, a record it is frankly now impossible to envisage ever being broken.

Legend has it that the seeds of Tottenham Hotspur FC were sown on the spot that is now a set of traffic lights on the corner of the High Road and Park Lane, outside what is now the White Hart Lane stadium. Here, in the late 19th century, a group of local teenage schoolboys decided to amuse themselves after the end of the cricket season by organising an association football team. Having already adopted the name Hotspur Cricket Club for their summer sport, Hotspur Football Club was duly selected as a name, with subscriptions first received on 5 September 1882, thereafter officially regarded as the club's formation date. The name Hotspur was taken from Sir Henry Percy, son of the Earl of Northumberland (a family which owned land in the local area now known as Northumberland Park). Sir Henry Percy was referred to as 'Harry Hotspur' by William Shakespeare in *Richard II* and *Henry IV Part I*, fittingly splendid heritage for a member of English football's aristocracy.

As the popularity grew of the team in particular and the sport in general, so the history of the club gradually evolved. The first recorded game ended inauspiciously in defeat, by two goals, against Radicals, on 30 September 1882. In 1885, seeking a means to avoid receiving correspondence meant for a different side called London Hotspur, club secretary Sam Casey decided, in a moment of laudable inspiration, upon the name 'Tottenham Hotspur Football and Athletic Club'. Spurs joined the Football Association in 1889, turned professional on 16 December 1895, and the following year, having had their Football League membership application rejected, joined the Southern

League. After dabbling variously in blue and white quarters, brown and gold, and even, in some moment of wild delusion, red shirts and blue shorts, impeccable judgement was exercised within the corridors of power as the colours of white shirts and blue shorts were settled upon, in 1898. The club moved to White Hart Lane at the start of the 1899-1900 season, marking the move by winning the Southern League that season.

As would be the case with the Double winners of 1961 and the great team of the early 1980s, the 1901 FA Cup victory was the culmination of several years of progress. These were sparked at the beginning of the 1898-99 season, with the appointment as player-manager of John Cameron. The 27-year-old Scot had proved his credentials as an inside-forward at Ayr, Queen's Park and Everton, while displaying his administrative abilities in the capacity of secretary of the Association Footballers' Union – the forerunner to the PFA. Cameron brought more Scots to the club, in the form of inside-left John Copeland and left-back Alexander 'Sandy' Tait, while Irish winger John Kirwan, goalkeeper George Clawley, defender Tom Morris and diminutive centre-half Jim McNaught had also been added to the ranks by the turn of the century. These men joined a side already containing veteran Welshman and club captain Jack Jones, as well as another Scot, Harry Erentz, and flying right-winger Thomas Smith, to form what was to be the first great Spurs team in history.

The final piece in the jigsaw was the addition, at the start of the 1900/01 season, of Alexander 'Sandy' Brown (so nicknamed as an abbreviation of his forename, rather than any reference to his hair colour). Another of Tottenham's Scottish brigade, Sandy Brown was born in Beith, in April 1879, and earned the nickname 'Glenbuck Goalgetter' for his goalscoring feats as a teenage striker for Glenbuck Athletic. He made his professional debut as a 17-year-old for Edinburgh-based St Bernards before moving south of the border to play for Preston and Portsmouth, ahead of his transfer to Spurs. He moved back to Portsmouth after just a single season at Spurs, but his prowess in front of goal and value to the team were indubitable, and his is the name inextricably linked to Tottenham's historic Cup success in 1901.

Spurs had made a solid but unspectacular start to the season, winning half of their 14 Southern League games by the time the FA Cup got underway in February 1901. The competition – then commonly known as the English Cup – had been delayed until February because of the death of Queen Victoria, but was well established as the most prestigious event in the national football calendar. As stated in the *Daily Mail* after the First Round matches: 'In football circles nothing else is talked about at the moment but the results of the matches played on Saturday in the First Round of the competition proper for the Football Association Cup', while a later edition of the paper referred to the FA Cup trophy as 'emblematic of the national championship at Association Football.'

The draw for the First Round of the competition did not exactly lavish good fortune upon Spurs, as they found themselves facing Preston North End – their conquerors at the same stage of the previous season's competition. In one of the numerous curious asides that can be gleaned from the archives of the day, although they were the home side Spurs adopted an alternative kit of blue and white stripes for the game. Preston took a first half lead, and Tottenham were just seven minutes from elimination when the head of Sandy

Brown rescued them, converting a cross from Kirwan. It was a sight that was to become increasingly common as the competition continued. However, the *Daily Mail* account of the game, while suggesting that Spurs had performed sufficiently well to earn a draw, delivered a withering assessment of the team's goalscorer:

'Tottenham Hotspur did not quite succeed in beating Preston North End and earning the right to enter the second round of the F.A. Cup competition, but with a little luck they would have won comfortably enough. McBride however, gave a wonderful exhibition in the Preston goal, and thus saved his side from defeat, as he did just a year ago at Preston. Rather than to the goalkeeping of McBride, excellent as it was, the non-success of the Hotspurs may, however, be ascribed to the comparative failure of the three inside Hotspur forwards, who very seldom did the right thing. Tom Smith and Kirwan were all right in the extreme wings, and Copeland at times worked well with Kirwan, but Cameron and Brown had an off day. Had Brown taken two chances which went to him during the game there would be no need for the team to journey to Preston to decide which of the pair shall enter the next round.

In spite of the fact that the game was not a scientific one, it was always interesting and exciting, and the crowd – there must have been about 20,000 present – surged and swayed about in the wildest excitement. At the start Preston were all over their opponents… Gradually, however, the Tottenham forwards began to feel their feet, and thereafter it was "pull devil, pull baker" all the time.

Both goalkeepers had a tremendous amount of work to get through in the first half, and both made some wonderfully fine saves, and at times very lucky ones …The equalising point was scored about seven minutes from the close. Brown heading through from a lovely pass by Kirwan.'

Four days later however, Spurs deservedly prevailed 4-2 in the replay at Deepdale, with a hat-trick from Brown seemingly helping him to take some steps towards redemption in the eyes of the same newspaper, which also conveyed the general impressiveness of the team as a whole, as well as the growing excitement of the supporters:

'The victory of Tottenham Hotspur in the replayed Football Association Cup tie at Preston yesterday was complete and decisive, and not one of the seven thousand spectators would deny that the 'Spurs' play on the famous enclosure was value for even a greater margin of goals than the score (4-2) represents. As a matter of fact, there never was any comparison between the play of the teams, for from the moment, five minutes from the kick-off, when Cameron opened the scoring, North End became a feeble, bewildered team in the face of the tricky passing and the occasional long crosses from wing to wing which characterised the Tottenham attack.

The outstanding feature of the game was the play of the London forwards. Perhaps chiefly because the Hotspur defence was seldom subjected to any serious strain, Tom Smith, on the extreme right, was persistently fed during the first half. After the left wing had drawn the attention of the Preston backs Smith was able to drop in quite a succession of lovely centres. At first most of these went to waste, mainly through over-anxiety on the part of the left wing, but presently Kirwan and Brown warmed to their work, and McBride, grand goalkeeper though he is, had a terribly exacting task.

Tottenham's second point came from a free kick against McMahon for putting his knee into Copeland's ribs, the ball being headed by Brown out of McBride's reach ... McBride had no chance with the third goal, which Brown put on from a six yards range after an extremely pretty run by the Spurs' left wing ... Brown notched number four goal, and although twenty minutes remained to play the spectators were satisfied and they melted slowly away.

As a match the game was too one-sided to be exciting. While McBride performed finely in the Preston goal, not another member of the defeated team played even moderate football ... In direct contrast to this, the whole visiting team moved like a well-oiled machine ... the halves played an untiring game, tackling with pluck and feeding their forwards with great coolness. This coolness was the feature of the forwards' play, which reminded them a great deal of the style of the old days. The capital work of Smith and Brown, both old North Enders, evoked many expressions of wonder that they had been allowed to go south ...The Bury team, who have to visit Tottenham in the second round, watched the game from the stand, and ungrudgingly acknowledged that the Spurs had played grand football.

The splendid news was published in the High Road, at Tottenham, at 5pm exactly. At first the people would not believe that the Spurs had scored such a decisive victory, but when the telephoned result was confirmed by telegraph there was much running to and fro and excited shouting. Naturally, local hopes run high that the Hotspur team will, at the very least, get into the semi-final round of the competition. The wiser among the supporters of the Tottenham Club counsel a discreet silence until after the game with Bury on Saturday week ... We heartily congratulate the directors of the Tottenham Hotspur club, and the thousands who support it, on the unexpectedly splendid form shown by their men. There is still a long, rough row to hoe, but cheerful spirits, in conjunction with extreme care and the keenest determination, can do much.'

Unfortunately, Spurs' reward for progression in the competition was more akin to punishment, the draw for the Second Round pitting them at home to Cup-holders Bury, a side unbeaten in their travels in each of their four previous Cup ties. English football was at the time dominated by teams from the north of the country, no southern club having won the FA Cup since 1882. Tottenham's triumph over Preston had therefore captured the imagination, with the *Daily Mail* noting on the day of the clash with Bury that 'the hopes of the South of England hang upon four clubs,' Spurs being joined in the Second Round by Kettering, Reading and one other side, at that point still loyal to their south London roots, going by the name of Woolwich Arsenal. The charmingly antiquated preview of Spurs' game ran thus: 'Football riddles have become fashionable in the north of London. The latest query is "Will the Spurs bury Bury or Bury bury the Spurs?"'

Spurs conceded early, but the Smith-Brown combination worked once in each half to see the team through, Brown's brace taking his goal-tally in the competition to six. Newspaper reports offered differing opinions of the decisive factors in Spurs' win over Bury, *The Times* suggesting that the match was lost by the visitors rather than won by the hosts:

'In gaining their victory the Hotspur team showed the greater smartness in getting to the ball, and, considering that they had a goal scored against them in the first few minutes, they may be congratulated on their triumph. But they were lucky in finding the Bury eleven quite off form. At no time did the visitors settle down, combination among the forwards being sadly lacking, and they were not to be recognised as the same set of players who took so prominent a part a year ago.'

The *Daily Mail* by contrast was a little more gracious in its acclaim of the victors:

'Although only a margin of a single goal separated the teams at the finish of the game, the holders of the Football Association Cup were beaten in such a decisive manner that a surplus of three goals would scarcely represent the afternoon's work in the field. It is usual to exclaim "Hard luck!" on behalf of the losers, but in the match under notice this would scarcely be fair, for the home side battled all the time in most resolute fashion against what odds chance could put in the way of their opponents.

The Tottenham forwards were always better together than their rivals … Brown was clever in the centre, and though he missed chances galore in the first half made amends by scoring two good goals and another couple which were disallowed.

It was a magnificent display of football in which both the science and the stamina of the home team were better than that of the holders of the Cup. The Tottenham players when once warmed to their work, played a great game all round, and finished as freshly as they started. It is almost impossible to imagine a better side on the display they gave on Saturday.'

Following such complimentary words on Spurs' performance, further cheer was proffered by the headline which followed directly beneath: 'Arsenal's Hopes Blighted – Defeated By West Bromwich Albion After A Poor Game.'

Spurs' Third Round opponents were Reading. Any sense of déjà-vu, or indeed plain exasperation, amongst the players would have been understandable, given that the two sides had already squared up six times that season – twice in friendlies, twice in the Southern League and twice in the Western League (producing three draws, two Tottenham wins and one Reading victory). If Spurs had earned their early successes through hard work and *élan*, they undoubtedly led a charmed life in the Third Round. For a start, in Reading they drew the only remaining fellow non-league side. For the third time in three Rounds they fell behind, but equalised when Kirwan pounced after Brown's initial shot had been parried. In the second half however, Lady Luck bestowed an outrageous favour upon Spurs, when defender Tait 'wilfully usurped the place of the goalkeeper and used his hands in order to prevent the ball from going into the net', according to the *Daily Mail*. The moment was missed by the officials, and Spurs lived to fight another day.

In that first game against Reading, Sandy Brown, 'although tricky in the open, seemed to lose his nerve in front of goal,' wrote the *Daily Mail*. However, a two-goal salvo in the replay had the same publication drooling:

'The particular gem of the collection of the twenty-two players was Brown. This player never spared himself, and as a consequence he put the ball into the net no fewer than four times.'

While two of these were disallowed for offside, two stood, alongside one from Copeland:

'One of the goals scored by Brown was a decidedly brilliant effort, and he could not have complained of the meed of applause which the spectators gave him.'

Spurs, now the only representative of Southern England left in the competition, had 'a very wide circle of friends and admirers.' They had reached the semi-final of the FA Cup for the first time in their history, their opponents West Bromwich Albion, to be faced at Villa Park, a choice of venue which rather stretched the definition of neutrality. For Sandy Brown in particular it was to prove a memorable occasion, for he scored all of the team's goals in a 4-0 victory. The club's wide circle of friends and admirers was again in evidence, with the *Daily Mail* reporting:

'The Hotspur's victory was so complete, so decisive, so convincing, that even the supporters of the local club, as they hurried into the street at the close of the momentous and most exciting game, could not restrain their desire to applaud the victors.'

This summary also gave some clarification to the newspaper's headline of: 'Tottenham to Fight in the Final for the Cup – Their Scientific Play Beat West Bromwich Albion'.

While the scoreline was eventually emphatic, the outcome might have been quite different, as Spurs struggled in a goalless first half, despite having had a gusty wind behind them. As noted in *The Times*, during the first half, 'The Tottenham forwards were not idle, but the rushing tactics and indefatigable vigour of their opponents prevented them from settling down to effective play.' The *Daily Mail* delivered an eye-catching précis of Spurs' first half performance: 'They were never at ease, and most certainly were never very effective, for the simple reason that most of them were as nervous as schoolgirls.'

It is difficult to imagine that, with such a propensity for the original and evocative, the media of 1901 would ever indulge in football's more inane clichés, but this it seemed was an early instance of the archetypal game of two halves. Three minutes into the second half, Kirwan broke down the left – with 'a pretty touch' – and crossed for Brown to nod home the opening goal. As noted in *The Times*:

'This success inspired the Tottenham players, and they asserted their supremacy, settling down to an accurate short passing game, and, keeping the ball low, they outmanoeuvred and outpaced their opponents, and in less than a quarter of an hour two goals were added. Both came from Brown, though they were carefully worked for by the whole line.'

Kirwan and Smith provided the ammunition, and Brown pulled the trigger, becoming the first man in history to score four goals in an FA Cup semi-final. While he may have had his limitations as an all-round footballer, he was undoubtedly the right man for the system purveyed by John Cameron's Tottenham, benefiting particularly from the talents of the team's wingers. Although not necessarily the quickest of forwards, Brown was the perfect focal-point for the Tottenham of 1901, his shooting and heading abilities providing a lethal cutting-edge to complement the team's approach-play.

There can be little doubt that there would have been those who saw in Brown a player whose abilities barely extended beyond goalscoring. Such a perspective brings to mind a comment made several decades later by Spurs manager Bill Nicholson, about his star striker Jimmy Greaves, after one particular game: "All he did this afternoon was score those four goals." Nicholson perhaps, had been trawling the archives, for after Brown's four-goal salvo against West Brom, the *Daily Mail* wrote:

'It is true that Brown got all the goals, but deadly shot as he is, and therefore deserving much praise as the possessor of a unique ability, it must not be forgotten that the others made the opportunities for him.'

Spurs fans, however, are willing to forgive a myriad of sins if they see in a player natural goalscoring ability, and, as Greaves would do later, so Brown merrily carved his name onto the club honours board.

And so to the 1901 FA Cup final, staged at Crystal Palace on 20 April in front of football's first ever crowd of over 100,000.

The match was billed as a clash of Tottenham's 'speed and trickery', against the 'more robust and callous' Sheffield United. Indeed, United were well fancied, and had been in fact since dispatching Sunderland in the First Round, while their victims also included a strong Aston Villa side in the semi-final. They had won the League two years earlier, and included in their line-up nine internationals, amongst them legendary goalkeeper William 'Fatty' Foulke, who reportedly weighed 21 stone.

Sandy Brown was to maintain his astonishing record of scoring in every Round of the competition, but, in developments some 100 years ahead of their time, the headlines were grabbed by refereeing controversy and, slightly incredibly, one of the first instances of the debate surrounding goal-line video technology.

On a sunny, windy afternoon, neither team gave a particularly good account of themselves, the magnitude of the occasion having a detrimental effect. As now seemed customary, Spurs conceded early, but after falling behind in the tenth minute they upped their game, threatening from both wings. Midway through the first half, Brown, inevitably, equalised, heading home from a free kick, before giving Spurs a second half lead in one of the best moves of the match. Jones, Kirwan and Cameron combined to release him, and he fired a rising shot in off the underside of the bar. Brown, according to *The Times*, had been subject to some fairly rigorous man-marking from United's Morren, but 'never lost either his form or his temper.'

However, barely a minute later United were level, in highly controversial circumstances, as a shot from Bert Lipsham was parried by Spurs keeper Clawley, and then scooped behind as attackers converged. United players appealed for a corner, Clawley for a goal-kick; but to the bemusement of all concerned, the referee, a Mr Arthur Kingscott of Derby, awarded a goal. As it happened, the incident was captured on film, the game being the first FA Cup final to be filmed by *Pathé News*, and Mr Kingscott's dubious call was granted immortality on celluloid. Spurs had had the better of the game, but following their outrageous good fortune against Reading earlier in the competition, they now found themselves on the receiving end of the whims of that fickle mistress Lady Luck. Scenes of players surrounding the referee, their faces contorted with rage, were conspicuously absent, and Spurs were forced to settle for a replay.

The replay was held at Bolton's Burnden Park, but with only half of the anticipated 40,000 spectators turning up – precious few of whom were from London, given the cost of transport, and the fact that the Bolton rail station was undergoing redevelopment – the occasion gained notoriety for vast amounts of food prepared for fans having to be thrown away, unsold and uneaten, resulting in the occasion being nicknamed The Pork Pie Final. With the pitch itself noticeably sloping, as well as being barren of grass in some places, the choice of venue did not elicit an overwhelming chorus of approval.

The game promised to be another tight affair, with the *Daily Mail* noting beforehand that 'Brown in the centre can be relied upon to score if he is only given the opportunity.' However, on the day itself Tottenham dominated from start to finish, winning 3-1:

'The score of three goals to one very nearly represents in figures the superiority of Tottenham Hotspur over Sheffield United. To be exact the London players were three clear goals, possibly four, better than their opponents. It is no exaggeration to say that they were all over their rivals during the first twenty-five minutes of the game … The play of the Hotspur forwards was of the most bewildering description. In and out they dashed – feinting, passing, dodging, centring, in fact, doing everything imaginable in football science, but score'

As the pattern of the game became thus established, United resorted to a more agricultural approach to stem the Tottenham tide:

'Sheffield's centre half-back [Morren], knowing full well the deadly accuracy and force of Brown's aim, almost literally clung to the feet of his man … Naturally, with such a severe handicap as Morren, and occasionally Johnson, Brown did not play his usual clever, self-reliant game during the opening period. However, he made full atonement in the second…'

And despite all this, yet again Spurs conceded first, late in the first half. However, undeterred by either this or the turnaround that left them playing into the wind in the second half, they continued to assert their superiority, making a tactical change that saw their wingers tuck infield. Player-manager Cameron scored an equaliser ten minutes into the second half, Smith gave Spurs the lead and, after having one effort saved by Foulke, and dragging another just wide, Brown finally rounded off a sensational season in the competition by heading in Tottenham's third, inside the final ten minutes. Captain Jack Jones was presented the trophy by FA President Lord Arthur Fitzgerald Kinnaird, but not before an FA Cup tradition was begun by the wife of Tottenham director Morton Cadman, who tied navy blue and white ribbons to the trophy.

A tradition of another type was the alcohol-fuelled post-match celebration indulged in by players, staff and supporters alike. As reported in The Tottenham and Edmonton Weekly Herald, and reprinted on spurshistory.com:

'Great was the enthusiasm in Tottenham that night when the team were welcomed home by a crowd of 40,000 people who dragged them in two broughams from the South Tottenham Station. The celebrations continued on the Monday evening, when thousands visited the Spurs ground and were treated, amongst other entertainments, to a kinematograph show including pictures of the cup-tie. A Tottenham bricklayer was the first local man to fill the cup. He begged Mr Roberts [Charles Roberts, club Chairman from 1898 until his death in 1943], at Bolton, to allow him to hold the coveted trophy. Before Mr Roberts could realise what had happened, the "brickey" had filled it at his own expense. On the train, journeying homeward, Lord Kinnaird, president of the Football Association, drank from the cup, although a total abstainer.'

As well as his Cup exploits Brown also scored 10 goals in 20 League appearances that season. Such a healthy strike-rate renders all the stranger the fact that he left Spurs on 1 May 1901, just 11 days after the FA Cup triumph, and the very first day of the close season. The circumstances of his departure are shrouded in mystery, swallowed by the passage of time. For any player of that era to spend just a single season at a club was highly unusual, the peculiarity in the case of Brown heightened by the level of success he had enjoyed at Spurs. The fact that he returned whence he had arrived, to Portsmouth, suggests that his ties to the South-coast club had not been fully severed in the first place, while the promptness of his move, literally as soon as the 1900/01 season had ended, gives reason to believe that the deal had been in place for some time.

Brown went on to earn an international cap, playing for Scotland in a 1-0 defeat to England in 1904, continuing his domestic career with Middlesbrough, Luton Town and Kettering Town, before returning to Scotland to play for Nithsdale Wanderers and Ayr United. Thereafter however, the life and times of Sandy Brown largely disappeared from public view, to such an extent that neither the place nor year of his death are known by the club he fired to FA Cup glory. Spurs, for their part, struggled without his finishing ability. The team's fortunes gently subsided after his departure, and the club ultimately had to wait two decades for further silverware.

Sandy Brown and his Tottenham team-mates had blazed a trail, establishing a tradition that was to grow over decades. With his 15 goals over just 5 rounds, compared to the modern-day 6, Brown established a record that will require a monumental effort to surpass. The club had profited undoubtedly from the tactical nous of player-manager Cameron, the bravery of goalkeeper Clawley and the speed and thrust of wingers Kirwan and Smith, yet without Brown it is reasonable to suggest that the club simply would not have won their 1901 FA Cup. He provided exactly what the Tottenham team of 1901 needed, that most vital commodity in football. His goals helped Spurs win the first of their magnificent haul of FA Cups, and have earned him Cult Hero status.

BILL NICHOLSON

'BILL NICK'

1938-1955
1958-1974

SPURS CAREER

Games	314
Goals	6
Caps	1
Manager	832

MAGIC MOMENT

Managing Spurs to the League and Cup 'Double' in 1961, ten years after winning the League with the club as a player

ON 15 May 1963 Tottenham Hotspur became the first British club ever to win a European trophy, doing so in gloriously emphatic style with the 5-1 routing of Atlético Madrid in the European Cup Winners' Cup final. Two goals apiece from Jimmy Greaves and Terry Dyson, and one from John White, confirmed a victory which made Tottenham the pride of England, while the magnitude and style of the win had observers across the continent gasping in awe. It was the crowning glory of the 'Super Spurs' team, which, having proved their pedigree domestically with the League and Cup 'Double' in 1961 and FA Cup in 1962, saw Europe as the final frontier to be conquered, the *pièce de résistance*. While Dyson's was the name in lights following his bravura performance, and the names of all the players who donned the gleaming white strip that night have rightly been etched into the annals, the victory stands as a testament to one man in particular, for in the space of five years since taking charge at White Hart Lane, manager Bill Nicholson had elevated Tottenham Hotspur to heights of which the fans had not dared dream.

At the helm when Spurs won the Double in 1961, and also in the team as a player when they had won the League Championship for the first time in their history, ten years earlier, the enormity of his contribution to the history of Tottenham Hotspur FC is unparalleled. Nicholson's association with the club spanned six different decades from ground-staff boy to club President, in which time, as well as his success as a player, he garnered eight further major trophies in becoming the most successful manager in Spurs' history. However, as he himself recalled in Jeremy Novick's *Winning Their Spurs*, 'Perhaps the greatest game was winning the Cup Winners' Cup.'

As a player alone, Nicholson achieved practically deific status at White Hart Lane, being an integral member of the first ever Spurs side to win the title, in 1951. Aptly enough for a man whose dislike for the trappings of fame bordered on revulsion, his route to Tottenham was low-key and unspectacular. He had joined the club from his hometown of Scarborough in 1936, after receiving an invitation for a trial, but has recalled that the invitation, sent by the club's then chief scout Ben Ives, took him completely by surprise. Even though Ives mentioned in the missive that he had spoken to the 17-year-old Nicholson, the man himself – then just a boy – had no idea how he had been scouted. In fact, in a rather charming prelude to the arrival of another club legend half a century later from the exotic shores of Argentina, Bill Nicholson confessed to not even knowing where Tottenham was. However, whereas in 1978 Ossie Ardiles arrived at the unfamiliar destination of White Hart Lane clutching a newly-gained World Cup winners' medal, Nicholson's beginnings were considerably humbler. One of nine children, he was brought up as the son of a hansom-cab driver, and carried such modesty with him through life, pursuing perfection on the pitch rather than glitz and glamour. For evidence of his priorities in football, one need look no further than the fact that, even when one of the most successful managers in the country, he continued to live in an end-of-terrace house just around the corner from White Hart Lane stadium; while one of the contributory factors in his eventual departure from the club was his dismay at the persistent requests of players for better salaries, when he considered that the privilege of playing for the club ought to have been sufficient payment in itself.

On arriving at the club he became a ground-staff boy, rolling up his sleeves to undertake such glamorous duties as painting the stands and rolling the pitch, while training two afternoons a week, and becoming a member of Spurs' 'nursery' club, Northfleet. The adage suggests that behind every good man is a woman, and as Nicholson adjusted to the bright lights of London he spent much of his time at the house of a friend three doors down from his own digs, where he met his future wife. The future Mrs Nicholson was known as 'Darkie' because, although christened Grace, she had a fairer twin sister, nicknamed 'Angel'. The pair married in 1942 and had two daughters.

In 1938 Nicholson signed professional forms, incidentally on the same day as another White Hart Lane legend, Ron Burgess. A wing-half, Burgess captained Spurs for eight successive seasons after the end of the Second World War, including the title-winning season of 1951. Nominally a defender, Burgess, in the finest Tottenham tradition, was imbued with an instinct to attack, an ability that made him one of the driving forces of the famous 'push-and-run' Spurs team of that era.

As for Nicholson, his first-team debut came in a 3-1 defeat away to Blackburn Rovers, on 22 October 1938. There followed 17 further appearances that season, impressively so for a 19-year-old within a squad of 46 professionals. However, the onset of war temporarily halted Nicholson's Spurs career, as he was called up to be an Army instructor. While football continued, results were obviously of little consequence. Indeed, Spurs were one of many clubs somewhat speciously expelled from the Football League during the war, for refusing to adhere to schedules which meant long-distance journeys at a time when player availability was nigh on impossible.

Six years later Nicholson went straight back into the post-war first-team at Spurs, as the conflict had prevented the emergence through the ranks of any younger players. Indeed, at 26, Nicholson was himself, effectively, one of the younger players in the post-war era. He found his niche within the Tottenham team as a reliable right-half, his robust and uncomplicated playing style matching his gruff persona.

While Arthur Rowe is credited with the creation and management of the push-and-run title-winning team of 1951, caps ought to be doffed in the direction of Joe Hulme, Rowe's predecessor and the man who initially sowed the seeds of this success. Taking over the managerial reins immediately after the war, Hulme assembled personnel including inside-forwards Eddie Baily (later to become a key member of Nicholson's management team) and Les Bennett; Ted Ditchburn (who was to make over 400 appearances in goal for the club), and Channel Islander Len 'The Duke' Duquemin, in attack; as well as Burgess and Nicholson. Rowe became manager in May 1949, and on inheriting this talented group of players instilled into them confidence, organisation and, most famously, the push-and-run philosophy. Essentially this involved short, quick passes from a player who would then immediately move into space to avail himself for a possible return pass. The moniker 'push-and-run' was not one with which Rowe himself was entirely at ease, considering that it did an injustice to the style of play, but as he was to point out, the philosophy accorded impeccably with the playing tradition of the club. The principle was not only adhered to by Nicholson on the pitch, but was to become a fundamental tenet of the Tottenham team he later managed to glory.

Another aspect of management introduced by Rowe and later aped by Nicholson was the use of pithy, punchy catchphrases around the Tottenham camp. 'Make it simple, make it quick' was a favourite, while 'A rolling ball gathers no moss' and 'He who stops is lost' were also trumpeted across the training ground *ad infinitum* by Rowe, with a view to making such principles second nature to the players.

Years later, the ghost of Rowe hovered above the Tottenham training pitches as players under Nicholson had drilled into them such catchphrases as 'If you're not in possession get in position'.

The push-and-run system found a spiritual home at White Hart Lane, willingly adopted and then perfected by the Tottenham team of the late '40s and early '50s. Beginning at the back, rather than kick long upfield, goalkeeper Ditchburn would innovatively roll the ball short to full back Alf Ramsey. Push-and-run became second nature to the players, who were, crucially, blessed with the fitness, technique and awareness to implement it. Ramsey was another nominal defender who loved an offensive foray, but with Nicholson offering solid cover behind him a platform was created for Spurs to rove forward, with their often mesmeric multi-pass attacks. Rowe's Spurs team won promotion from the Second Division at a canter in his first season in charge, following an unbroken nine-month stint atop the table.

By the summer of 1951 the Tottenham players were therefore champing at the bit ahead of their return to the First Division. While their best-laid plans went wildly awry in their first game back amongst the elite – a 4-1 defeat at home to Blackpool – wrongs were quickly righted, and a run of 8 successive victories, scoring 28 and conceding just 6 between September and November, helped the team establish their title credentials. Ironically, Nicholson's one Spurs goal that season came in the 3-2 defeat to Huddersfield which signalled the end of Spurs' early run of eight consecutive wins. Huddersfield were to prove a curious nemesis, beating Spurs home and away in the league, despite finishing 19th, and also knocking them out of the FA Cup.

By New Year's Eve Tottenham had reached the top of the First Division for the first time in 17 years. A run of five victories and two draws during a packed March fixture list proved decisive, and when Sheffield Wednesday were despatched at White Hart Lane in the penultimate game of the season, Tottenham Hotspur became First Division champions for the first time in their history. Nicholson was well established as a mainstay of that history-making team, having appeared in all but 1 of the team's 42 league games that season.

It was a magnificent finale to the season, and while the term 'fairytale ending' would probably have been met with disdain by a gruff, unassuming Yorkshireman like Nicholson, the campaign nevertheless ended on an indisputable personal high, as two weeks later he was awarded his sole England cap, against Portugal at Goodison Park, on 19 May 1951. The occasion saw Nicholson make history, as he scored spectacularly from long-range after just 19 seconds, the fastest goal by an England player on debut. However, like flies to wanton boys are we to the footballing gods, and having the misfortune to play during the same era as legendary Wolves right-half Billy Wright, Nicholson was unable to add to that first appearance.

The following season Spurs finished second, the push-and-run style often hampered by quagmires of pitches in the winter months. In the years thereafter the side that had won successive Second and First Division titles struggled to maintain their form. That most persistent and relentless of foes, Father Time, ground them down, hampering their efforts to play the slick brand of football which relied so heavily upon off-the-ball movement. The problem of a glorious Tottenham team growing old together was one Nicholson would himself have to face as manager a decade later when the stars from the Double-winning team of 1961 began to fade.

Nicholson's personal fortunes came to symbolise those of the team in the early 1950s. After sustaining a knee injury in the 1953/54 season, he informed Rowe that his playing days were numbered, and retired after 342 games and 6 goals for Spurs. His decision signalled the end of one era at the club; but another was to follow immediately, as Rowe signed one Robert Dennis Blanchflower to replace Nicholson at right-half.

Nicholson's achievement as a member of the Championship-winning team of 1951 should not be underestimated, for the achievements of that side elevated Spurs to their rightful place amongst the elite of English football. However, in a side boasting Ditchburn, Bailey, Burgess and crowd favourite Les Bennett, Nicholson was but one of a number of stars. There can be little doubt that it was for his incredible array of achievements as a manager that Nicholson has become revered as a Cult Hero at Spurs. Curiously, Nicholson did not ever receive a contract for his role as manager. As he himself reasoned, in his typically trenchant northern style, "If I was good enough to do the job, they'd keep me. If I wasn't good enough they'd sack me." The Tottenham board, in their infinite wisdom, opted to keep rather than sack Nicholson.

Upon his retirement Nicholson took up a coaching role at White Hart Lane, progressing to become first-team coach in 1955, assistant manager in 1957, and manager in October 1958. It was a logical progression for him, having previously gained invaluable experience of such roles during his period of military service. This had first comprised infantry training in 1939, before he become an instructor in the Physical Training Corps at Brancepeth. Other roles included a post in the Central Mediterranean Forces based in Italy, where he taught coaching in a number of sports to men who themselves went back to their bases and passed on the instructions to their own troops. Such experiences were undoubtedly critical to Nicholson in his education as a football manager. As he recalled, in Ken Ferris' *The Double*, 'It was invaluable … [It] taught me how to handle people and how to talk to people. It deviously taught me how to get players fit.'

Motivated by his experiences in the Army, he immediately began attending FA coaching courses at Birmingham University. The courses had been founded by England manager Walter Winterbottom, who was later to take Nicholson with him to the 1958 World Cup in Sweden. Nicholson had gained his Full Certificate at the first time of asking, and during the Championship-winning 1950/51 season had even undertaken management of the Cambridge University side, noting, as quoted in *The Double*, 'Being intelligent young men the Varsity players were receptive to ideas and I enjoyed my time with them.'

After Spurs had finished in the top three in the previous two campaigns, Nicholson took over with the club 16th in the First Division, 1 point above the relegation zone having gleaned just 9 points from their first 11 games of that 1958/59 season. The record books suggest that the new manager made quite an impact, his first match in charge at White Hart Lane providing one of the most memorable scorelines in the club's history. Tottenham Hotspur is nothing if not an entertaining team, and goalless draws are fairly anathema to the club. Yet even by these standards, a 10-4 victory ranks as extraordinary. Thus, however, did Nicholson's long and illustrious managerial reign begin, as Spurs defeated Everton at White Hart Lane. One of the stars of that game, Tommy 'The Charmer' Harmer, is famously reputed to have noted to Nicholson immediately after the game, "We don't score ten every week you know," while *The Times* reported the game in an understandably enthusiastic manner:

'Perhaps this resounding triumph … will prove a turning point this season for Spurs. Certainly nothing could be more encouraging for Mr Nicholson, their new manager, who has been coaching the side for the past few seasons.'

However, given his relentless pursuit of perfection it is barely conceivable that Nicholson would have allowed himself an iota of complacency about the result, obsessive scrutiny of the four goals conceded far likelier. The next week saw Spurs beat Leicester 4-3, but 2 defeats followed, with the team shipping 15 goals in Nicholson's opening 4 games in charge. It is a measure of the bold pragmatism of Nicholson and courage of his convictions that in his debut season in management he was able to take the decision to relegate from the team Danny Blanchflower, in response to the wing half's too frequent neglect of his defensive duties. Nicholson was a huge admirer of Blanchflower, later restoring him to the team and the captaincy, and giving him *carte blanche* to attack within the well balanced Double-winning and Cup Winners' Cup-winning teams of the early 1960s. With Spurs fighting relegation however, the situation demanded a different approach. As Nicholson put it, as quoted in Phil Soar's *Tottenham Hotspur: The Official Illustrated History*:

'In a poor side Danny was a luxury. That's why I dropped him. But in a good side his creativity, his unorthodox approach, was priceless – a wonderful asset.'

Tottenham muddled through, avoiding relegation, with an 18th-placed finish, but conceding 95 goals in the process. It hardly required the managerial expertise of Nicholson to identify that defence was a cause for concern. However, by this time he was already exercising his uncanny knack for negotiating the transfer market. Crucially, his first buy was Dave Mackay, acquired from Hearts in March 1959 for £32,000, making him Britain's most expensive half-back. It immediately proved money well-spent, as Spurs went unbeaten in the League in the remaining eight games of the season following Mackay's arrival. The manner in which Nicholson would slide out of White Hart Lane in pursuit of signings, his intended destination rarely known to anyone, has become the stuff of legend. Indeed, when he left London on a train to sign Mackay, his staff at White Hart Lane had expected him to return to North London with Swansea's Mel Charles in tow.

Further signings followed. Scottish international goalkeeper Bill Brown was signed in the summer of 1959, while one of the final pieces of the Double-winning jigsaw was completed that autumn, when John White was bought from Falkirk, for £20,000. On this occasion Nicholson had asked his captain Blanchflower to testify to White's ability, Blanchflower having opposed White in a Northern Ireland game against Scotland. Blanchflower promptly gave the move his seal of approval, and when Nicholson discovered that White was a national-standard cross-country runner his last doubt was shed, and the signing completed.

That Nicholson was prepared to act on the confirmation of Blanchflower says much about the level of mutual trust and respect that existed between manager and captain, a relationship unsullied by the fact that Nicholson had seen fit to drop Blanchflower just months previously. Blanchflower was to become an increasingly influential figure at the club, not only delivering and carrying out Nicholson's orders as on-pitch lieutenant, but also given his manager's blessing to make his own on-pitch tactical decisions as he saw fit. Such a healthy if unorthodox relationship formed the backbone of the magnificent Spurs team of the early 1960s. One wonders whether it is any coincidence that when the next great Spurs team emerged, around 20 years later, winning domestic and European trophies, it too had at its core a strong relationship between manager and captain, with Keith Burkinshaw and Steve Perryman constantly in contact, the former allowing the latter to make on-pitch decisions as appropriate.

At the end of the 1958/59 season, Nicholson made the rather unusual decision to take his players on an end-of-season tour to Russia. Although presumably bemused, the players entered into it whole-heartedly, and were ultimately to reap the benefits. The tour involved rigorous, daily training sessions, and three friendly games (Spurs recording two victories and a defeat), as well as spare time in which to take in some of the curiosities of life behind the Iron Curtain. Nicholson considered the trip a success, quoted in *The Double* as saying:

'I was glad of the opportunity of getting the players together … We trained hard and we played three matches. I cannot overstate the value of that trip in terms of getting things together.'

It is an opinion with which winger Cliff Jones concurred ("That's where we saw the signs"), and the ultimate vindication of Nicholson's judgement in hauling his players to Russia was the evidence of the White Hart Lane trophy cabinet, soon to brim with silverware.

Nicholson signed striker Les Allen from Chelsea in late 1959, but the improvement in defence was the most noticeable difference made in his first full season in charge. With Mackay now offering protection, the switch from right-back to centre-half of big Maurice Norman helped Spurs shore up at the back, and the figure in the 'Goals Against' column was almost halved to 50, as the team finished third, just two points behind champions Burnley. Said Nicholson, in *The Double*, 'The third in the League table was a boost. We were getting it together…'

The Tottenham side circa 1960/61 by no means replicated the style of the 1950/51 team, for while Arthur Rowe's push-and-run team would not even trap the ball, looking instead to play one-touch football, Nicholson's Tottenham adopted a slightly more controlled approach, with the man in possession often taking several touches. However, off-the-ball movement remained integral, as Nicholson preached the importance of creating space and providing options at all times.

Prior to the 1960/61 season, Nicholson imbued these principles into the team, making them second nature to the players, as all manner of training drills were devised to encourage the players to work passing triangles automatically into their play. Fitness levels were also high on the agenda, in order to facilitate this style of play, while countless hours were also dedicated to set-pieces, including Dave Mackay's long-throw routines and John White's deep corners for Cliff Jones to meet at the far end of the penalty area. Of course, as well as the philosophy, training routines, fitness and camaraderie, there were the slogans. Where Arthur Rowe had gone ten years previously, now Bill Nicholson followed. Cliff Jones recalls Nicholson drumming into the heads of his each team mantras such as, 'If not in possession, get in position', while other choice Nicholsonisms included 'The man without the ball makes the play', and 'Time equals space'.

Whatever the tedium of leaving training day after day with such slogans ringing in their ears, the football produced by the players suggests that the messages were appreciated, subliminally if nothing else. Spurs started the season in irresistible fashion with 11 successive victories, their style of play enthralling neutrals across the country as well as their own fans. As Dave Mackay recalls in Jeremy Novick's *Winning Their Spurs*:

'We didn't think, "Oh no, we're two down, we'd better play it tight at the back or something." We never played like that. We just played good open football all the time, attacking and trying to entertain.'

However, this cavalier attitude was known to backfire on occasions. On 3 December 1960, Spurs raced into a 4-0 lead after just 36 minutes against reigning champions Burnley, but astonishingly contrived to throw away the lead and draw 4-4. Spurs fans of a more recent vintage may not be entirely surprised to hear of such a collapse from their team, but at the time Nicholson was far from impressed, remarking in disgust, "We scored eight and still drew."

While statistics alone do not do justice to the team, ranking as they do alongside lies and damned lies, they still make for impressive reading. As well as the 11-match winning streak, Tottenham were unbeaten in their first 16 games, amassed a record-equalling 33 points from away games and a record-equalling 11 'doubles' of beating clubs both home and away, whilst also becoming the first club to reach 50 points in just 29 games.

There were undoubtedly big names within that Tottenham team, but Nicholson's achievement in winning the Double lay in creating a whole greater than the sum of its parts, for a very good group of players was turned into a sensational team, purveying an exquisite brand of football the like of which had fans and pundits alike drooling in admiration. As *The Times* reported, following Spurs' 4-1 demolition of Manchester United in their fifth game of the season:

'For the first half-hour on Saturday Tottenham indeed were flawless. If the match had ended at that point – with Spurs already two up – it would have been sheer perfection ... In those opening phases Spurs played the sort of football that might even have had Real Madrid thinking and moving a bit quicker. They seemed to come close to the ideal, blending the continental and British styles subtly and finding the best of two worlds.'

Et cetera; yet Nicholson, one suspects, would only have taken note, with furrowed brow, of the paragraph which reported: 'To maintain such a standard over the full 90 minutes comes within the range of few, if any, sides. Even the great Hungarians in their hey-day, or Brazil, the reigning world champions, or Real Madrid, found that the real secret is to pace a match, turning on the tap of inspiration in bursts. Tottenham tried to keep the flow going too long and though they finally emerged the most handsome of victors they paid the price after half-time.'

Bill Nicholson was of the school of managers who much preferred to be on the training ground, working with players, rather than stuck behind a desk ("I would tell the directors that they could get me in the office before a quarter to ten. After that I would be out with the team, coaching," he once remarked, according to *Tottenham Hotspur: The Official Illustrated History*). The reason he opted to live throughout his managerial career in a house a stone's throw from the Tottenham stadium was to save travelling time. It therefore should surprise no-one to discover that he was meticulous in his preparation for games, for example ensuring immediately prior to the 1961 FA Cup final that each of the Spurs players took a ball out with them when they inspected the Wembley pitch beforehand, so that they would get an idea of how the turf would play.

Nicholson's obsessive pursuit of improvement and, ultimately, perfection, made him quite the innovator. While it is a common sight now for managers to watch games from up in the stands, Nicholson was one of the first to adopt the technique. In February 1961 he even had a telephone cable installed underneath the Spurs dugout, so that he could communicate to first-team trainer Cecil Poynton at touchline level, while he himself remained in the stands. On the pitch he was just as forward thinking, making Tottenham one of the first teams to use overlapping, attacking full backs, when he encouraged Joe Kinnear on the right and Cyril Knowles on the left to augment attacks at every opportunity, in the mid-1960s.

Nothing but the best satisfied Nicholson when he managed Spurs – and even then, such was his perfectionism, the best was not enough for him. When Spurs wrapped up the First Division title under his auspices in 1961 with victory over Sheffield Wednesday, he was not content, wanting the club to go on in their final three League games and achieve the three points necessary to break the record held by Arsenal for points gained in a single First Division season. As it happened, two defeats in their final three games meant that this feat was not achieved, a source of great frustration to Nicholson. Incredibly, even victory weeks later in the FA Cup final, to complete the historic Double, was considered unsatisfactory. There is little doubt that Spurs performed underwhelmingly in the final, achieving their 2-0 victory in rather nervy, laborious fashion against a Leicester team cruelly reduced by injury to 10 men (in an era before substitutes were allowed) after just 19 minutes. Nicholson could not disguise his disappointment with the performance, with Dave Mackay recalling in *Winning Their Spurs*, 'Bill was disappointed with the FA Cup final because we didn't put on a good show.'

Nicholson's disappointment was even greater the following season, when Spurs were ground down by the quest for glory on three fronts, and, fatigued by their European Cup exploits, failed to repeat their Double success, winning 'only' the FA Cup in 1962. As Nicholson recalled, in *The Double*:

'Looking back, the Double was fabulous, but there was also disappointment for me when we did not put our Double feat right out of anybody's reach – remember that Arsenal caught up with us ten years later – by doing it for a second year in succession. Which we should have done.'

Years later, the personnel may have changed in the Tottenham ranks but the message remained the same from a manager still obsessively demanding the highest standards. Nicholson is widely reported to have greeted Spurs' 1972 UEFA Cup victory by announcing to his charges that he had just been into the dressing room of beaten opponents, Wolves, to tell them that the better team had lost.

However, good praise rarely bestowed is therefore worth more the earning. Thus, when Nicholson applauded flying winger Cliff Jones after his majestic hat-trick helped inspire the 8-1 demolition of Gornik Zabrze in the European Cup Qualifying Round Second Leg in September 1961 – memorably the first ever European match at White Hart Lane – Jones was understandably somewhat taken aback, as quoted in Matt Allen and Louis Massarella's *Match of my Life*:

'After that game, after scoring a hat-trick, he came up to me and said "Well done, son". I couldn't believe it. "A pat on the back, Bill, what have I done to deserve this?" And he looked at me and said, "A pat on the back is only a couple of feet away from a kick up the arse."'

The European campaigns of the 1960s beginning with that tie against Gornik, continued the elevation of Nicholson's team to the status of legends – and his own education as a manager. He typically opted for a slightly surprising, if understandable, degree of caution in away legs, generally opting to omit forward Les Allen and select an extra body in defence, in the form of Tony Marchi.

Spurs reached the semi-final of the European Cup in their debut season in European competition. Nicholson's extensive preparations involved a scouting trip to see opponents Benfica, as well as the other semi-final in which Real Madrid beat Juventus – notable commitment in the days before low-cost airlines. Convinced that Spurs would beat Real if they reached the final, he set out his stall for the away Leg – Marchi drafted into the side in place of Allen – only to see some questionable refereeing leave Spurs chasing a 3-1 deficit. In the return Leg at White Hart Lane, disallowed goals and several rebounds off the woodwork left Spurs cursing their luck at a 2-1 victory, which saw them exit the competition 4-3 on aggregate. Looking back, Nicholson ruefully recalled, "I lost count of the near misses."

That same season, Spurs sought at least to emulate their domestic success of the previous year by winning the League Championship again. The main rivals for the crown were Ipswich Town, managed by Alf Ramsey – alongside whom Nicholson had worked so effectively in Spurs' Championship-winning side a decade earlier. While Nicholson would earn his rightful place in the history books as manager of the first Double-winning team of the century, Ramsey would himself go on to make history as manager of England's World Cup-winning team of 1966. The two most talented managers of their time had both been in contention to manage Spurs, and had both coveted the job once their playing careers had ended, but Nicholson had got the nod and Ramsey had gone to Ipswich.

Ramsey's Ipswich had only won promotion to the First Division in 1961, and took the top-flight by storm, their innovative use of deep-lying, unorthodox wingers frequently confounding opponents. Nicholson had wanted to counter this threat by changing Spurs' formation, but eventually bowed to the wishes of his players to retain the playing style with which they were familiar. Spurs lost to Ipswich both home and away. The four points thereby ceded proved crucial, as Ipswich won the title with 56 points, while Spurs amassed 52. As if to prove the point, in the following season's Charity Shield game Nicholson enforced the changes he had previously planned, and Tottenham won 5-1 – but the dream of a second consecutive Double had not been realised.

After the European triumph of 1963 the Spurs team gradually disbanded, its members having reached their peaks, and Nicholson therefore set about building a new one. This he did, and although not of the same class as the Double-winners at the beginning of the decade, the team was strong enough to bring home more silverware, in the form of the 1967 FA Cup. Only Mackay – by then club captain – and unused substitute Jones remained of the Double-winning team. Frank Saul and Joe Kinnear were the only home-grown players in that side; the others, including Jimmy Greaves, Pat Jennings, Mike England and Alan Mullery, had been bought by Nicholson.

As the new decade started, more blue and white ribbons were needed, as Spurs won the League Cup when the year ended in '1', with Martin Chivers scoring both goals in a 2-0 win over Aston Villa. By then, however, the wonderful flowing football pioneered by the push-and-run team, and recreated by Nicholson's Double-winners, was being usurped as the template for the English game by the unsightly long-ball approach. The following season Spurs won their second European trophy, beating Wolves 3-2 in the two-legged final of the 1972 UEFA Cup, while 1973 brought another League Cup triumph, Ralph Coates enjoying his finest moment in lilywhite with the only goal of the final against Norwich City. Yet more silverware beckoned in 1974, but this time Spurs were unable to maintain their 100 per cent record in Cup finals, losing over two Legs of the UEFA Cup final to Feyenoord.

However, that infuriating trend honed by so many Spurs teams since was beginning to emerge, as the side were simply unable to replicate such success in the League. In one-off Cup games the players raised their games, but lacked the consistency to challenge for the League Title over the course of a season, as evidenced by final standings of eleventh, third, sixth, eighth and eleventh in the first seasons of the new decade. Moreover, off-field problems were beginning to mount. Player disputes over pay were becoming more common; the dressing-room frequently echoed to the sound of rows between Nicholson and surly star striker Martin Chivers; and the 1974 UEFA Cup semi-final Second Leg in Rotterdam, against Feyenoord, was marred by hooliganism from the travelling Spurs contingent. Four consecutive defeats at the start of the 1974/75 season proved enough for Nicholson, and after 38 years, including 15 as the most successful manager in the history of the club, he resigned.

It was not a wholly unexpected development, as he had originally planned to step down had Spurs won the previous season's UEFA Cup. Unfortunately, his exit was tinged with bitterness, as he took offence at the decision of the club to overlook his recommendation of Danny Blanchflower as his successor. However, the reign of new Spurs manager, Terry Neill, was short-lived, and when Keith Burkinshaw took over, in 1976, Nicholson willingly accepted a position back at White Hart Lane as scout, where his finds were to include non-league player Graham Roberts, who would go on to captain the side to UEFA Cup victory in 1984.

Spurs achieved more success with the year ending in '1', winning the 1991 FA Cup final in the same month in which Nicholson was appointed club President. There could be no more fitting appointment than the man who was to give over 60 years service: "It's been my life, Tottenham Hotspur, and I love the club."

Such was the reverence with which Nicholson was held at the Spurs that tributes to him over the following years included the erection of a bronze bust of him in the main reception of the ground; naming a suite at the stadium after him; and even in 1999, the naming of the road leading to the entrance of the stadium as Bill Nicholson Way.

Bill Nicholson died on 23 October 2004. At a memorial service held at the Paxton Road end of the White Hart Lane pitch, 85 white doves were released, to celebrate his 85 years. The service was packed with players from the contemporary squad, as well as players and staff from the numerous Tottenham teams he had managed over the years, while eulogies were delivered by such club legends and Nicholson protégés as Jimmy Greaves, Cliff Jones, Martin Chivers, Glenn Hoddle and Gary Mabbutt.

No single man has done more to put the club on the proud pedestal it today occupies in football history. He ensured that the wonderful artistic playing style became a trademark of the club, masterminded an era in which repeated success confirmed Tottenham's status as one of the greats of the game, yet throughout it all retained a laudable sense of humility and dignity. A true gentleman, he would remind his players of their obligation to the fans, as Cliff Jones recalls:

"He made you aware of your responsibility to the community because the football club is part of that community and the lives of the supporters."

It was fitting that this sense of respect was reciprocated by the fans prior to the home game against Stoke City, in October 2009, when a packed White Hart Lane stood to give Nicholson a full five-minute ovation, on the fifth anniversary of his death. It is to be hoped that his dignity continues to be remembered by all who support and play for the club.

DANNY BLANCHFLOWER

1954-1964

SPURS CAREER

Games	382
Goals	21
Caps	56

MAGIC MOMENT

Captaining Spurs to both the First Division Championship and FA Cup in the 1960/61 season

'DANNY BOY'

WHEN Spurs clinched the First Division title on 17 April 1961 with a 2-1 victory at home to Sheffield Wednesday, the delirious White Hart Lane crowd left nobody in any doubt as to who they considered their hero, invading the pitch and raising the roof with repeated choruses of "We want Danny! We want Danny!" It was indicative of the impeccable judgement of the Tottenham fans, for Robert Dennis 'Danny' Blanchflower was soon to be named Footballer of the Year, for the second time in four years. The man himself obliged the request, leading his team to the White Hart Lane directors' box to receive their ovation from the awe-struck throng of 57,000. Three weeks later the fairytale season concluded at Wembley, as Blanchflower led his team to victory over Leicester, and up the 39 Wembley steps, to receive the FA Cup and complete the famous Double. The image of the slender Spurs captain hoisted on the shoulders of Ron Henry and John White, holding aloft an FA Cup bedecked in white and blue ribbons, is etched in the mind's eye of many a Spurs fan – those of generations hence, as well as those privileged to have witnessed the Double-winners.

Some players are best remembered, and their achievements best summed up, by one particular career-defining moment on the pitch. In the case of the club's greatest ever captain, the only Spurs man to lift both League and FA Cup in the same season, and the first Spurs captain to lift a European trophy, his Tottenham career is epitomised by this particular quote:

"The great fallacy is that the game is first and last about winning. It's nothing of the kind. The game is about glory. It's about doing things in style, with a flourish, about going out and beating the other lot, not waiting for them to die of boredom."

Danny Blanchflower was a man with a gift for delivering the *mot juste*, and these words epitomised the romantic notion of the game evinced by his play – graceful, elegant, but always with bristling attacking intent.

Not only did Blanchflower's vision of the glory game define his own approach, his words have been adopted at Tottenham Hotspur as an unofficial motto of the club. They encapsulate everything the style of the club should be, to this day, forming the bedrock upon which the much of the club's glorious tradition has been built, and setting a standard to which every Tottenham team has since aspired.

The signing of Danny Blanchflower will go down in history as the final great legacy bequeathed to Tottenham Hotspur by Arthur Rowe, a man whose name had already been immortalised in the White Hart Lane corridors for bringing the League title to the club for the first time in its history, with his 'push-and-run' team of 1950/51. By 1954, however, it appeared that Rowe had taken Spurs as far as he could. The history-making team he had assembled to win the Second and First Division titles, in successive seasons at the beginning of the decade, had disbanded. Spurs finished 16th in the league in 1953/54, and mid-way through the following season, with the pressures of management clearly taking their toll on his health, Rowe stepped down, to be replaced by Jimmy Anderson. While he had been unable to replicate the success of the 1951 side, a compelling case can be made for Rowe's contribution to the even greater success reaped by the club in 1961, through his decision to bring Blanchflower to White Hart Lane.

Blanchflower is not the only Spurs cult hero whose very signing for the club almost failed to materialise – nor was he the only, unthinkable though it seems today, who might have ended up at Arsenal, had events transpired differently. In September 1954, the 29-year-old Blanchflower was suitably disillusioned by what he perceived as a lack of ambition at his team, Aston Villa, to submit a transfer request. While some teams baulked at the £40,000 price tag slapped on him, Arsenal and Tottenham stayed in the hunt. Spurs boss Arthur Rowe reached a gentleman's agreement with his Highbury counterpart, Tom Whittaker, to settle upon a £30,000 upper limit and let the player decide if necessary, so as not to become embroiled in an auction. Blanchflower had been swayed towards the red half of North London, but when the Arsenal board refused to offer in excess of £28,000, Rowe stepped in, and Blanchflower began to warm to the idea of continuing his career at White Hart Lane. The game in England was undergoing something of a revolution, following the defeat of the national team by Hungary's 'Magical Magyars' the previous year. As a progressive thinker himself, Blanchflower saw in Rowe's Spurs, which had swept to glory with the push-and-run style in 1951, a team capable of further progression. In December 1954 he therefore opted for the blue and white half of North London, enabling Spurs to celebrate one of their most significant ever victories over their rivals.

To report that Blanchflower was captain at Spurs would be to utter a truth, but to neglect so much more, for his role extended to that of on-field manager, acting on the pitch in lieu of Bill Nicholson. As Cliff Jones put it in Matt Allen and Louis Massarella's *Match of my Life*, Blanchflower 'bridged the gap between the boardroom and the dressing room'. Famously, however, Blanchflower did not simply act as on-pitch conveyer of the wishes of his manager, for many a time and oft the irrepressible Irishman took matters into his own hands. The first hints of this penchant for spontaneous, unverified tactical decision-making first emerged at Aston Villa, as, inspired by 2-0 and 3-0 defeats to Tottenham in the 1953/54 season, he attempted to instil Spurs' push-and-run philosophy upon his team-mates on the Villa Park training ground. At a team already steeped in tradition, this approach did not exactly meet with universal approval. 'I was a banana case wanting to change things,' recalled Blanch-flower, as quoted in Ken Ferris' *The Double*. This frosty reception to his ideas was one of the major catalysts in his decision to request a transfer.

While Spurs' playing style fitted Blanchflower like a glove, if anything his tendency to take on-pitch matters into his own hands increased once at White Hart Lane, spurred on by the increased responsibility he had been handed as Northern Ireland captain by national manager and personal mentor Peter Doherty. In an FA Cup quarter-final tie against West Ham in 1956, with Spurs trailing 3-1 in the latter stages, Blanchflower took it upon himself to send hulking central defender Mo Norman into attack. The change paid dividends, as Spurs forced a replay in which they triumphed, and Blanchflower's inter-vention was therefore greeted without demur by Tottenham's influential Board of Directors. However, in the semi-final Spurs faced another make-or-break situation, trailing to Manchester City. Again, Norman was directed forward by Blanchflower, but this time to no avail, as Spurs lost 2-1. A similar, ultimately futile alteration, in a 2-1 defeat to Huddersfield towards the end of the campaign, succeeded only in incurring the wrath of then-manager Jimmy Anderson, who saw such impromptu changes as undermining his authority.

Blanchflower could perhaps be better considered an innovator rather than necessarily a tactical genius. His decisions as captain were always bold, and at times revolutionary, and one obscure but noteworthy piece of trivia is that he can be credited with setting up the game's first 'defensive wall' against a free kick, in an international match for Northern Ireland against Italy in 1957.

A key ingredient to Blanchflower's character as a footballer was his ego. 'He thought a lot of himself,' recalled Bill Nicholson in *The Double*, 'and I thought a lot of him.' A man oozing confidence in his own ability, Blanchflower would constantly demand the ball and then dictate Tottenham's attacking play, becoming the brains of the Double-winning side. Back in 1956 however, his audacity was decidedly less well received. Spurs' League form had slumped dramatically following their Cup exit, and the club needed a point from their final two games to ensure top-flight survival. Then-manager Anderson dropped Blanchflower from the squad, telling the press that his captain had picked up an injury. Although he was reinstated for the final game of the season, Blanchflower was stripped of the captaincy.

The relationship between Nicholson and Blanchflower was a fascinating one, with Nicholson, despite his obvious football nous, frequently judging it expedient to cede to the ego and authority of his skipper. Undoubtedly the most famous such occasion was in the changing room immediately prior to the 1963 European Cup Winners' Cup final. Nicholson dolefully went through the teamsheet of opponents Atlético Madrid, despondently eulogising about each player, before Blanchflower, unable to contain himself, interrupted. As Jimmy Greaves recalls in his autobiography *Greavsie*, Blanchflower proceeded to give his own team talk, claiming:

'If their centre-half is big and ugly, then ours is bigger and uglier. If their striker can cause problems in a penalty area then Jimmy G can cause ten times as many problems. If they have a fast winger called Jones [which, bizarrely, Atlético did] then ours is so fast he can catch pigeons'.

Nicholson, to his credit, had the humility to accept that this was a more suitable preamble to the biggest game in the club's history – and Spurs promptly took to the pitch and destroyed their opponents, 5-1.

However, as Cliff Jones affectionately recalls in *Match of my Life*, Blanchflower's words in the dressing room were not necessarily always so inspirational:

'He did go on a bit at team talks. Bill would ask if anyone had questions at the end of our meetings and Danny would always stand up – "Just one thing Bill". We would think, "Oh no," and he would go on and on, talking for hours. We wouldn't know what he was talking about either.'

While even his most ardent loyalist would struggle to make a tenable case for pace ever having been his forte, such was this man's myriad other talents that he did not appear to need it. Blessed with grace, balance, an eye for the perfect pass and the technique with which to deliver it, he was an artist, and the football pitch his canvass.

Having been dropped in 1956, the irrepressible Blanchflower bounced back in style, his performances in the 1957/58 season earning him the first of two Footballer of the Year awards.

Many consider that his performances that season surpassed even those of the Double-winning season of 1960/61, when he again picked up the individual award. Bill Nicholson took over the managerial reins at Tottenham in 1958, and while the Nicholson-Blanchflower combination was to prove the making of the finest period in the club's history, it began with a rift that proved almost irreparable. Spurs found themselves on a downward slide following the managerial change, and with Nicholson of the opinion that Blanchflower's neglect of his defensive duties as wing half were largely responsible, the Irishman was once again dropped, in early 1959. A run of four victories ensued, seemingly vindicating Nicholson's decision; but Blanchflower, unwilling to watch from the sidelines at the age of 33, requested a transfer. In recent years the phrase 'What if…?' has been uttered wistfully by Spurs fans, wondering what successes might have been, but looking back to 1959, the hypothetical can be dismissed with relief. Blanchflower later suggested that his transfer request was as much to clear the air as actually to move away from the Lane. When the club's board of directors rejected the request, the matter was put to bed. On 7 March 1959, Blanchflower was restored as captain for a game against Wolves, following a run of four home games without victory, and by the following week Blanchflower was back to his superlative best in a 6-0 demolition of Leicester.

Danny was the first piece in the Double-winning jigsaw, but long before the puzzle had been completed the Irishman was entertaining a belief tantamount to certainty that the feat could be achieved. In the modern era this may not seem particularly notable, but back in the 1960s the League and Cup Double was something of a holy grail for the country's elite. The Double had proved tantalisingly close in the years preceding Tottenham's glory season. In 1957 Manchester United had won the League but surprisingly lost the Cup final, while in 1960 Wolves slipped up at the last in the League – ironically, with defeat to an out of form Tottenham – before winning the Cup at a canter. Many saw an insurmountable psychological barrier preventing any team from repeating the achievement, last managed by Aston Villa in 1897. Given his enormous reserves of self-confidence, however, it is unsurprising that such doubts were completely alien to Blanchflower.

As early as the summer of 1958 Blanchflower was predicting that such glory was possible for his Spurs team, insisting as much to an obsessive degree on the plane journey home from Northern Ireland's World Cup campaign in Sweden, according to fellow passenger, the late Joe Mercer.

Bill Nicholson remained more cautious – "Who knows about the Cup? One or two little things going the opposite way and bingo! You're gone" – but Blanchflower was absolutely adamant that the dream would be realised. As Spurs set off like a runaway train in the 1960/61 season the belief began to spread to team-mates, John White concurring at Christmas, and Cliff Jones finally coming round to the notion only prior to that season's FA Cup semi-final.

By the time Bill Nicholson had taken up the reins from Jimmy Anderson, various members of the Double-wining team of '61 had already been brought to the Lane. Legendary names in the White Hart Lane pantheon included Maurice 'Mo' Norman, Bobby Smith, Cliff Jones and Terry Dyson. However, the fulfilment of Blanchflower's potential at Tottenham, as well as the transformation of the club itself into a genuine title contender, was only to be truly catalysed by the signing of Dave Mackay in March 1959. When Blanchflower had arrived at Spurs he had played in front of the giant Norman, who was stationed at right-back. Later to become an integral central defender in the Double-winning team, Norman was hardly the most mobile, and with Blanchflower's attacking instincts taking him forward at every opportunity, Norman was often left lacking support. Peter Baker assumed the role of right-back from the 1956/57 season, but faced a similar problem playing behind Blanchflower. However, the arrival of Mackay had a liberating effect upon Blanchflower, for only then was he finally able to enjoy unfettered licence to indulge his creative instincts. The Mackay-Blanchflower axis was the vital ingredient in the Double-winners' success, blending creative nous and steely defence.

Blanchflower's romantic notion of how the game should be played was as evident off the pitch as on it, his romantic style of play matched by talents as a wordsmith that earned him the moniker 'The Wilde of White Hart Lane'. Eloquent, verbose and often outspoken, he makes a candidate for a scrapbook of quotations as well as a highlights reel of footballing prowess. Not for him the soulless clichés that litter modern-day press conferences and interviews, for no matter the occasion or the company, he was always armed with razor-sharp wit. When presenting his team to the dignitaries at Wembley before the 1961 FA Cup final, the Duchess of Kent pointed out to him that the opposing team, Leicester, had player names on their track-suits. Blanchflower replied: "Yes Ma'am, but we know each other." Jimmy Greaves recalls Blanchflower being asked by a reporter his opinion of George Best, and replying: "George makes a greater appeal to the sense than Finney or Matthews did. His movements are quicker, lighter, more balletic. George offers grander surprises to the mind and the eye. He has ice in his veins, warmth in his heart and timing and balance in his feet."

While such a lyrical style ought to have made him a media superstar, he became better established as a newspaper columnist than a television pundit, writing for the *Daily Mail*, the *Observer* and *Sunday Express*. However, his refusal to toe the line rather militated against him in the commentary box. In one game as a pundit, he opined, "These teams can't play", prompting a producer to suggest into his earpiece that he "Accentuate positive truths rather than negative truths". Blanchflower promptly corrected himself: "These teams positively can't play".

Although he was one of the footballers who pioneered product endorsement, famously Blanchflower became the first person to refuse to appear on the television programme *This Is Your Life*, citing personal reasons (and riposting, when asked to explain them, "If I told you any more they wouldn't be personal"). Blanchflower's way with words, when married to his forthright views, made him unpopular amongst some in the higher echelons of the game, particularly in an age in which, as members of the working class, footballers were very much expected to be seen and not heard. His on-pitch tactical changes had invoked the wrath of some in the Tottenham hierarchy, while he once said of the President of the Football League, "He's a self-made man who worships his creator." Given his refusal to compromise his views in order to conform to the opinions of those in the corridors of power, it is all the more impressive that he twice won the Footballer of the Year award.

Blanchflower led by example throughout the Double-winning 1960/61 campaign. While his team laboured to convert superiority into goals on the opening day of that season at home to Everton, he remained undeterred throughout, an endlessly scheming genius at the hub of all that was creative about Spurs. As *The Times* put it, 'Blanchflower, full of impish tricks and ideas, drove his forward line to its limits', and five minutes from time the pressure told, as he helped create a goal for Les Allen. This was swiftly followed by a second from Bobby Smith in a 2-0 victory.

The visit of Manchester United to White Hart Lane a fortnight later saw Blanchflower, aided by John White and insured by Mackay, run rings around the opposition in a 4-1 victory that could be considered Spurs' first official declaration of their intent and confirmation of their early season title credentials. As reported by *The Times*:

'There is no doubt where the main glare of the spotlight now rests – at White Hart Lane … For the moment Tottenham Hotspur remain the paramount chiefs of all the tribes in the Football League.'

Of Blanchflower's six goals that season, few were better than that struck in the 4-0 victory away to Wolves in early October, in Spurs' record eleventh consecutive win since the start of the season. As *The Times* put it:

'Blanchflower, almost with a smile on his face, beat an intended Wolves offside trap by flashing a 25-yard shot into the top corner of the net when everyone expected a pass.'

However, his abundance of talents were best utilised as a creator rather than scorer of goals, typically playing the role of orchestrator as Spurs' attacking play swamped opponents. On one occasion in mid-February 1961, Aston Villa tried to mark Blanchflower out of the game, and by the end of a goalless first half appeared to have succeeded, but Blanchflower's creative spirit broke free of the shackles and ran riot in the second half. Ever the romantic, he had reacted to Villa's stultifying approach by espousing to his team-mates during the half-time break the virtues of the 'push-and-run' mentality which had seen Spurs win the First Division title in 1951. Come the second half, Blanchflower, 'Back on his old stamping ground and clearly enjoying every minute of it', according to *The Times*, once again eased into the role of principal string-puller, and masterminded a 2-1 victory for Spurs, silencing critics who had dared to suggest, albeit in hushed tones, that two defeats over the preceding month had hinted at a stalling of the Tottenham juggernaut. In dealing with adversity by reverting to the basic tenets of the beautiful game, Blanchflower illustrated why his name is so synonymous with the famous Tottenham tradition of glorious football, and indeed illustrated why his was such a vital role in helping to shape that tradition.

However, Blanchflower's contribution in that most famous of seasons was not just in carving apart opponents. As pressure mounted on Tottenham, having become the scalp craved by all and sundry, Blanchflower also demonstrated the nous and capacity to draw the sting out of opposing teams. As he said in Phil Soar's *Tottenham Hotspur The Official Illustrated History*, 'I could change the rhythm, change the pace, slow it down if necessary'. Jimmy Greaves elaborated on this point in his autobiography, *Greavsie*:

'Danny was a cerebral player who dictated the pace of a game and it was his ability to dictate the tempo of a match that was crucial to Spurs' success. When opponents seemed on the point of seizing the initiative, Danny would put his foot on the ball and slow the game to suit Spurs. There would follow a seemingly meaningless interchange of passes in the midfield, between Blanchflower, White and Mackay that would lull the opposition. Then, when Danny sensed an opening, the telling pass would be made and Spurs would immediately spring into life and attack to devastating effect.'

Spurs wrapped up the First Division title with three games to spare, going on to complete the Double with victory in the FA Cup final a month later. It makes an interesting footnote to recall that, ever the romantic, Blanchflower – in common with his manager – was slightly underwhelmed by the nature of the Cup final victory over a Leicester side reduced by injury to ten men early in proceedings.

The following season Spurs embarked upon a triple-pronged quest for glory, seeking to repeat their Double-winning feats whilst also chasing glory in the European Cup. If anything, the team were victims of their own success, the rigours of three combined challenges ultimately sapping energy from the side as it fell short in the defence of its First Division crown. In Europe, the players learnt on their feet, adapting to European competition – and particularly away legs – by playing a more restrained game, with added responsibility consequently falling to Blanchflower as the creative spark. The European flame was extinguished in agonising fashion at the semi-final stage, as Spurs sought to overturn a 3-1 first leg deficit against Benfica. The Portuguese scored early in the Second Leg, but after a Jimmy Greaves goal had been debatably disallowed for offside, Bobby Smith finally pulled one back for Spurs. The noise at White Hart Lane in the club's debut European season lives long in the memory of all involved, with fans as well as players appreciating the particularly unique atmosphere created by the floodlights, crisp night air and foreign opponents. Blanchflower himself spoke warmly of the noise created by the White Hart Lane crowd on such nights, as they exhorted their heroes with renditions of 'Glory Glory Hallejuah', as quoted in *Tottenham Hotspur The Official Illustrated History*:

'The sound came from everywhere. It was marvellous. A local vicar used to complain that the whole thing was like a substitute for religion, and I suppose it was in a way.'

Spurs were trailing 4-2 on aggregate to Benfica, when the classy John White weaved his way into the Portuguese penalty area but had his legs swept from him, and referee Aage Poulsen pointed to the spot. With the crowd suddenly muted in breathless anticipation, and tension reaching unbearable levels, Blanchflower demonstrated remarkable *sang froid* when his team needed him most. He stepped up to slot away the penalty with all the insouciance of a man jesting in a training session, *The Times* writing of it:

'Blanchflower faced perhaps the most difficult moment of his career. The ball on the spot; Pereira 12 yards away and so much hanging by a thread. This truly was face to face. But Blanchflower, cool as ever, sold a dummy perfectly.'

Ultimately however, it would prove insufficient, and despite a bombardment of the Benfica goal, Spurs were beaten 4-3 on aggregate.

The consolation that season was a second consecutive FA Cup final, in which Blanchflower again displayed unflappable coolness from the penalty spot, sending goalkeeper Adam Blacklaw the wrong way as Spurs beat Burnley 3-1. Again, however, the occasion struck Blanchflower as anti-climactic, this time because of the thought of the glories that had slipped by so agonisingly in the preceding weeks.

Older and wiser, Spurs entered European competition again the following season, in the European Cup Winners' Cup, but by this time, if anything, age was beginning to take its toll on the Blanchflower legs. A cartilage injury sustained in the Second Leg of Spurs' opening European tie of the season, against Glasgow Rangers, ultimately meant that he missed 22 games that season – having been present in all 49 of Spurs' games in the Double-winning season of 1960/61. Amidst his silky skills and appearance of poetry in motion, it is easy to forget the steely resolve of Blanchflower, for despite jarring his knee on the day of the semi-final Second Leg against OFK Belgrade, he played with a painkilling injection in a 3-1 win. The same troublesome knee, which was ultimately to put paid to his career, threatened to keep him out of the final, two weeks later, against Atleticó Madrid. Quite frankly, however, history demanded that he play, and be the man to lift Spurs' first European Trophy. That team, pieced together in the late '50s, to emerge as the Super Spurs in the early '60s, was as much Blanchflower's as Bill Nicholson's. This was to be the last great night for the Double-winners, and the skipper simply had to be there, to lead them out before the players began to go their separate ways. Moreover, at 37 years of age, Blanchflower knew that the match was almost certain to be his last major Cup final. Spurs were already without Dave Mackay, also injured, but before the teams had even taken to the field, Blanchflower was able to rouse his troops with his legendary pre-match team talk. Spurs romped to a 5-1 victory, the first British team to win a European trophy. As was *de rigeur* when Spurs made history, Blanchflower was at the head of the team.

Tottenham led the First Division for much of the first half of the following season, 1963/64, but form understandably slipped away following a seismic double-blow that winter. Dave Mackay was to break his leg in a game at Old Trafford in December, and just one month later Blanchflower called time on his magnificent Tottenham career, his final game also against Manchester United. It was a measure of the rapport enjoyed by Blanchflower and Bill Nicholson, and the respect held by manager for captain, that on stepping down as Spurs manager in 1975, Nicholson recommended Blanchflower as his successor (a recommendation overlooked by the Tottenham board which, staggeringly, opted instead for Arsenal man Terry Neil). His only forays into management were brief spells at the helm of Northern Ireland and Chelsea.

Danny Blanchflower died on 9 December 1993, aged 67, a piece of Tottenham Hotspur dying with him. To this day, fans of the team do not simply crave success, they demand that success is achieved playing 'the Tottenham way'. This was defined, both in his words and in his sumptuous style of play, by the club's most celebrated captain, Danny Blanchflower.

CLIFF JONES

1957-1969

SPURS CAREER

Games	378
Goals	159
Caps	59

MAGIC MOMENT

Scoring a hat-trick in Spurs' first European match at White Hart Lane

'JONESY'

WHITE Hart Lane has proudly staged many memorable nights of European action, but the template for such glories was set on Wednesday 20 September 1961, in Tottenham's first ever European tie. The side ran rampant that night, emphatically laying down a marker for all great Spurs teams of future generations with an 8-1 demolition of Poland's Gornik Zabrze. Amongst the glittering array of heroes who imperiously bestrode the turf, as continental ambassadors of the club for the first time, one man's star shone particularly brightly. Cliff Jones marked the occasion by scoring what is reverentially known in football parlance as 'the perfect hat-trick' – finding the net with right foot, left foot and head. That momentous treble, struck in stunningly quick succession in the first half, stands as a fitting tribute to Jones, for he was blessed with outrageous ability with each outlet – as comfortable on the left wing as the right, and fabled for his prodigious heading ability.

Jones has described that game as his most memorable for Spurs, and has paid tribute to the contribution of the club's supporters that night, recalling in Matt Allen and Louis Massarella's *Match of my Life*:

'The noise hit me like a wall. I've played at Wembley, the Maracana, Hampden Park and Ninian Park, but nothing matched the atmosphere of White Hart Lane that night'.

With the floodlights on, Spurs playing in the famous all-white strip, and the cold night time air 'a lot sharper somehow', Jones' memories of the European nights at White Hart Lane are ones to which generations of Spurs fans can relate.

The mauling of Gornik could be added to an ever-lengthening list of achievements of the rampant League and Cup Double-winners of 1960/61. The team had everything: dependable defence; a midfield axis – of Blanchflower, White and Mackay – for all seasons; and goalscorers in Allen and Smith. But the jewel in the crown, the man who added that *je ne sais quoi* going forward, was Cliff Jones. Before a flying, goalscoring winger from Portugal dazzled England's premier division in the early 21st century, the original flying, goalscoring winger was a modest Welshman called Jones. Blessed with electric pace, a regular goalscorer and a man of incredible bravery on the football pitch, Jones injected additional zest into the Tottenham team as they conquered all before them in the early 1960s.

Jones learnt his trade in modest surroundings in his native Wales, spending a season in the Welsh League, two in reserve football and then two in the Swansea first team in Division Two, before becoming the most expensive player in the country, in 1958, when signed by Bill Nicholson for £35,000. Having been courted by Arsenal (for whom his uncle Bryn had played 20 years earlier), his debut, inevitably, came against the North London rivals. The game was drawn 4-4, but within a struggling Spurs side Jones failed to make a positive impression in his early days at the club. Given the size of his price tag, a vocal contingent amongst the passionate but notoriously fickle White Hart Lane faithful began to question his talent. The pattern thereby established was one that was to follow many future illustrious Tottenham wingers, for players of the ilk of Chris Waddle and even David Ginola would also have their doubters early in their Tottenham careers. Jones needed a change in fortune, but his worst enemy would not have wished upon him the break he quite literally received when he fractured his leg in the 1958/59 pre-season, in a clash with Peter Baker, during one of Tottenham's famously full-blooded training games. However, the silver lining to this cloud was that the lay-off allowed Jones his first rest period in almost two years of non-stop football. His absence also gave him some respite from the fans, who proved vastly more supportive when he re-entered the fray midway through the season.

Jones was joined by Dave Mackay, as that most reverentially regarded list of names, the 1961 Double-winners, was gradually assembled. Curiously however, one of the most important events en route to the creation of this historic Tottenham Hotspur side was a visit to the ballet in Russia.

At the end of the 1958/59 campaign, in which Spurs had ended up scrambling to stave off relegation, Bill Nicholson organised a 12-day team trip to Russia. The itinerary included friendlies against Torpedo Moscow, Kiev and the Russian Olympic team (games won 1-0, 2-1 and lost 3-1 respectively), as well as an evening at the Bolshoi Ballet – an excursion at which any cynicism amongst the players quickly dissipated, as they were left marvelling at the fitness of the ballet dancers. Whatever the thoughts of the players before the trip – and it is fair to assume that there might have been a few raised eyebrows – none doubted its value by the time they returned home, and hindsight has only emphasised its importance. Nicholson had succeeded not only in helping the team to bond, but also in preparing their performances for the standards they would need to reach in winning the title. Jones recalls, in Ken Ferris' *The Double*, 'That's where we first saw the signs. That's where we really started to play.'

The seeds had been sown, and a hint of glories to come was provided in the 1959/60 campaign, as Spurs improved their final League position from 18th to 3rd, and Jones scored 20 goals in 38 League appearances. As such he became the club's second-highest scorer that season, establishing himself within a team that had evolved into genuine title contenders. The club finished only two points behind champions Burnley in 1960, and would have won the title had not Jones himself missed a crucial penalty in a 1-0 defeat to Manchester City that April. The incident was to prove a highly controversial one. The penalty had been awarded at the very end of the first half, and on taking the kick Jones saw his effort saved by City goalkeeper Bert Trautmann, but promptly followed up to slot home the rebound. However, the referee did not allow the goal to stand – having made a decision, astonishing and courageous in equal measure, to blow for half-time immediately after the save, before the rebound shot was taken. Understandably, the call prompted bewilderment, amongst protagonists and spectators alike. Jones recalls, in Jeremy Novick's *Winning Their Spurs*, 'At the time nobody really knew what was going on – when the referee pointed to the centre circle, people thought it was a goal, but it was just for half-time'. Similar confusion was conveyed by *The Times*:

'The referee blew his whistle and pointed to the centre. The 50,000 crowd roared its relief and settled back. Spurs, it appeared, at long last were ahead. It was only a mirage. In a trice it transpired that the referee's actions merely heralded half-time rather than a goal. The crowd's roar now took on a rising and angry note: Blanchflower [Tottenham's captain] pleaded the Tottenham case as the players left the field amid all the hubbub, the uncertainty, and the unanswered question marks.'

Spurs went on to lose the game, and a chastened Jones handed penalty-taking duties to Danny Blanchflower. Another home defeat the following week left them wondering what might have been, come the season's end. They were not to be denied for long, of course, for under Bill Nicholson a Spurs team had been assembled that was ready to challenge for honours.

Jones' potency from either wing was fully utilised by Nicholson. Having spent much of his time at Spurs on the left, he was switched to the right wing in place of Terry Medwin for the final two games of the 1959/60 season, scoring in convincing wins against both Wolves and Blackpool, as Terry Dyson took the left wing slot. While Jones had presumed the move just a temporary one, Nicholson saw the alteration as answering the only real selection decision he faced, going into the 1960/61 season.

Although of diminutive stature, Jones was absolutely fearless, unflinchingly diving in with his head where angels feared to tread. It is a testament to his astonishing prowess in the air that, although only five feet eight inches tall, he established a reputation as a regular scorer of headed goals. The man himself attributes this prolific aerial record to his on-pitch perspective as a winger, noting in *Match of my Life*:

'I always had an advantage because I had a knack of seeing the ball as it came across and the defender at the same time, from my wing position'.

However, Bill Nicholson highlighted a more prominent contributory factor to this talent when he said of Jones, as quoted in *The Double*, 'There was no braver player in the game than Cliff.' Jones' face frequently bore the scars of flying boots, fists and heads. Indeed, as long-time Spurs fan Bill Clark recalls, "One of his last matches was a 7-0 drubbing of Burnley in 1968; Jones scored two. One of his goals was scored after he hit the post. He actually *hit the post with his head*, crashing into it following a diving header. Incredibly brave from what I remember..."

Jones' penchant for playing without shin pads was further indicative of his fearlessness, and with such abandon, straddling the gap between daring and recklessness, he inevitably incurred a number of injuries. In the very first game of the Double-winning season he sustained ankle ligament damage after an agricultural challenge from Everton's Alex Parker – a long-time friend – and was ruled out for a month. In fact, as Spurs began that season like a runaway train, registering a record 11 consecutive wins, Jones made only 3 appearances.

Nevertheless, his was a crucial role in that Double-winning season. As the heavy winter pitches took their toll on wearying legs, and the pressure began to mount from challenging on two fronts, Spurs went three League games without a win in the spring of 1961, and a total of 190 minutes without a League goal, before Jones finally scored to open the floodgates, in a 4-2 win over Chelsea, as reported in *The Times*:

'Tottenham, having dominated but failed to score in a first half at White Hart Lane yesterday that was ominously like the Newcastle nightmare of last week, overcame the psychological pressure that gnaws their composure these days with a delightful exhibition to rout Chelsea in the second half ... Bitter-sweet memories of the first half ... were swept aside within four minutes of the resumption. Jones, eluding the attentions of Bonetti and Sillett, shot in to the net and broke into a dervish dance of delight.'

The very next day, as Spurs entertained Preston, Jones was on hand to apply the *coup de grâce* to a sumptuous team goal, the 100th of Tottenham's incredible season, as part of a hat-trick in a 5-0 win.

By this time he had matured into the finest winger in the land, and indeed was regarded by many as the best in Europe at that time. Affirmation of this notion is provided by the £125,000 bid from Italian champions Juventus in the summer of 1963, after he had turned in a virtuoso performance against them in a pre-season friendly. The salary cap on footballers, only lifted in 1961, meant that a number of British players had already tried their luck overseas, including two team-mates of Jones during his time at White Hart Lane, Tony Marchi and Jimmy Greaves, as well as fellow Welshman John Charles, of whom Jones would have been a team-mate if the move had gone ahead. Bill Nicholson, however, was vehemently opposed to the move, and his word being law, Jones stayed at Spurs for another five years.

While he had all manner of weaponry in his arsenal, perhaps Jones' most crucial asset was his pace. He said in *Winning Their Spurs*, 'I loved dribbling, and I loved taking players on', but he was not the sort to produce fancy footwork and dizzying step-overs; instead his potency lay in his ability to glide by defenders, darting one side of them or t'other in the blink of an eye. While a generation of defenders left chasing shadows would presumably beg to differ, fans recall feeling a buzz of excitement whenever Jones set off on a gallop towards goal. As one supporter, Richard Early, remembers:

"The sight of Cliff Jones in full flight, steaming down the wing, leaving defenders littered in his wake, was more thrilling than I can put into words."

It is mildly ironic that this archetypal 'flying' winger was himself a nervous flyer during Tottenham's glorious European campaigns of the early 1960s, although as Jimmy Greaves recalls, in his autobiography, Jones reasoned that, 'Flying doesn't frighten me really; it's the thought of crashing that puts the fear of God into me.'

Typically, the only means by which opponents felt able to stop Jones were illegal ones, vagrant legs missing the ball and chopping at the player. Indeed, the memory of him hurtling to the ground after being tripped by a desperate opponent is just as indelibly ingrained an image as that of him on the run, as long-term fan Geoff Harrow recollects:

"I had the pleasure of watching Spurs in the early 60s and Cliff Jones was one of my favourites. To a young lad – as I was at the time – he seemed to me to be unbelievably fast. The pitch then was surrounded by a red shale path and then a low white wall topped with half-hoops through which we boys would watch the game, having been passed through to the front by all the adults. My spot was on the touchline towards the northeast corner of the Lane. I can remember more than once, when Cliff Jones was tripped when running at full speed. He would skid off the pitch and across the shale before thumping into the wall. Up he would get, white shirt stained red from the shale and back into the fray."

Spurs wrapped up the First Division title in April 1961, with victory at home to Sheffield Wednesday, before travelling to Wembley the following month as overwhelming favourites to win the FA Cup final and complete the historic Double. On that occasion however, with the weight of history on their shoulders, and even neutral fans hoping to see the fabled team play to their full potential, Tottenham flattered to deceive, a collector's item in that Double-winning season. Captain Danny Blanchflower, so often the hub of all that was good in Tottenham's play, was below par, while the usually dominant Dave Mackay also struggled to wield his influence. As Ken Ferris recalls in *The Double*, on Cup final day, 'Jones was the only bright spark for Tottenham'. The match proved one of the occasions on which the Welshman was regarded as something of a pressure release and attacking outlet by his team-mates, who made no secret of the fact that, as appropriate, they were prepared to feed him the ball and let him go haring upfield when they needed respite. As Dave Mackay once told him:

"Spurs won't have any trouble when they want to get rid of you – they'll just give you the ball, set you running, open up all the gates and you'll disappear up the High Road."

With the team struggling to fire on all cylinders in the Cup final, the turning point in the game was a wretched one, when Leicester right-back Len Chalmers was accidentally injured by Spurs forward Les Allen, and rendered effectively useless, after just 18 minutes. It was an era in which substitutes still were not allowed, and for the seventh time in nine years a side was forced to carry an injured player in the Cup final. Ironically, when substitutes were eventually allowed in Cup finals, the first beneficiary was Cliff Jones himself, who collected a winners' medal as an unused substitute in Tottenham's 1967 Cup win.

Chalmers' injury was undoubtedly detrimental to the game as a spectacle, as Leicester thereafter struggled to make inroads, while Spurs adopted something of a low-risk, safety-first approach, determined to avoid mistakes in the knowledge that with a man advantage the win would eventually come. In truth, it was a disappointing approach – if understandable, given the tension of the occasion – far-removed from Tottenham's traditional style, which had won them so many admirers in the Double season. The mentality was not assumed on managerial orders, but instead reverted to almost automatically by some of those on the pitch, who suddenly realised just what a golden opportunity lay before them to achieve their aim. As Spurs full back Ron Henry recalls, in *Winning Their Spurs*, 'I took it on myself. The manager never told me that, I just felt it myself.'

Jones, however, continued to offer a threat, and appeared to reap his reward shortly before half-time, when he burst to the far post to drill a Terry Dyson pass into the net from close range. However, even as he began his celebration, the linesman's flag was being raised, and referee Jack Kelly disallowed the goal. *The Times* labelled it, 'What looked a reasonable enough goal,' while Jones himself was understandably more forthright, recalling in *Winning Their Spurs*, 'It was a ridiculous decision. Dyson played the ball and I was fully four yards onside'.

Spurs did finally break the deadlock well into the second half, with a goal from Bobby Smith. Thereafter, the shackles of tension released, the players were able to express themselves, Jones continuing to menace the defence of ten-man Leicester and Dyson eventually adding the second goal. To a man, Brown, Baker, Henry, Blanchflower, Norman, Mackay, Jones, White, Smith, Allen and Dyson, as well as reserves Medwin, Saul and Marchi, carved their names in the history books. When listing Spurs' cult heroes it is no particular exaggeration to suggest that any and indeed all of the above would merit inclusion, for each was a vital component in the finest team in the club's history.

Jones was a particularly close friend of another attacker pivotal to Tottenham's Double success, a young Scot by the name of John White. Quite how many worlds White might eventually have conquered will never be known, for he was tragically killed, struck by lightning on a golf course while sheltering under a tree, on 21 July 1964, aged just 26.

Jones and White were amongst the most mischievous members of the squad. High jinks included a recreation of the film *Spartacus*, which the team had been to see together, whilst staying in a hotel in Sheffield prior to a game, with each man using half a table-tennis table and long ash-trays as impromptu props. Later, when Spurs stayed in a foreign hotel ahead of a European tie against Benfica, Bill Nicholson was woken at 2am, with the news that two of his players were fighting – only to find Jones and White armed with swords from the hotel foyer, re-enacting fight scenes from Errol Flynn's *Robin Hood*. Jones it seems, always had a glint in his eye and an irrepressible gift for the deadpan one-liner, recalling in *Match of my Life* that during the tour of Russia in the summer of 1959, when he shared a room with Dave Mackay, he had asked Bill Nicholson for a translator – 'Not for Russian, a Scottish one. I can't understand a word Mackay's saying to me.'

After the celebrations of 1961 the 'Super Spurs' began the following season looking to replicate the feat and also add European glory. The European Cup campaign had begun with that Qualifying Round tie against Gornik Zabrze of Poland, but before the glory of Jones' 'perfect hat-trick' the team had travelled to Poland in the First Leg and found themselves 4-0 down in the first half. Although Jones and Terry Dyson clawed back a couple of goals to take into the return match, Spurs did not play well that night, a fact that did not go unnoticed by the nation's press. What might euphemistically be termed the 'physical' approach of Bobby Smith drew particular criticism, as well as incensing the Polish crowd. Bill Nicholson was also unhappy with the performance, so the side therefore felt they had a point to prove, as well as a deficit to overturn, in the Second Leg. That they did in some style, demolishing the Poles, and looked good to go all the way, despatching Feyenoord and Dukla Prague, before controversially losing out to Benfica at the semi-final stage.

Gallingly, Spurs also fell just short of retaining their crown as First Division champions, ultimately paying the price for two defeats to eventual champions Ipswich, as they finished third in the table, four points behind the Suffolk outfit. Jones, however, maintains that the team of 1961/62, augmented by the arrival of Jimmy Greaves, was even stronger than the Double-winning team of the previous season. In the estimation of many observers a repeat of the Double was only prevented by the mounting fixture list.

Spurs did however retain the FA Cup in 1962. Jones was again prominent in the run to Wembley, scoring in the Third and Fourth Rounds, as well as the quarter- and semi-finals. His quarter-final strike at home to Aston Villa was a typical, full-length flying header, while his semi-final goal in the 3-1 defeat of Manchester United was even more impressive, as he cut in from the left wing and danced through seemingly the entire United defence before firing home. Two such moments of magic summed up so much of what Jones brought to the Tottenham team, and few were more deserving of their winners' medal that year.

The FA Cup victory of 1962 earned Spurs another crack at European competition, in what was then, in a pre-Champions League era, the highly prestigious European Cup Winners' Cup competition. Glasgow Rangers, Slovan Bratislava and OFK Belgrade each fell victim to the swaggering Tottenham Hotspur side, with Jones turning creator, particularly in the home leg of the tie against Slovan. With big Bobby Smith having made his presence felt amongst the Slovan back-line early in the game, Jones was able to bombard the visitors' area with bedlam-creating crosses, on which Greaves and Smith duly gorged themselves. Jones himself got on the scoresheet in that night's 6-0 win.

In the famous defeat of Atlético Madrid 5-1 in the final of the 1963 Cup Winners' Cup in Rotterdam, Terry Dyson deservedly took the plaudits for a sensational performance – Bobby Smith famously advising him afterwards to retire immediately – but not for the first time Jones was integral to making the breakthrough and settling the team, haring down the right before whipping in a cross for Greaves to side-foot home from close range. While Jones recalls the victory over Gornik the previous season as his greatest moment in a Spurs shirt, it is entirely apt that he was to be one of the match winners in the club's historical first European trophy win.

The Double-winning team gradually broke up after the European triumph of 1963. Thereafter, the club struggled to rekindle former glories, as key personnel such as Blanchflower and White were lost. Once poetry in an absolute blur of motion, the limbs of Jones now began to creak. By 1967, when a Spurs team fit to challenge for honours had once again been assembled under the auspices of Bill Nicholson, Jones was no longer an automatic choice, watching the team's FA Cup triumph that year from the substitutes' bench. And so, ultimately, in October 1968, Cliff Jones became the last member of the Double-winners of '61 to depart White Hart Lane, moving to Fulham, and bringing down the curtain on a glorious era in the history of Tottenham Hotspur.

DAVE MACKAY

1958-1968

SPURS CAREER

Games	318
Goals	51
Caps	22

MAGIC MOMENT

Captaining Spurs to victory in the 1967 FA Cup final

'THE REAL MACKAY'

IT is unquestionably one of the most iconic images in the history of Tottenham Hotspur, and indeed the wider English game: a snarling Dave Mackay storming towards the whimpering Billy Bremner of Leeds, grabbing a handful of the latter's jersey and, if the picture captures the moment correctly, preparing to kill him. While Spurs have a long tradition of ball-playing teams and individuals with the silkiest skills, fans retain a particularly special place in their affections for those players who exude such commitment they appear willing to run through brick walls – and then crawl over broken glass – just for the privilege of wearing the famous lilywhite shirt. Mackay played for Spurs as if his life depended on it, his commitment almost costing him his very career, as the scars of his twice broken left leg testify. The enduring black-and-white photograph in question was taken in the 1966/67 season, and Mackay, having only just risen like some snarling, barrel-chested phoenix from the flames of the second fracture, was understandably unimpressed by Bremner's attempts to inflict further damage upon that same leg.

The accolades lavished upon Dave Mackay read like a canticle of worship to a deity, a testament to the qualities he brought to White Hart Lane and the magnitude of his contribution in helping to create one of the greatest teams of the century. Spurs' highest ever goalscorer, Jimmy Greaves, describes Mackay as "The greatest player ever to wear to have worn a Tottenham shirt". Team-mates in the 1961 Double team are similarly effusive, Cliff Jones describing Mackay as "The best player I've ever worked with", while Ron Henry once called him "The perfect player. He would bring you back to life". Legendary Portuguese forward Eusebio said of Mackay, after Spurs' European Cup clash with Benfica in 1962, that he was the best wing-half he'd faced in the world. However, possibly the most glowing tribute to Mackay was that bestowed upon him by Bill Nicholson, describing him as "My greatest ever signing".

How might the course of Tottenham Hotspur's history have transpired had Nicholson succeeded in signing one of his other primary transfer targets, Swansea's Mel Charles, the younger brother of fabled Welsh international John? Nicholson set off to travel north, with staff at White Hart Lane expecting him to return with the Welshman in tow. However, Charles chose Arsenal instead, and while his career faded to obscurity Nicholson resumed his pursuit of a previous target, Hearts' Mackay. Nicholson had first noticed Mackay when taking temporary charge of the England Under-23 team against Mackay's Scotland, and considered the player to be in the mould of the great Ron Burgess, captain of the first ever Spurs team to win the League, in 1951. High praise, but as would soon be borne out, entirely merited. Negotiations with Hearts were concluded swiftly, the Scottish club considering that Mackay's history of injuries rendered it good business to complete his sale for £32,000, the highest sum ever paid for a British wing half (eclipsing a record previously held by his new captain at Spurs, Danny Blanchflower). Again, however, hindsight bears witness to the fact that Tottenham were the overwhelming beneficiaries, the signing of Mackay proving one of the most influential in the club's history.

Mackay arrived at White Hart Lane in March 1959, during what is typically referred to in football parlance as a transitional period for the club. Earlier in the campaign Jimmy Anderson had stood down as manager, allowing Bill Nicholson to take over the reins.

After successive top-three finishes, Spurs found themselves struggling to avoid relegation in 1959. The memories of the 1951 League Championship-winning Spurs side had been unceremoniously barged out of the frame by the realities of a survival scrap, and while Nicholson was looking in the long term to fashion a new team of challengers, the immediate priority was maintaining top-flight status. Into such a parlous situation strode the indomitable Mackay, and his impact was immediate. As Nicholson himself recalled, as quoted in Ken Ferris' *The Double*:

'The first day he arrived at our training ground after I bought him, the other players were shaken by his drive and commitment. They looked at each other as if to say, "What's happening here?" We had a bunch of seasoned professionals, most of them internationals, and Mackay was able to stir them all up.'

Mackay's attitude galvanised his colleagues. His abhorrence of defeat was ingrained within him, as evident in casual games of snooker, golf or cards as it was on the football field. It goes without saying that his fiercely competitive nature was evinced in training sessions, as Terry Venables was to discover on his very first day as a Tottenham Hotspur player, when a robust 'welcome' from Mackay ended in the pair coming to blows, as he recalls in *Venables: The Autobiography*:

'As I tried to go by him, Dave hit me right in the balls with his fist. I folded over in agony and fought to get my breath...'

The pair later settled their differences and put the world to rights over a couple of pints, as Mackay was wont to do, but far from having any concerns about the impact of Mackay's attitude upon dressing room harmony, Nicholson embraced the presence of a man with such a ferocious sense of competition:

'He brought a new surge into every aspect of club life, particularly in training. Suddenly training became just as important as the matches. Six-a-side games and full-scale practice matches assumed a greater importance. In practice games he had to be a winner. His barrel chest would be thrust out and he would emerge on the winning side, no matter what the odds.'

Mackay himself suggests that his attitude stemmed from his size as a child, recalling in *FourFourTwo* magazine: 'As a kid I was very small; slim as well.'

It can hardly be considered coincidence that with Mackay added to their ranks, Spurs' results instantly improved. He made a dream debut in a 3-1 win at home to Manchester City, in which his every touch seemed a successful one, as even his mis-kicks flew to team-mates. Noted *The Times* of the match:

'The advent of Mackay, Scotland's captain, at left-half, now gave the whole defence a sensible balance ... Mackay, under the microscopic gaze of English judges, quickly asserted his command.'

The man himself has rather modestly attributed the success of his first Spurs appearance to luck, but given the vigour and determination he brought to the team, the very least one could say would be that in this instance fortune favoured the brave. Niggling injuries meant that Mackay featured in only four of Tottenham's final eight games that season, but his arrival and very presence lifted the players, as they won six and drew two, to finish in the relative safety of 18th. His short-term impact had been undeniable in helping Spurs to avoid relegation, but his long-term influence was to prove instrumental in the most successful period in the club's history.

Mackay struck an instant on-pitch rapport with Danny Blanchflower, the former providing defensive nous to complement the latter's attacking instincts, *The Times* writing of Mackay after his debut, 'Cool, sensible, and poised, a perfect foil to Blanchflower's airier touches'. As a pair they formed the axis upon which the Double-winning Spurs team was built. Mackay's contribution was as readily recognised by the fans as the players, with long-time supporter Alan Granville, recalling:

"His skill rivalled the legendary Blanchflower. To say he had a 'never say die attitude' is an understatement. I always felt with him on the field we just couldn't lose."

Nicholson saw Mackay as the heartbeat, while rating Blanchflower as the brains of the team. Pity then poor Tony Marchi, re-signed in the summer of 1959 from his loan spell at Juventus for £20,000, but destined to earn the reputation as the game's 'finest reserve', as, despite his undoubted quality, he was unable to win a place ahead of Mackay and Blanchflower.

In Mackay's first full season at White Hart Lane Spurs' fortunes improved to the extent that their 1959/60 title challenge fell only at the final hurdle, as the club finished two points behind champions Burnley.

Famously, 1960/61 brought unbounded success. While the campaign is often remembered for feats such as the astonishing run of 11 consecutive wins, and the history books suggest that with 115 goals and 66 points the team was near-invincible, the glory of League and Cup triumph owed much to the contribution of Mackay in some of the crucial, tighter games of the season. In February 1961 Spurs travelled to Villa Park twice in one week, first in the League and then the FA Cup Fifth Round. The League fixture was a tight affair, with pressure mounting on Spurs to maintain their title assault, and both sides also sounding each other out ahead of the Cup clash. However, after a goalless first half Mackay was a central figure in the second, as Spurs registered a 2-1 win ('Mackay, that great chest of his thrust out, with every justification, one might add,' noted *The Times*). There then followed a typically inspirational Mackay performance in the Cup, as his boundless energy left Villa chasing shadows in a 2-0 Spurs win ('It was also a day of mud and thunder, whence Mackay emerged joyfully like some Christy minstrel', was *The Times'* summary of his impact).

Perhaps the most crucial game of Tottenham's league campaign in the Double-winning season was the trip to Sheffield Wednesday in April. Wednesday were the closest challengers to Spurs (eventually finishing second), and had been the first team to beat Tottenham that season. While defeat would not have meant concession of the title, it would most certainly have made for a nervy finale to the campaign – not an occasion for the faint-hearted. Mackay duly rolled up his sleeves and got stuck in as his team required, the early caution he received for his troubles neatly epitomising his attitude to the challenge at hand. Spurs came from behind to win 2-1, and in doing so virtually guaranteed that the title would return to White Hart Lane.

While Mackay's drive and determination were unparalleled, it is worth stressing that his style of play, though hard, was also fair, as a matter of great pride. Jimmy Greaves has emphasised that he adhered to a strict code of conduct, describing him in his autobiography as 'a lawmaker rather than a lawbreaker.' Recalled Bill Nicholson, in *The Double*:

'He brought many players tumbling to the ground with the ferocity of his tackling, but was always scrupulously fair, always going for the ball. He had a strict code of conduct. He tackled robustly but always fairly, and expected similar treatment from himself. But if anyone went outside the rules he became very angry indeed.'

In the case for the defence of this claim, Exhibit A would presumably be *that* Mackay-Bremner photograph. The picture is considered by generations of Spurs fans to epitomise the man's ferocious aggression and competitive nature, although Mackay himself has pointed out, in *FourFourTwo* magazine:

'I don't like the picture because it portrays me as a bully – he's smaller than me and I'm picking him up. I'm not a bully and I don't like bullies, but he kicked the broken leg and that really annoyed me. I could've killed him that day.'

While Mackay undoubtedly added an edge to Spurs, for him to be remembered as an uncouth and agricultural spoiler – due to the photograph of him about to devour Bremner – would be a fallacy, for Dave Mackay was a hugely talented footballer. Opponents would typically be treated to the sight of Mackay emerging from the players' tunnel and out onto the pitch with a ball in his hands, which he would hurl high into the air, and then trap perfectly with his instep, as if laying down the gauntlet. Terry Venables is one of many to recall that he would even offer the ball to opponents before a game with the words, "You'd better have a kick now" – a taunt later to be repeated by no less a magician of the game than Glenn Hoddle.

Tales also abound of Mackay's exquisite skills on the training ground. Bill Nicholson has recalled the players being asked to volley a ball against a wall continuously, alternating feet, and not letting the ball touch the ground, saying in Jeremy Novick's *Winning Their Spurs*, 'If a player does between 12 and 15 he's doing well. Mackay will get 20 to 25'. Venables again has spoken of Mackay making mincemeat of some of the more convoluted exercises set by coach Eddie Bailey, as team-mates struggled to cope, while Mackay himself recalls competitions with Cliff Jones and John White to play keepy-uppy with coins, saying of the art of flicking a coin into his top pocket, "It's quite difficult..."

Mackay had almost missed the FA Cup final of 1961, having sustained a leg injury while playing for Scotland without shin pads. His fearless attitude meant that injury lay-offs were a frequent blight on his career. When Spurs sought to defend their League crown in 1961/62, Mackay missed numerous early season games, and the team managed just five wins from their first ten games. As the season wore on, glory beckoned in the club's debut season in Europe, as they reached the semi-final of the European Cup. Following a controversial first leg in Portugal, in which they had two goals questionably disallowed for offside, and hit the woodwork three times, Spurs brought Benfica back to White Hart Lane facing a 3-1 deficit. In the dying seconds of the return leg, Spurs had forged ahead 2-1, and therefore trailed 4-3 on aggregate, when a Mackay shot rattled the woodwork and flew back out, as reported by *The Times*:

'Mackay, that roaring lion, was left shaking his fist at the skies as that last shot of his ricocheted with a sickening thud off the Benfica crossbar.'

Pity those skies which felt Mackay's wrath. Few familiar with that season's competition doubt that Spurs would have gone on to claim the ultimate prize had they won the semi-final (as it happened Benfica beat Real Madrid 5-3 in the final), but instead of being the hero of the hour, Mackay, along with his team-mates, was left to rue what might have been. Going out to Benfica, he says, in *Winning Their Spurs*, was 'My biggest disappointment in the game.'

Despite the defeat to Benfica, Tottenham at that time were a mighty force, and the spirit amongst the players was buoyant. Tony Marchi recalls in *The Double*, 'The camaraderie was brilliant – everyone used to have a go at each other.' Mackay himself recalls the atmosphere in the squad being a happy one, and was himself evidently one of the key social officers in the camp. In an era, perhaps never to return, in which players and fans regularly mixed, Mackay was often to be found chatting to team-mates and fans alike, after games or training, in the Bell and Hare pub near the ground. Indeed, fan Matt Fletcher recalls:

"My memory is not from his playing days but from merely two or three years ago. I was in The Corner Pin pub in the corner of Park Lane and in walked Dave Mackay. A table was given up to him (ironically with *that* famous photo above it) and he held court, chatting to people, shaking hands and signing whatever came to hand."

Mackay's mischievous contribution to the general bonhomie in that greatest ever Spurs team is almost as legendary as his on-pitch impact. Here was a man who, before a game, would tease his giant defensive team-mate Maurice Norman with the words, "What's going to happen today love? Are you going to be alright?" Come Spurs' crucial league encounter against Sheffield Wednesday, in April 1961, with the League title at stake, Mackay's sense of mischief still came to the fore. Running back with the ball towards his own goal, he drew his foot back as if to blast the ball at his own goalkeeper, a prank seemingly pulled with the sole purpose of prompting coronary failure amongst his team-mates and the White Hart Lane faithful. In that same game, as reported in *The Double*, journalist Ken Jones (cousin of Spurs winger Cliff) recalls Mackay preparing to take one of his trademark long throws, then turning to him to say "You can have 6-1 that Smithy won't get his head on this". It may seem slightly incongruous that a man so driven towards winning could display such a sense of humour in the midst of battle – but nobody in their right mind would ever question Mackay's attitude. He, it seems, was that particularly rare beast; a man who could be both fiercely competitive, yet retain a sense of perspective.

Spurs went on to win the 1962 FA Cup final, and consequently had another stab at European glory the following season, in the European Cup Winners' Cup. While the 'Super Spurs', as they were popularly nicknamed, are best remembered for winning the Double, the team, still based upon the Mackay-Blanchflower axis, enjoyed one final season of success in 1962/63, before it gradually began to disband. After a barnstorming start to their league campaign, in which they scored 4 goals or more in a dozen different games before Christmas, a particularly severe winter created a fixture backlog, and just 3 wins from their final 10 league games meant they finished second. For the Super Spurs, the last chance of glory was the European Cup Winners' Cup.

Mackay was to play another pivotal role in this campaign, and it is some measure of his performances during the 1962/63 season that he was named runner-up in the Footballer of the Year awards, to Stanley Matthews. In the First Round Cup Winners' Cup tie he created the opening goal for Jimmy Greaves, which silenced the feverish Ibrox support and smoothed Spurs' passage. In the following Round the level of responsibility on Mackay's shoulders was heightened by the absence of the injured Blanchflower. Two decades later, when Spurs went on to record another famous European triumph, they did so without their regular skipper, Steve Perryman, suspended for the 1984 Uefa Cup final, and renowned hard-man Graham Roberts assumed the captain's armband and rose to the challenge.

In 1963, the example was set by Spurs' original defensive enforcer, as Mackay led the team on the pitch in the absence of the regular captain. Under his auspices Spurs triumphed 6-2 on aggregate over Slovan Bratislava, to reach the semi-final against OFK Belgrade. The first leg, in the imposing Red Army Stadium in Belgrade, was to prove one of the classic Mackay performances, for Jimmy Greaves had been sent off after 55 minutes, leaving Spurs to battle with ten men. The Belgrade players would presumably have been buoyed by the sending off of an opponent, but the situation thereby created was the sort Mackay relished. He duly rolled up his sleeves and inspired a magnificent defensive performance to hep Tottenham take a 2-1 lead back to White Hart Lane. He then scored the first goal of the second leg, as Spurs eventually ran out 5-2 aggregate winners, to qualify for the final.

Tottenham became the first British team to win a European trophy when they beat the holders Atlético Madrid on 15 May 1963, but they did so that day without their inspiration en route to the final; in a cruel twist of fate Mackay was forced to miss out due to a pelvic injury sustained in the line of national duty.

It is desperately unfortunate for Mackay that injuries sustained in the heat of battle played such a significant role in his Spurs career. Recalled Cliff Jones, prior to that Cup Winners' Cup final, as quoted in *Tottenham Hotspur The Official Illustrated History*:

'With Dave in the team we feel we can match anyone … Without him, the odds change.' Fortunately however, Spurs produced a superlative performance, with Terry Dyson playing a starring role in a glorious 5-1 victory. Nevertheless, it would be a travesty to overlook the talismanic contribution of Mackay in helping Spurs win the Cup, and few would dispute that the trophy, and the glory of Tottenham's first European triumph, was as much his as his team-mates'. It was a momentous night, and an achievement which continues to resonate several decades on. Legend even has it that as the team paraded the trophy on a lap of honour, Mackay was seen to shed tears.

That victory however, was to prove the end of an era. Terry Medwin was forced out of the game that summer through injury, and Blanchflower's retirement followed in November. Mackay was the obvious choice to replace Blanchflower as captain – indeed, Bill Nicholson regularly stated that Mackay would already have been captain had it not been for the presence of the Irishman. However, just a month after Blanchflower retired,

Mackay's injury curse struck again, as he sustained a double break to his left leg after 20 minutes of a league match against Manchester United. It was a blow sufficiently significant to end the season, even for a warrior of his ilk, and it was 16 weeks before he even had his cast removed. Nine gruelling months of recuperation followed, but cursed with outrageous bad fortune, his determination to return saw him launch himself into a typically full-blooded challenge on his return match – for Spurs' reserves against Shrewsbury – and he broke the same leg.

Spurs had begun the 1963/64 season well, and indeed had led the First Division at various points before Christmas, but the sudden loss of both Mackay and Blanchflower proved seismic blows, and understandably the team faltered, finishing sixth, and then, again without Mackay for much of 1964/65, eighth. Nicholson re-built, and Mackay returned, moving back into defence. After the injury-plagued anguish of missing the 1963 Cup Winners' Cup final, and breaking his leg twice, few could begrudge Mackay one final moment of glory at Tottenham. It arrived on 20 May 1967 as he joined select band of Tottenham legends in becoming only the fourth man to skipper the team to victory in the competition to which the club has its fondest links, the FA Cup.

Mackay represented one of the last vestiges of the Double-winning team, for while Cliff Jones was an unused substitute in the 1967 final, every other member of the 1961 team had departed. By 1967 Mackay's Spurs team-mates included Jennings, Knowles, Mullery, England and Gilzean. The team enjoyed a degree of good fortune on the road to Wembley, meeting lower-league opponents in each of the third, fourth, fifth, and sixth rounds, before overcoming high-flying Nottingham Forest in the semi-final. However, silverware was the least the team merited, given that they had embarked on a remarkable 28-game sequence after Boxing Day, in which their only defeat was to eventual champions Manchester United. They finished a creditable third in the League, and Wembley then hosted its first ever all-London final as Spurs faced the glamour-boys of Chelsea. After Jimmy Robertson had given Tottenham a first-half lead, Frank Saul doubled the advantage in the second half, after a trademark long Mackay throw, a technique likened by Jimmy Greaves to a dead ball delivery for accuracy and potency. Chelsea scored a late consolation goal, but when referee Kenneth Dagnall blew for full-time, he confirmed a fifth FA Cup victory for Tottenham. As well as a triumph for the club, it was a fitting personal reward for Mackay, after the injury hardships he had had to endure, to lead the team up Wembley's 39 steps – or 'John Buchan way', as he dubbed them – and lift the FA Cup for Spurs.

It effectively proved the finale to Mackay's Spurs career, and the following summer he left White Hart Lane. At 33 years of age, the decision of Nicholson to release him was understandable, the ravages of time having seen him move from midfield to defence, and it was widely expected he would return home, north of the border, to Hearts. Instead however, he was picked up by Brian Clough at Derby County, and immediately appointed club captain. Mackay duly led his new team to the Second Division title in his debut season, also collecting the Footballer of the Year award. Such an astonishing Indian summer to his career is, on reflection, unsurprising for one of the game's born winners, but it nevertheless raised the issue of whether Tottenham had been premature in letting him go, particularly as Spurs themselves struggled to replace him and recapture the glory years of the early 1960s.

The fact that he later managed Derby to the First Division title in 1974/75 raises a further question, of whether he ought to have been considered the man to succeed Bill Nicholson at White Hart Lane, rather than Brian Clough at the Baseball Ground. Certainly the issue of managerial succession at Tottenham was a messy affair, the outgoing Nicholson having sought to have Danny Blanchflower involved, while the board eventually opted, somewhat bizarrely, for Terry Neill. One wonders whether Mackay might have proved the more successful option, but such thoughts reside firmly in the realm of the hypothetical.

At Spurs however, the Scot remains a hero, as cheery a gentleman off the pitch as he was tenacious on it, whilst also blessed with natural skill in abundance. It is a lament passed from one generation to the next, that Tottenham Hotspur have had no other player quite like Dave Mackay.

JIMMY GREAVES

'GREAVSIE'

1961-1970

SPURS CAREER

Games	379
Goals	266
Caps	57
Goals	44

MAGIC MOMENT

Scoring a hat-trick on debut for Spurs, a sure sign of things to come

THREE minutes into the 1962 FA Cup final, the first major final of his career, Jimmy Greaves made his mark. Having collected a Bobby Smith header, Greaves found himself forced away from goal some 20 yards out, but gambled on an early surprise shot. It was not an immensely powerful effort; rather, he seemed to caress the ball goalwards. It was a touch ordained from on high, however, stroked between a melee of legs and beyond goalkeeper Adam Blacklaw, a convoluted path seemingly too small for a golf ball, let alone a football. Nevertheless, the conclusion was that of 265 other occasions – Greaves had scored for Spurs. It was the first in a 3-1 victory, as Spurs won the FA Cup for the fourth time in their history. That he should have scored from what could barely be classified a 'half-chance' merits little more than a shrug of acceptance, for an air of inevitability hung even over half-chances when Greaves was the recipient. That afternoon, the greatest stage in the domestic game was the platform upon which were showcased the talents of the greatest goalscorer in the history of Tottenham Hotspur FC, and, in the opinions of many, the history of the English game.

What does one add to the team that has everything? That was the question facing Bill Nicholson after Spurs destroyed all-comers in romping to the Double in 1961, the first team to do so that century.

Nicholson could have been forgiven for casting a cursory glance upon his forward line, giving a nod of satisfaction and moving on to examine other areas of the team, for goals were hardly in short supply. In winning the First Division that season Spurs had recorded their highest ever total in a single League campaign with a staggering 115 goals, as well as a further 21 en route to their FA Cup triumph. They had flown in from all angles, with an attack comprising Bobby Smith and Les Allen, amassing 50 League goals between them, while Cliff Jones, Terry Dyson and John White had also reached double figures. And yet, despite this, Nicholson's decision was that the only player capable of making the best even better was James Peter Greaves.

Given Spurs' feats in the preceding season, when Greaves arrived at White Hart Lane he was under some pressure to prove that he was worthy of such exalted company, both to fans, enjoying a strict diet of success, and new team-mates alike. His pedigree was certainly impressive, even then, at the tender age of 21. From his debut at Chelsea as a 17-year-old in August 1957, to his departure to Italy at the end of the 1960/61 season, he had scored 124 goals in 157 games for the club, finishing as the top scorer in the First Division twice in the process.

The fact that Bill Nicholson, a manager whose judgement of both the quality and temperament of a player was of the highest order, should identify Greaves as worthy of joining the all-conquering Spurs, ought in itself to have been sufficient commendation to doubters. Nicholson had apparently been alerted to the possibility of Greaves signing for Tottenham while the striker was still a Chelsea player, in the middle of negotiations over his move to Milan. Nicholson has recalled meeting Greaves at a dinner at London's Café Royal, when the latter mentioned how, hypothetically, he would have loved to have played in the Double-winning Spurs team. Fast-forward a few months, and word was beginning to emerge of Greaves' unhappiness in Italy. While the early indications were that his eye for goal remained as keen as ever (he ended with 9 goals in 12 games for Milan), as an East End boy with a young family he had found it difficult to adjust to life in Italy, and Nicholson duly seized the moment.

The Tottenham manager had gone to some lengths to ease the pressure on the shoulders of his new charge. To the delight of pub-quiz enthusiasts the world over, Greaves arrived at White Hart Lane for the peculiar price tag of £99,999, a sum stipulated by the manager in order to avoid saddling Greaves with the reputation as the first player to command a six-figure transfer fee.

Greaves has stated in his autobiography that he received a 'polite but guarded welcome' on walking into the Tottenham dressing room for the first time in December 1961. The Tottenham squad was a close-knit one of just 17 players who had become the best team in the land and knew it. That they wondered why they needed a new player in their ranks, and particularly why a striker, given their sensational goalscoring form the previous season, is understandable. In time of course, such reservations seem laughable, and are now consigned to the annals, replaced by glowing tributes. Dave Mackay has described Greaves thus, in *Match of my Life*:

'Without doubt the most natural goalscorer that I ever played with during my football career … We knew that when Jimmy was one on one with a goalkeeper it was a goal. Other players, if they were through on a keeper six times would maybe score four. Jimmy would score all the time. If we were under pressure, often the ball would be knocked up to Jimmy 40 yards out; he'd take the defence on and score a great goal.'

Initially, however, the players reserved judgement. The fans, by contrast, were more swiftly won over, Greaves taking just 90 minutes to allay any concerns. Having already scored a brace for the reserves in a victory at Plymouth – that first game in Tottenham colours attracting a staggering 14,000 spectators – rather inevitably for a man who was to score on debut for every professional team for which he played, he found the net in his first Tottenham game proper – and in some style. Spurs fan Michael Grayeff takes up the story:

"It was against Blackpool, the last Saturday before Christmas, December 1961, and we had our usual spot 'Behind the Boards' (later known as the Shelf), level with the Park Lane penalty area. To be quite honest, for 30 minutes Greaves just ambled around, contributing little to the match. Then: a throw-in from the right, helped on and Greaves with an overhead scissor kick into the back of the net! We screamed ourselves hoarse, banging the wooden planking with our hands, delirious with excitement…"

Greaves went on to complete a hat-trick, a suitable portent of the astonishing feats his White Hart Lane career would bring. For Spurs fans it was love at first sight, the 5-2 final score that day a mere footnote. He quickly became renowned as a striker so prolific he simply belied comparisons, with spectators buzzing in anticipation every time he received the ball. That famous scissors-kick with which Greaves opened his Tottenham account has been widely hailed by press and spectators alike as one of the all-time greats, with *The Times* reporting:

'It was Greaves who showed the way with as electrifying an effort as one has seen all season. As Medwin, lurking at inside left, headed on a long throw-in by Mackay, the ball sped across the Blackpool area some three or four feet off the ground. Greaves, all alone, was surrounded by tangerine. Leaping horizontally, like a high jumper performing the western roll, he volleyed the ball left footed to the roof of the Blackpool net from some 10 yards. Walters [Blackpool's goalkeeper] could have only heard the ball. It was quick as light, an act only within the range of men like Pele, of Brazil, Koesis in his Hungarian days, or perhaps Charlton of a few seasons ago. The crowd rose as one.

The ground was a sea of waving handkerchiefs, scarves, hats and arms, a rich salute for a special goal.'

Even Greaves himself typically mentions it when asked to recall his career favourites – and this from a total list of 465. However, such acrobatics were unusual for him, as was the headed effort with which he also scored that day. His reputation was not forged on spectacular crashes and bangs, for he was instead blessed with uncanny positional sense and anticipation, and an almost psychic awareness of the whereabouts of the goal. He did not blast in many long-range efforts. Merely caressing the ball into the net was sufficient, because the hard work had typically been done already in his movement, control, pace and awareness. It has frequently been said of Greaves – not least by the man himself in his autobiography – that his finishing style was that of placing the ball, rather than hammering it:

'Whenever I was presented with an opportunity, I never hit the ball with all the power I could muster because I didn't have to. When I saw an opening, I would simply "pass" the ball through the space knowing no one could reach it'.

It was a description he had attached to a goal in his early Chelsea career, but it might as well have been the opening gambit in a thesis on his career-long scoring technique.

That Greaves had such wondrous natural ability was just as well, for his work-rate – or lack thereof – gained some notoriety. This, after all, was a man of whom an exasperated Bill Nicholson once said "All he did this afternoon was score those four goals." Looking back on his career, in an interview with the *Daily Telegraph*, Greaves delivers one of the great understatements of our time: 'I didn't go along with coaching. My job was to score goals, that's it, the rest of it didn't affect me,' while in an interview with the *Guardian* he is even more trenchant: 'Training was a pain.'

The lifestyle of Greaves would have had modern-day nutritionists spluttering into their isotonic drinks, for his pre-match meal typically comprised a full roast and his visits to the dressing-room toilet would invariably see cigarette smoke rising from the cubicle, while his fondness for the bottle, as is well-known, eventually degenerated to a full-blown alcoholism he worked hard to conquer. Martin Chivers recalls in his autobiography, *Big Chiv*, how one morning at pre-season training, as the players sweated their way through one of Nicholson's infamous cross-country excursions, Greaves thumbed down a lorry and hitched a lift all the way back to the training ground.

The notion of Greaves opting to avoid an arduous training session by hopping on the back of a lorry when his manager's back was turned will surprise few who remember him in his Tottenham days, for as well as being a goalscorer *par excellence*, much of his popularity also stemmed from his celebrated and irrepressible sense of mischief. Greaves played the game with a smile on his face and a twinkle in his eye. As former team-mate Terry Venables recalls, in *Venables The Autobiography*: 'Jim never seemed to take football seriously ... Nothing seemed to bother him on the pitch.'

Another former team-mate, Alan Gilzean, recalled in *Tottenham Hotspur 101 Great Goals*:

'He was a great character, Greavsie, there was never a dull moment. Team meetings, on the park – even in the tensest of moments he always found the funny side of it ... No matter how tense it was Greavsie always enjoyed it.'

It was therefore little surprise that, during England's crunch World Cup game against Brazil in 1962, when proceedings were interrupted by a dog making its way onto the pitch and waltzing around all attempts at capture, Greaves was to be seen getting down on all fours to entice the animal to him (and doing so successfully). Seemingly always on the look-out for an opportunity to cause mischief, he became renowned as one of the primary instigators of practical jokes in a jovial Tottenham camp. He had reliable sidekicks in the form of Messrs Venables, Mackay and Gilzean, and team-mates who let their guard down could typically find themselves on the receiving end of some training ground prank, as Greaves recalls in his autobiography:

'We were forever playing tricks on one another and having a lark ... One popular prank was to squeeze shampoo on someone's head as he was in the process of rinsing his hair of the shampoo he had already applied. We'd be in fits watching Frank Saul or Cyril Knowles frantically trying to rinse their hair wondering why on earth there was still so much shampoo.'

Nor did he have any qualms about selecting victims whilst on the pitch. During a game against Leicester City in 1965, as he waited to take a penalty, opposing goalkeeper Gordon Banks prepared for the kick by wiping his hands against one of the goalposts. Greaves took the opportunity to roll the ball into the empty net, as Banks remained by the woodwork, and in a strangely satisfying conclusion, the referee actually allowed the goal to stand. Naturally this incurred the chagrin of Banks, but, as Greaves recalls in his autobiography, the goalkeeper's protests were waved away by the commendably free-spirited official, who explained, "I played advantage ... best law there is".

Unsurprisingly, this impish trait further endeared Greaves to his fast-growing legion of worshippers. Just as, several decades later, another player of wondrous natural ability and irresistible cheek would take White Hart Lane by storm, in the form of the irrepressible Paul Gascoigne, so Jimmy Greaves effortlessly won over the public in his role as loveable rascal with incredible talent. Greaves' charm and razor-sharp wit later qualified him as a star of the small screen, in such television gems as *Saint and Greavsie*, and, more latterly, as a popular speaker on the after-dinner circuit.

Back in his playing days, Spurs began the 1961/62 season looking to defend their Division One crown. Ultimately, they fell just short, finishing third, four points behind eventual champions Ipswich. Statistically therefore, a 3-1 defeat at home to Ipswich (Greaves, inevitably, scoring the only Spurs goal) in March 1962 could be said to have cost Spurs the title, and psychologically too it was a defining moment, as the blow felt by Spurs was inversely proportional to the boost afforded Ipswich. More broadly, also to blame was a poor run of League form in the midst of which that defeat came, with the team recording just one League win between 1 January and 24 March. However, perhaps most telling in Spurs' unsuccessful defence of the title was the club's involvement in other competitions – the FA Cup and, for the first time, the European Cup.

The 1961/62 seasons marked Spurs' debut season in European competition, and Greaves' excitement at partaking in such occasions was that of a giddy child on Christmas morning. The European Cup was only seven years old, and no London team had at that point qualified for the competition. In an era in which song from the terraces was the exception rather than the norm, on those historic Wednesday nights a floodlit White Hart Lane would reverberate to the strains of a 60,000-strong chorus of "Glory, Glory Hallelujah", a cacophony which Greaves recalls had the hairs standing up on the back of his neck.

Having been an AC Milan player at the start of the tournament Greaves was ruled ineligible until the semi-final stage of the competition, when Spurs took on Benfica over two Legs, eventually losing the first Leg 3-1 whilst having two goals controversially ruled out. Greaves has long been adamant that the club suffered from officiating so poor it was downright suspicious, and while inclined, albeit through gritted teeth, to be phlegmatic about the generous attitude of the officials towards Benfica's ultra-physical approach, he has been unrestrained in his criticism of the decisions to disallow two Tottenham goals that night. The second was from Greaves himself, which was described by *The Times* as, 'A hairline decision indeed'. Instead of marking his European bow with a goal, Greaves was left cursing the officials, his anger only tempered by evident bewilderment, as reported in *Tottenham Hotspur The Official Illustrated History*: 'I beat the full-back before I scored and was still given offside.'

The bubbling atmosphere at White Hart Lane for the return leg epitomised all that Greaves loved about European nights at Spurs, as Tottenham set out to overturn the deficit to another deafening soundtrack of "Glory, Glory Hallelujah" from the White Hart Lane faithful. With the floodlights on and the stadium full to capacity, the stage was set for something momentous – yet while memorable, the night was to prove another one of intense frustration and disappointment, for the club in general and Greaves in particular. Benfica promptly tore up the script by scoring after 15 minutes, leaving Spurs facing a 4-1 aggregate deficit. Tottenham pulled one back ten minutes later through John White, before Greaves was then given fresh reason to vent his spleen at the officials. Smith crossed, Greaves stole between two defenders and the ball duly nestled in the net. However, after already awarding the goal, Swiss referee Aage Poulsen Esquire consulted his linesman – vigorously waving his flag – and disallowed the effort. Greaves, in his autobiography, describes in succinct and mildly comical style the clash of cultures – East End versus European – in the exchange which followed:

"King offside? Whatdya mean 'king offside?'

I was furious.

'Orf-side,' said Mr Poulsen.'

Greaves was left cursing the referee, ruing the day, and muttering that most famous Tottenham refrain, "If only..."

The defeat to Benfica marked the end of one part of the triple-pronged stab at glory in 1961/62. As remarked, Spurs' League challenge also floundered, but the season would nevertheless end with silverware, in the FA Cup. In contrast to the modern era, in which the importance of the FA Cup has gradually diminished beside the lucre of other competitions, in the 1960s it still held immense prestige and allure. Greaves himself described Cup competition at that time in his autobiography, as 'caviar', compared to 'the bread-and-butter' of League games, claiming, 'There was more glory attached to winning the Cup than the League Championship' – and intimating that Tottenham as a team preferred the glamour of those Cup games.

Just as Greaves' name is indelibly etched in Tottenham's European history, so he was to play an instrumental role in the illustrious FA Cup tradition so definitive of the club. He played in every game of Spurs' victorious 1961/62 FA Cup campaign, netting eight times on the road to Wembley, with a goal in every round bar the semi-final. Amidst the headlines of the eventual Wembley triumph, it is easy to forget such footnotes as the Third Round, but having trailed 3-0 at half-time to Birmingham City at that stage, Greaves' strike in that game, helping to earn a 3-3 draw and replay, was to prove as crucial as his later strike at Wembley.

The 1962 FA Cup final was against tough opposition, a Burnley side that had pipped Spurs to second place in Division One, but Greaves' early goal set Spurs on their way to a 3-1 victory, and their star striker to his first winners' medal with the club.

1962/63 was Greaves' first full season as a Tottenham Hotspur player, a watershed he marked by scoring the highest ever number of League goals for the club in a single season. Even by his own uniquely high standards, 37 League goals in one season was an astonishing figure. Notable amongst these was one of a brace in the 4-0 win at home to Leicester City, in November 1962, when he collected the ball near halfway and danced around seemingly half the Leicester team, plus goalkeeper Gordon Banks, before tapping the ball into the net. It was a masterclass in balance, control, stamina, speed and bloody-minded determination to score at the expense of all other considerations. A once-in-a-lifetime achievement – or so one would think, and for most other footballers it would indeed have been. For Greaves however, it was merely a prototype. He scored enough of these to turn it into a trademark of his career. A similar effort against Manchester United, in a 5-1 thrashing in October 1965, had him again easing past one opponent after another, seemingly gaining pace with the ball at his feet while opponents slowed down, before rounding goalkeeper Pat Dunne and passing the ball into the empty net. Leicester City were again the hapless lambs led to the White Hart Lane slaughter in October 1968, as Greaves embarked on a one-man demolition of his opponents. Long-time fan Gary Wright recalls:

"Pat Jennings kicked the ball to Jimmy standing on the halfway line, in front of the Shelf. Instant control on his instep took him diagonally towards the Paxton Road end goal. He beat the first man, and accelerated past the second with a deft swivel and dip of his right shoulder. He straightened his run on goal and dragged the ball back and away from the third defender. The crowd was now beginning to expect something special and an almost deathly silence fell as we held our collective breath. By this stage Jimmy was facing the goal. He drew the next defender and put him on his backside, as the next fall guy entered the frame. In a split second Jimmy slid the ball past him to face Peter Shilton. The young goalkeeper made his move towards Jimmy's feet – too late. Jimmy casually slid the ball past the prone Shilton, and it rolled sublimely into the net just inside the post on the Shelf side."

It is a goal remembered by many as possibly his finest, with another fan John Peddubriwny pointing out:

"Although the TV wasn't there that day, the press snappers got a picture of the goal. There was a line of Leicester players each down on one knee with their other legs stretched out. That was how quick it was."

Greaves had a penchant for rounding the goalkeeper and slotting the ball home, as fan Tony Marken puts it, "like he was playing a game in the local park". When asked, on a recent BBC question and answer session, why such a style is rarely seen in the modern game, Greaves quipped, "Strikers just haven't got the ability to do it these days!"

Greaves' form in 1962/63 had brought him 24 goals in 24 games by Boxing Day, at which point Spurs were second in the First Division. However, the fixture list was then thrown into disarray by the weather, with thick snow resulting in just two League games and one FA Cup match played by the club from that point until early March. Tottenham were to finish the season second in the First Division, with Greaves' 37-goal haul the platform for a total of 111 League goals by the team that season, the highest by any club in the Football League that campaign. Again, a realistic tilt at the Championship had suffered for Cup commitments, but on this occasion the European trail was to provide ample compensation, as Greaves' love affair with European fare at the Lane continued.

Spurs actually only played three ties in reaching that season's European Cup Winners' Cup final. Greaves scored in the away Leg against Glasgow Rangers and in the home leg against Slovan Bratislava, before reaching a career lowlight in the semi-final First Leg away to OFK Belgrade. In a contest the feistiness of which was typical of contemporary European away days, tempers flared and blood flowed. After one mid-pitch free-for-all had already ensued, another difference of opinions led to Greaves aiming a punch at one Blagomir Krivokuca, in the opposition ranks. For the record it was one of the few occasions in his career in which Greaves missed his intended target, but the referee nevertheless took a dim view of such attempted pugilism, and Greaves became the first Tottenham player since Cyril Poynton in 1928 to be sent off. While Greaves recalls in his autobiography that an early bath in the in the Belgrade changing room was impossible – 'the water had just been run and was like molten lead' – he had to sit out the rest of the game and the Second Leg. However, the team triumphed in his absence, and he was restored to the line-up for the final, in Feyenoord's Rotterdam stadium, against Cup-holders Atlético Madrid.

Greaves has frequently described the game as the greatest in which he ever played, and it certainly ranks as one of, if not the, finest result in Tottenham Hotspur's history. Atlético were highly competent – second in the Spanish Primera League – but no match for a rampant Spurs, who were to triumph 5-1. While Spurs' record goalscorer featured twice on the scoresheet (breaking the deadlock with a penalty area poacher's goal, before converting a Terry Dyson cross in the second half), the hero of the hour was to be Dyson, who scored a brace, as well as creating two and generally slicing Atlético to ribbons.

The result was hugely historic. As the first British team to win a European trophy Spurs immeasurably boosted the profile of the British game on the continent, but the very achievement of winning the trophy itself is not to be underestimated. Unlike in the modern era, in which the Cup Winners' Cup was eventually discontinued with the cream of European club football competing in the creatively-named Champions' League, in the 1960s the Cup Winners' Cup still featured many of the continent's greatest club sides. Although only three years old, the competition ranked alongside the European Cup in terms of quality. Greaves has written that the memories of European nights, good and bad, at White Hart Lane, are amongst his most cherished, on account of the atmosphere created by all those connected to the club, willing the team to victory. However, Tottenham's own proud European heritage is itself due largely to the contribution made by their star striker in those nascent years of European competition. As with so many others, on the chapter in Tottenham Hotspur history on European glory nights, the name Jimmy Greaves is writ large.

It was a glorious time, the side of 1962/63 comparing in quality to the Double-winners of 1961. Any player would have revelled within such a team, and Greaves certainly benefited from playing in such a formidable Spurs line-up. Alas, *sic transit gloria mundia*, and following the glory of Spurs' Cup Winners' Cup triumph in 1963, the all-conquering team was gradually dismantled, and the side underwent several seasons of transition. After the second-placed finish in 1963 Tottenham finished fourth and sixth in the following seasons – yet Greaves' goalscoring prowess remained undiminished, as he amassed 35 and 29 League goals respectively in these campaigns, ending as the First Division's top goalscorer in each. By this time the perfect attacking foil for him had arrived at White Hart Lane, in the form of Scottish striker Alan Gilzean, and the pair would form a lethal partnership affectionately bestowed by fans with the moniker 'The G-Men'. Greaves has professed that he was never happier than when playing with Gilzean, and the sense of admiration was evidently mutual, the Scot noting in *Tottenham Hotspur 101 Great Goals*:

'The fella was a great player, he was gifted by God, he could turn so quickly … In the box he always had time, he had a split-second more than any other player, and that is the difference between an ordinary player and a great player.'

The 1965/66 season culminated in England's victorious World Cup campaign, a bittersweet experience for Greaves, as has been well documented. Having begun the tournament as England's first-choice striker, a challenge from France's Joseph Bonnel in England's third and final group game left Greaves needing 14 stitches in his left leg. Although he was back to fitness by the time of the final, manager Alf Ramsey understandably did not at that stage want to alter the team, and Greaves was left to witness England's finest hour from the sidelines.

Perhaps less well known is the Herculean effort made by Greaves even to make the England team at all for the World Cup. Seven months before the start of the tournament he had been struck down by hepatitis, and although he returned to action in February 1966 he faced a race against time to achieve optimum fitness and force his way back into the international reckoning. However, 15 goals in 29 appearances for Spurs that season earned him a place in the England squad for a World Cup warm-up tour of Scandinavia, where a four-goal haul against Norway made it impossible to omit him from the World Cup squad. Greaves finally received a World Cup winners' medal in June 2009, and boasts the phenomenal scoring record of 44 goals in just 57 international appearances.

In the 1966/67 season Greaves netted 25 goals in 38 First Division appearances as the rebuilt Spurs team climbed from the previous season's eighth to third, but again the FA Cup proved the route to glory for the club. Only Greaves, Cliff Jones and Dave Mackay survived from the club's previous FA Cup triumph of 1962. If anything, in that interim period Greaves' goals had papered over the cracks of the evolving team, but the triumph of 1967 was well-deserved by a side beginning to gel and play the Tottenham way. Greaves scored six goals en route to Wembley that year, the most notable of which was his opener against Nottingham Forest in the semi-final. Poacher's goals were the man's trademark, the majestic 'pass' into the net his signature and the occasional mesmeric lengthy solo run not unusual, but his goal against Forest that afternoon at Hillsborough was a real collector's item – a long-range half-volley, after being teed up by the head of Gilzean. As reported by Geoffrey Green in *The Times*:

'But for a single stroke of genius that changed the course of the match – a 20 yard volley, left foot, from Greaves that went home like greased lightning off the inside of a post – every major role might have been changed.'

Greaves may be idolised at White Hart Lane, but his name is probably banned from utterance at the City Ground, Nottingham, given his record of 24 career goals against Forest. Spurs won the semi-final by the odd goal in three, and travelled to Wembley to face Chelsea. While Greaves wrote of a happy, tight-knit atmosphere in the Spurs camp that season, buoyed by the Cup-run, the mood in the Chelsea dressing room was widely reported to be considerably less jovial, and in the run-up to the final stories emerged of disagreements and disputes within the camp. Goals from Frank Saul and Jimmy Robertson were enough to give Spurs a 2-1 win, making it five FA Cup final wins in five appearances, and a second winners' medal in the competition for Greaves.

It was to prove his last piece of silverware at the club. Spurs made an early exit from the following season's European Cup Winners' Cup, and finished seventh in the

League, Greaves recording 26 League and Cup goals. In 1968 he retired from international football aged just 28, a decision which ought to go down as one of the darkest moments in the history of the national team, but the loss of Alf Ramsey's England was undoubtedly the gain of Bill Nicholson's Tottenham, as that season he recorded 4 hat-tricks on the way to a tally of 27 League and 9 Cup goals, including his 200th for the club.

The 1969/70 season was Greaves' final one at White Hart Lane. With Bill Nicholson looking to give youth its head the team finished in its lowest League standing for over a decade, ending the campaign in 12th. In January 1970 the FA Cup, so frequently at the hub of the club's achievements during his Tottenham career, was to prove a depressing finale to Greaves' time at White Hart Lane. A single Crystal Palace goal in the fourth round tie, from Gerry Queen, consigned Spurs to a 1-0 defeat, prompting the *Daily Express* headline: 'Queen is King at the Palace'. For Greaves, however, his time upon the White Hart Lane throne was over. He was one of a number of players dropped after that game, and was not to play another first-team game for the club. With a doleful symmetry, his last appearance in lilywhite was the same fixture as his first – for the reserves, against Plymouth Argyle. It marked a slightly inauspicious end to his Tottenham career, before he moved to West Ham United in March 1970, his increasing disaffection with the game highlighted in peculiar fashion by his decision to participate in a London-to-Mexico Rally Drive before that season had ended.

Statistics might keep company with lies and damned lies, but in the argument that Jimmy Greaves was the greatest goalscorer in the English game, Exhibit A would probably consist of the record books. When his 'goals scored' column is juxtaposed with 'games played' it produces a ratio so impressive as to be scarcely believable, his 220 league goals coming in just 321 appearances. With a further 46 in all other competitions for the club over the course of seven seasons, Greaves is comfortably Tottenham's greatest ever goalscorer. In 1962/63 he became the club's highest ever League goalscorer in a single campaign, with 37. He was the leading goalscorer in the old First Division in four different seasons with Spurs, including consecutively during the 1962/3–1964/5 seasons. To these can be added 124 goals in 157 appearances for Chelsea, before arriving at Spurs, including another two seasons as the First Division's leading scorer. Even Greaves' record of 9 in 12 for AC Milan merits the raising of an impressed eyebrow, this promising start in Italy coming in spite of the ultra-negative and frankly soporific *catenaccio* style of play fashionable at the time in the country, essentially loading the dice in favour of defence and typically generating low-scoring fare. Numerous other statistics can be trotted out to support his status as a goalscorer supreme – 25 hat-tricks or more, 100 League goals at the age of 21, and so on – but bare statistics alone do not justice to his talent.

However, just as telling a barometer of his achievements is the unanimity with which he is recognised as the finest purveyor of his trade. Statistics can be dispensed with by those who have seen him play, for seemingly every member of this privileged band have been cast under his spell, without hesitation or demur naming him the greatest goalscorer there has ever been in English football. Within the pantheon of the game's greats, few compare to Jimmy Greaves for natural goalscoring talent, while his irrepressible cheek endeared him to the masses even further. On the roll of honour of Spurs' cult heroes Greaves is arguably the most popular.

PAT JENNINGS

'BIG PAT'

1963-1977

SPURS CAREER

Games	590
Caps	119

MAGIC MOMENT

Saving two penalties in the same game at Anfield

IN March 1973 Spurs travelled to a Liverpool side sweeping aside all-comers en route to winning the First Division title. Bill Shankly's men swarmed forward putting the Tottenham rearguard under immense pressure and were awarded a first half penalty in front of the Kop, a decision which sparked a dispute between Kevin Keegan and Tommy Smith as to who would shoulder the responsibility. The argument was won by the former, but when he eventually took the spot-kick Pat Jennings in the Tottenham goal flung himself low to his right to make firm contact on the ball with his famously enormous hands, and push it away to safety. One penalty save at Anfield is enough to write any goalkeeper's name into legend, but five minutes from the end of the game Liverpool were awarded a second spot-kick. This time Smith made sure that the duty fell his way, but the burly defender's side-footed effort was saved again, this time Jennings diving to his left and gathering. It prompted a punch of the air with two clenched fists from Jennings, quite a collector's item, for the normally ice-cool Irishman rarely displayed any emotion – but as he recalled in BBC documentary *Big Pat* even the referee was swept up by the drama: "I can still see … the referee, he's got his hands up waving it on, a big smile on his face."

BBC commentator John Motson, with typical restraint, gasped, "It's Liverpool against Jennings – and Jennings has won!" Meanwhile, Geoffrey Green of *The Times* wrote of the match: 'Jennings, the Tottenham goalkeeper, had saved two penalty kicks taken by Keegan and Smith as part of a whole series of brilliant saves. There is no goalkeeper better than Jennings in the British Isles and perhaps even on the Continent.'

The sentiment was confirmed, at least as far as was possible, by the presentation of the Football Writers' Association Footballer of the Year award to Jennings at the end of that season. However, perhaps Jennings' greatest achievement was nothing to do with silverware. Instead it is a feat of which Ban Ki-Moon or even Barack Obama would be proud of, for few men in history have been able to unite such fierce rivals as the tribes of Spurs and Arsenal. Yet having spent 13 trophy-laden years at White Hart Lane, followed by 8 at the enemy, Pat Jennings to this day continues to be lauded by fans at both ends of the Seven Sisters Road. It certainly wasn't a transition Sol Campbell managed particularly smoothly, while manager George Graham was at best accepted at White Hart Lane rather than celebrated. But Jennings managed to cross this deep divide, winning over both sets of supporters with his glowing smile and wistful Irish charm.

Pat Jennings never really did things the orthodox way. Not for him the usual career progression of a football-mad childhood, matches against older children and the signing of schoolboy forms in his early teens. In fact, when he left school at 15 it was not to pursue a football career at all but to work, first as a factory-hand and then as a labourer in a timber gang, felling trees. Growing up in Newry, in Northern Ireland, Gaelic football rather than Association was the sport of choice. As events would transpire, this background was actually to prove of considerable benefit to Jennings in preparing him for his future career, for, as he is quoted on the National Football Museum website as saying: 'You have to withstand knocks, and all the time you are leaping to catch the ball against opponents who are also using their hands.' The one-handed catch; the willingness to brave a crowd jumping for the ball; the huge kick – such crafts of his eventual trade were established in his days as a Gaelic footballer in Newry.

When he eventually tried his hand as goalkeeper, after watching a local team in action, Jennings' rise to prominence was nothing short of meteoric, as he reached the top flight of English football within just 18 months of first assuming his position between the sticks. He began with Newry United, and after one season in the juniors and six months with the seniors he represented the Northern Ireland youth team in a tournament in Bognor Regis. During this time he was spotted by Second Division Watford, earning a £6,000 transfer in May 1963. The following June saw him transfer to Spurs for £27,000, at 19 years of age, and with only 48 professional games behind him. Spurs' history may be liberally sprinkled with glamorous big money signings, both domestic and foreign, but in Jennings there lay proof that players could arrive at the club in a low-profile, unheralded manner and proceed to become all-time greats. While it can hardly be considered a tradition of the club, it is interesting to note that the trick was repeated a decade and a half later, when Graham Roberts was plucked for a pittance from the lower reaches of the domestic game and thrust into the first team, going on to captain the side to UEFA Cup glory. The notion of such a transfer policy being pursued by any major football club in the modern era seems to be wedged firmly within the realms of fantasy.

One tradition of which Jennings most certainly was a part, however, was that of magnificent goalkeepers at the Lane. Jennings signed at a time when double-winning goalkeeper Bill Brown was between the sticks, but before either of them had come the legendary Ted Ditchburn. An agile shot-stopper and accomplished gatherer of crosses, Ditchburn played a key role in the Tottenham side which made history by winning the League Championship for the first time in 1951. His contribution was not limited to repelling the opposition, for by pioneering the short roll-out to his full back, he helped set in motion the push-and-run style for which that team became famed. Ditchburn eventually made a then record 452 appearances for the club, despite having missed 6 years during the war, and also became an England international. Ditchburn has famously been rated by Terry Venables as the best goalkeeper in Tottenham's history, and the Ditchburn-Jennings debate is one to which many long hours and countless column inches have been dedicated. The passing sands of time mean that the argument is now framed in yesteryear, inconclusively perhaps, as few remain who are able to compare the two from first-hand experience. That there even exists a debate at all ranks as some compliment to Jennings' career at Spurs, reflecting particularly favourably upon the manner in which he rose to the challenge on joining Tottenham.

While Jennings confesses to some disbelief at the way in which his career was progressing, he is typically modest and phlegmatic about the way in which he coped with his rapid ascension, stating on the Tottenham Hotspur official website: 'People just kept on putting me on another rung of the ladder and I managed to respond to it.'

In keeping with the unorthodox manner in which he had joined the game, Jennings' development as a goalkeeper was similarly far-removed from the norm. As he himself put it in Hunter Davies' seminal work *The Glory Game*: 'I've never had any coaching in my life. When people get on to me, trying to make me do something a certain way ... I can't do it. I'm just as likely to say "bollocks" if someone tries to tell me what to do.'

In an era before specialist goalkeeping coaches and pro-zone statistics, Jennings and his fellow keepers would typically tackle the complexities of their trade by wandering off to a corner of the training field and practise amongst themselves, with their team-mates' shooting drills the only organised training in which they participated. However, another aspect of the era was the fact that football was very much still a contact sport in the most literal sense of the word, goalkeepers of the time being afforded far less refereeing protection than in the modern era. Once again, Jennings's history within the hurly-burly of the Gaelic football field was to work in his favour, preparing him for the aggressive nature of goalkeeping in the '60s and '70s.

Should any Spurs fan from Jennings's halcyon playing days close their eyes and try to recall the big Irishman in his pomp, it is likely that they will picture in their mind's eye the unmistakeable sight of him leaping above a crowd to gather the ball with just one hand – albeit one that seemed the combined size of two possessed by mere mortals. The one-handed catch became Jennings' trademark, and is the most obvious visual testament to the fact that he was not afforded coaching, for no coach in his right mind would espouse such a risk-fraught approach. Yet in the same way that the club's most skilful outfield players – the likes of Greaves and Hoddle – were blessed with innate, unteachable qualities, so Jennings in goal was possessed of a quite remarkable natural ability when it came to plucking crosses from the air as simply as if grabbing an apple from a branch. He was no doubt aided in this unusual technique by the fact that he possessed unfeasibly large hands, each seeming approximately the size of a shovel.

Terry Venables has pointed out that there is method in the madness of Jennings' one-handed takes – "You can get a slightly longer reach with one hand" – while the man himself has made no secret of his philosophy, as quoted in *CNN Sports Illustrated*: 'People think I catch it one-handed. I don't. I take the ball with one hand when I have to. My hand just stays with the ball, travels with it, slows it down, just as if I was controlling it with my foot. It's the exact same skill. My hand is travelling at the same pace as the ball.'

A further quirk of Jennings's style was his knack of saving with his feet. Indeed, he was prone to use whichever part of his huge frame was most suitable, but can certainly be considered something of a pioneer of the art of goalkeeping with his legs. Now the norm, it was an innovation when used by Jennings, again reflecting the fact that he had essentially invented his trade as he went along. The sight of Jennings rushing towards an attacker and spreading himself to block a shot was to become a familiar one to Spurs fans.

Jennings is fondly remembered as going on to become the best goalkeeper in the world, notably starring for Northern Ireland in their heyday at the 1982 World Cup in Spain when they qualified for the second round and beat the host nation, but it is worth noting that his earliest performances at Spurs were far from convincing. In the first two years of his career he was unable to make the number one jersey his own, instead sharing duties with Bill Brown, the Double-winning keeper. As long-time Spurs fan Gary Wright recalls: "Big Pat was a real nervous starter after he signed from Watford. In his early days he did not convince and there were plenty that doubted he would make it." Many of the club's greatest sons struggled to find their feet around that time, and consequently received what could euphemistically be described as an 'impatient' welcome from Spurs fans, used to silverware and success. Alan Mullery and Terry Venables were amongst those who took some time to win over the supporters in the 1960s, the latter recalling with typical cheekiness, "I wouldn't say they were impatient. They wait 'til the third game before they give you the bird."

The rocky start to Jennings' Tottenham career mirrored the club's fortunes at that time. Spurs' victory in the European Cup Winners' Cup final of May 1963 was the last hurrah of the great Double-winning team assembled by manager Bill Nicholson. But in the latter half of the decade a new team was being pieced together, and with Bill Brown departing in October 1966, Jennings became a central figure in the new side moulded by Nicholson.

As well as Jennings, the likes of Mullery and Venables, Mike England, Cyril Knowles and Joe Kinnear were added to the team, while Dave Mackay remained of the Double-winners, taking over as captain. The side may not have replicated the extraordinary success of their immediate predecessors, but they nevertheless were good enough to bring silverware back to the Lane, first of all, in the 1967 FA Cup final. On such occasions as Cup finals, neon lights the following day and forever more inevitably proclaim the name of an outfield player, typically the scorer of the winning goal, but in 1967 Jennings played his full part in Spurs's victory. Twice he denied Chelsea a crucial opening goal in the first half by diving full-length low to his right, to deny goal-bound shots from John Hollins (followed, inevitably, by a one-handed catch from the resulting corner) and then Charlie Cooke. Club skipper and archetypal hard man Mackay was suitably thrilled by the occasion to plant a smacker on Jennings' cheek as the players went on a lap of honour around Wembley.

It was the first of a glut of trophies for Spurs in the next half-dozen years, with Jennings providing a rock-solid base to the team. Tottenham won the League Cup in 1971, the UEFA Cup in 1972, and another League Cup in 1973, as well as losing the following season's UEFA Cup final, before heading into decline. Jennings' consistency in this period was nothing short of incredible. It is a truth universally acknowledged that while the mistakes of outfield players can be swallowed up in a match and forgotten, goalkeepers have no such margin for error – yet despite the microscopic scrutiny he underwent by virtue of his position, Jennings is widely regarded as the club's most consistent performer in this period.

Personal accolades provide evidence of this, with Jennings picking up the Footballer of the Year award in 1972/73 and PFA Footballer of the Year award in 1975/76. The game may have evolved over the years, but one truth which remains unaltered is the fact that goalkeeping is a far less glamorous trade than that at the opposite end of the pitch, and headlines then, as now, were most typically grabbed by outfield players. As Jennings himself put it, in Hunter Davies' *The Glory Game*: 'One mistake with a goalie and that's it. You can't redeem it the way a forward can. He can miss five and then score one and everyone's pleased.'

That Jennings could therefore perform at such a level as to win Player of the Year awards in two separate seasons gives some indication of the supreme standard he attained and maintained during his time at White Hart Lane.

Indeed, for more evidence of his popularity one need look no further than the 1971/72 season, in which Martin Chivers scored a quite remarkable 43 goals in all competitions – including two goals in the club's UEFA Cup final triumph – only to see Jennings beat him to the club Supporters' Player of the Year award. In 1973 Jennings was selected by England manager Sir Alf Ramsey to represent a British select XI, arguably confirming his status at the time as the greatest goalkeeper in Europe, if not the world.

Jennings was by now a seasoned international, having made his debut for Northern Ireland as an 18-year-old in 1964, in the same game as a certain George Best. The pair were to become room-mates, but remained rivals at club level, famously going head-to-head in the FA Cup in January 1968, as reported by Geoffrey Green of *The Times*: 'The poetry of movement was in him [Best] but the last beat of his pentameter eluded him as he tried to dribble past Jennings and walk the ball home to an empty net. Jennings, quick as a cat, saw the danger, dived at the winger's feet, blocked a sideways swerve, and in that movement rescued Spurs.'

While Best ultimately never had the opportunity to grace the world's greatest football stage, Jennings' longevity saw to it that he represented his country at the World Cup finals, both in 1982 and 1986, and he was to play a starring role in the former tournament.

In identifying particularly outstanding performances from Jennings' 590 Spurs appearances one is not simply spoilt for chance but absolutely flooded in a deluge of saves which seemed to stretch the boundaries of physics, such was the high standard he maintained week after week. However, amongst his finest displays was in a UEFA Cup tie away to Grasshoppers of Zurich in September 1973. Although the 5-1 scoreline forever etched in the annals could cursorily be glanced over as an emphatic Tottenham victory, the bizarre but indubitable truth was that Spurs were lucky even to have won at all, and would not have done so but for their keeper. Recalls Martin Chivers of the game, in his autobiography *Big Chiv*: 'In the dressing room afterwards Bill [Nicholson] said, "It might be 5-1 on paper but, to be honest, you all ought to give your bonus to Pat Jennings because he kept you in the game"' Although it was the truth, we had come to expect nothing less from Pat. We were just so confident that he was never going to make mistakes as he was so steady and completely unflappable.'

Jennings even famously once scored for Spurs, at no less a venue than Old Trafford. His enormous clearance in the 1967 Charity Shield against League Champions Manchester United bounced once, over red-faced opposite number Alex Stepney, and into the net. Coming in the opening game of the season, the strike briefly made Jennings the club's leading scorer for the campaign. Never normally one given to ostentation, Jennings takes particular pleasure in the fact that his goal was captured for all to see by the live television cameras, recalling that few games were televised in that era, and that a player could go his entire career without being seen by the armchair audience.

Aside from such incidents, however, Jennings was typically the calmest man in the arena, simply going about his business in understated but impeccably professional fashion. The club may have had – and still retain – a tradition for flair and glamour, but

Jennings was very much a steady, consistent influence within the team, dismissing as perfunctory those saves which had team-mates and fans alike rubbing their eyes in disbelief. The one-handed saves and use of his legs to block when players were sent through one on one with him were adopted because they were effective, rather than in any attempt to court the limelight, his inventiveness in such situations birthed by necessity. Similarly, the fact that in 1967 he married a showband singer should not be construed as an attempt to court the celebrity lifestyle and blaze a trail where Posh and Becks would later follow. Jennings married Eleanor Toner on a Monday, and was back at training on a Tuesday – as Spurs prepared to travel to Arsenal, for a game they would win 2-0.

As Jennings' trophy-strewn career mirrored Tottenham's successes of the late '60s and early '70s, so the messy and acrimonious nature of his departure encapsulated in a microcosm the downward spiral of the club by the middle of the decade. Bill Nicholson had resigned early in the 1974/75 season, having become disillusioned by the increasingly money-driven nature of the game and its players, as well as the hooliganism of those in the stands. Terry Neill took over the reins for two years which fell somewhere between nondescript and ignominious, and with the side firmly in decline, new boss Keith Burkinshaw was unable to prevent relegation at the end of his first season in charge, in 1976/77. (It should be noted at this juncture that an ankle injury meant that Jennings featured in only 23 of Spurs' 42 League games that season.)

The departure of Jennings to Arsenal ranks as one of the darkest days in Tottenham history, a horrendous culmination to a sequence of events which, in hindsight, seem all the worse for being so eminently avoidable. The contract of the 31-year-old hero was up, and although there was no animosity between Jennings and Burkinshaw, no effort was made to retain his services, with the manager viewing young Barry Daines as a capable replacement for Second Division football. Jennings was asked not to train with the team, for fear that he might embarrass the other goalkeepers who had been selected to usurp him. Bobby Robson's Ipswich seemed the likely destination, until an injury to a striker left them altering their transfer market priorities, but after returning to the ground to bid farewell to his colleagues, and finding himself ignored by the club's directors, Jennings determined to exit in a manner that would cause maximum embarrassment to the club, even though he has since professed that he remained 'Tottenham through and through'. Thus it came to pass that Pat Jennings joined the enemy.

Rejected by Spurs as being past his prime, Jennings signed a four-year contract at Highbury, ultimately staying for nine seasons. His sale was a ghastly mistake by Burkinshaw – one which, to his credit, he acknowledges as his worst in football – while Neill, then in charge at Highbury, gallingly, but understandably, rates it as, "One of the best transfer deals I made in my career as manager."

However, perhaps the ultimate compliment Jennings can be paid lies in the fact that his reputation amongst Spurs fans did not suffer for his move to Arsenal, even though its timing rubbed salt into the gaping wound of relegation. Others once adored at White Hart Lane have, rather infamously, been awarded less than wholly complimentary welcomes when returning in opposition colours. Such was the popularity of Jennings, however, that he holds the unique status of remaining a Tottenham legend even as an Arsenal player, one of the few men ever to receive a rapturous ovation from both sets of fans at a North London derby. Of course, he did his standing amongst the Spurs faithful no harm at all by making the mistake as Arsenal goalkeeper which ensured a Tottenham victory, in an FA Cup Third round tie at White Hart Lane in January 1982. Garth Crooks profited from that Jennings lapse, as reported by Vince Wright of *The Times*: 'Crooks shot with more hope than expectation but Jennings allowed the ball to roll under his arm and into the net.'

It was the only goal of the game, and set Spurs on their way to winning the competition for a second consecutive season. While nobody would dare to question Jennings' integrity, Spurs fans with a sense of romance – and there are many, for such a sentiment runs deep at the club – can be forgiven for considering that this was one last favour from the big Northern Irishman, helping the club win its favourite trophy in its centenary year…

Jennings re-signed for Spurs as goalkeeping cover in September 1985, attracting a crowd of several thousand just for his reserve team debut against Chelsea, and making one more first-team appearance in January 1986 in the Screen Sport Super Cup against Liverpool, before finally retiring following his appearance for Northern Ireland in the 1986 World Cup. Since then he has worked for Spurs in a coaching capacity and as a match-day hospitality host. Fan Doug Nash speaks for the masses when he says: "At his peak he was easily the best goalkeeper in the world. As well as this he was a very modest man, almost seeming embarrassed by his own brilliance. There's only one Pat Jennings and we'll never see anyone like him again."

Jennings' modesty, one suspects, dictates that he would sooner chop off one of those enormous hands than accept such glowing tributes, but nevertheless – time down the road excepted – his status as one of the club's great servants, one of the game's very greatest goalkeepers and a true Spurs Cult Hero is beyond dispute.

CYRIL KNOWLES

1964-1976

SPURS CAREER

Games	506
Goals	17
Caps	4

MAGIC MOMENT

Scoring twice in the final game of the 1974/75 season, to help Spurs to the victory which saved them from relegation

'NICE ONE CYRIL'

QUITE how such a parlous situation was reached is too wearying a tale to relate, but as the 1974/75 season reached its unbearable finale, Spurs found themselves eyeball-to-eyeball with relegation, and in desperate need of a hero. Cometh the hour, cometh Cyril Knowles, galloping forward from his rather ill-fitting abode of defence to hoist his team to safety almost single-handedly. The season had seen Tottenham lurch from one crisis to the next like some ghastly waking nightmare, beginning with the resignation of legendary manager Bill Nicholson and unravelling disastrously until the final-day resignation decider, in which nothing less than victory – against a Leeds United team which had just reached the European Cup final – would guarantee top-flight status. Knowles, however, was primed for battle. His early 20-yard free kick flew into the Leeds net; he kept his cool to slot home a second-half penalty; and had a hand in two further goals, as Spurs triumphed 4-2 to maintain their top-flight status.

Wrote Geoffrey Green of *The Times*: 'This was a ding-dong battle and nothing like the game one had expected to be, buckled and laced with fear from beginning to end. No doubt it was a flashing opening goal by Knowles – Tottenham's hero of the night – after only four minutes with a 20-yard free kick through the Leeds wall that released all the tensions and opened the floodgates. Nor was that the end of Knowles's contribution. He was involved one way and another in each of Tottenham's four goals...'

Fittingly, the two goals he scored that afternoon were his last League goals for the club he had joined over a decade earlier. Knowles had been a crucial member of the Spurs sides which had won the FA Cup, League Cup (twice) and UEFA Cup, in the late 1960s and early 1970s, but his contribution had never been quite as crucial as that made in keeping the team in the First Division that afternoon. Rarely had the choruses of "Nice one Cyril" rung out with quite such jubilant fervour around White Hart Lane.

That Knowles attained cult status at Spurs itself borders on the remarkable, for, ostensibly at least, he met few of the club's well-established criteria. Tottenham's history is littered with supreme goalscorers and outrageously gifted midfielders, while loyal and heroic captains also earn a special place in the affections of fans. However, one imagines that few Spurs young fans have grown up practising for countless hours with dreams of becoming, respectfully, the new Edinburgh or Edman – and fewer still would admit to it – for typically the left-back position is decidedly short on glamour. Yet despite all of this, within a team brimming full of internationals and star names, Cyril Knowles comfortably established himself as one of the most popular players of his era, his hero-status confirmed by that most absolute of markers, a terrace anthem in his personal honour (an anthem, indeed, which was eventually to gain even broader popularity).

Knowles was signed for Tottenham by Nicholson in 1964 for £45,000, after two seasons at Middlesbrough. He hailed from a footballing family, his younger brother Peter playing for Wolves, before leaving football to become a Jehovah's Witness. Prior to turning professional, Cyril had worked down the Yorkshire coal-mines, imagining that the opportunity of a football career had passed him by after rejections as a youth from Manchester United and Blackpool. The signing of Knowles was part of Nicholson's rebuilding of Spurs, following the break-up of the Double-winners. In fact, one of his first moves in piecing together a new Spurs team was wedging Knowles in place as one of the initial building-blocks. Knowles' 12-year Tottenham career would last – and eventually outlast – the entirety of Nicholson's post-Double tenure, and from the outset he sank his teeth into the role of heir apparent to the Double-winners with quite refreshing verve. His debut, in a 2-0 home win over Sheffield United, on the opening day of the 1964/65 season, had *The Times* purring, under the headline 'Zest of Youth in Changing Spurs', going on to say: 'In defence, where Knowles and [goalkeeper Pat] Jennings made their first appearances for this famous team, there was a crispness and cohesion that augurs well.'

A shrewd prophecy, for Knowles was to play in all but 4 of Tottenham's 46 games that season, making the full back berth his own and featuring just as regularly for over 10 further seasons.

With the team undergoing surgery, results were understandably underwhelming relative to the glory of previous years, the transitional period seeing Spurs finish sixth and eighth respectively in Knowles' first two seasons. Changes were afoot in more than just personnel, for Alf Ramsey's World Cup-winning England team of 1966 was to give national momentum to a tactical style which eschewed the use of wingers. This evolution was continued and the style modified at White Hart Lane, with Nicholson using it to create a gateway of opportunity for Knowles at left-back, and Joe Kinnear on the right, to overlap and attack. As Pat Jennings recalls, in *Match of My Life*: 'After the 1966 World Cup we were the first team to use Cyril and Joe as attacking full backs … Joe would be playing like a right-winger, Cyril as a left-winger.'

For Knowles, a left-back who had begun his career as a winger and whose default switch was still set permanently to 'attack', the move was manna from heaven. 'When he got forward he could cross as well as anyone,' recalled Steve Perryman, in tribute production *Nice One Cyril*. Any defender in whose veins coursed attacking juices would find a welcome home at White Hart Lane, for the flames of adventurous forward play have long burned bright at N17. As long-term fan Jill Lewis described him: "Swashbuckling and stylish, the best left-back I've seen for Spurs by a mile." Spurs' overlapping full back tactic bordered on revolutionary, but its success was due primarily to the ability of Knowles, as well as Kinnear, to execute it. Perryman has noted that, while the notion gradually gained acceptance in England, it typically took teams by surprise when unleashed on the continent. Indeed, Knowles' contribution as overlapping full back gained particular prominence on one of Spurs' most famous European nights, when they overcame AC Milan at the semi-final stage of the 1972 UEFA Cup, en route to winning the trophy. It had seemed an uphill task for Spurs, particularly when they conceded first against the Milanese, to whom the art of keeping clean sheets was, inevitably, second nature. However, as the visitors attempted to close out the First Leg tie at White Hart Lane, Knowles thrived on the left, a winger in all but name, providing ammunition for an attacking pair of renowned heading ability, in Martin Chivers and Alan Gilzean. The headlines were grabbed that night by Steve Perryman, whose two goals earned a 2-1 victory, and Alan Mullery, returning to captain the side after a lengthy absence. Naturally, the full back's was not the name in lights, but in refusing to be cowed after falling behind, and exerting pressure to force a victory, Tottenham had taken their cue and attacking dynamic from Knowles.

He was at it again in the Second Leg, steaming down the left as early as the sixth minute, enabling Chivers and Perryman to combine in setting up a goal for Mullery. However, that Second Leg also highlighted another, more unfortunate aspect to Knowles' game, for in him the ability to enthral walked hand-in-hand with the capacity to err, often in gruesomely spectacular style. 'Twas his lapse, in that Second Leg in Milan that led to the concession of a penalty, duly converted, to make the score 1-1 on the night, and cut Spurs' aggregate lead to 3-2. A nerve-shredding final 20 minutes duly followed, but Spurs ultimately progressed. Such is the lot of a defender however – remembered for mistakes as much as achievements, while few recall the errors in front of goal of the club's leading strikers.

Another moment painful to behold yet indelibly etched in the memory was Knowles' attempted clearance in the League Cup semi-final second leg against Chelsea, a wild fresh-air hack which left his goalkeeper Pat Jennings unsighted and resulted in the ball bouncing almost apologetically into the net. Rather unfortunately, it was to prove the decisive goal that night, dealing Spurs an aggregate 5-4 defeat in the competition they were defending. The error was all the more galling for being high profile, occurring as it did in a televised live game. The warning signs had been prominently displayed the previous week, Knowles having given the self-destruct button a good thump in the First Leg of the same tie against Chelsea, as reported by Geoffrey Green of *The Times*: 'Knowles tried to dribble [around Chelsea forward] Garland on the edge of his own penalty area with no one else in sight, only to stumble, lost the ball and leave Garland with a virtual open goal.'

However, like a tight-rope walker insouciantly dispensing with the safety-net, much of the thrill of Knowles' game was contained in such very acts of daring. While he paid the price for the errors against Chelsea, invited by Nicholson to indulge in a spot of personal reflection in the surroundings of reserve team football, his talent was too great to keep suppressed for long. He was swiftly restored to the starting line-up, eventually making 35 League and 12 Cup appearances that season, and featuring in both Legs as Spurs beat Wolves in the UEFA Cup final.

There are those – of, say, the George Graham School of Defending – who would have suggested that such mistakes were inevitable from Knowles, given his penchant not simply for tempting fate on the football pitch, but for making himself intimately acquainted with it and then antagonising it relentlessly. A born showman, at times he appeared to be a flamboyant attacker masquerading in the unconvincing disguise of a full back. As Martin Chivers noted in his autobiography: 'Cyril was a natural piss-taker on and off the field.' He relished japes at the expense of his team-mates in training, whilst on numerous occasions on the pitch could clearly identified to be teasing opposing strikers. The dribble inside his own penalty area against Chelsea, as detailed above, could hardly be deemed an isolated incident, and sometimes he even upped the ante by endeavouring to weave his way along his own goal-line. Such moments could give palpitations to managers, but for spectators – once they had exhaled in relief – such risk-laden bravado was part of the irresistible allure of the man, proving particularly popular when coolly concluded with an astute pass out of trouble, to the chagrin of the chasing opposition forwards.

Recalls fan Gary Wright: "My lasting memory is Cyril performing an outrageous dummy on our goal line against Everton. I have never seen anything like it before or since." That he could even consider such an approach says much for his confidence in his ability, whilst also providing an insight into Knowles' mischievous, fun-loving nature.

The man was renowned as one of the primary jokers in the Tottenham pack. A permanently cheery soul, he had an unmistakeable high-pitched laugh, and a twinkle in the eye that betrayed an infinite stream of practical jokes. Ralph Coates described Knowles in *Nice One Cyril* as 'Full of character, full of jokes' – and spoke as one who knew, having been treated to the full Cyril Knowles Welcome Experience on joining the club in the summer of 1972 (a process which involved being very straight-facedly assured that it was against club policy for any player to be allowed to wear the same shirt to training on consecutive days).

Knowles was the comic relief around the Tottenham camp, seemingly unable to suppress that mischievous streak even if he wanted to. Prior to the crunch relegation-decider against Leeds United in April 1975, manager Terry Neill took a step which, it is fairly uncontroversial to assert, may have prompted the raising of one or two quizzical eyebrows amongst his charges, by inviting a psychic to assist with the pre-match preparation. After individual sessions with each player, the psychic's invitation for a volunteer in front of the whole group of players was, naturally, met by Mr Knowles. While it seems rather unlikely, the tale told by those present at the time is that Knowles was laid out prostrate, with his feet on one chair and his neck resting on the other – then told by the clairvoyant to imagine that he was a steel girder. Knowles – so goes the legend– went absolutely rigid, not even budging when the hulking frame of Pat Jennings sat slowly down upon his stomach. It is difficult to know quite how to react to such a tale (although if Spurs had lost that game one imagines that the reaction greeting Neill may have erred on the downright savage) but the following day Knowles turned in one of his most famous performances in lilywhite.

While his proclivity for casually indulging in such heart-stopping fare as goal-line dribbles was well-known, as Bill Nicholson pointed out in *Nice One Cyril*, 'He knew when to laugh and joke. [But] he was very serious before all the matches. On a matchday he always suspected that this might be the game when he plays not so well, therefore he was always keyed up for every game.'

Ex team-mate John Pratt has also paid tribute to Knowles in *Nice One Cyril* for his willingness to talk him through games as he broke into the team, highlighting a level of maturity and sense of responsibility it would be easy to overlook. George Graham, a frequent adversary of Knowles in the pair's playing days, has described him as, "An outstanding left-back, with a very educated left foot," while Terry Venables refers to him in *The Greatest Ever Spurs Team* as, 'A good passer, aggressive tackler and outstanding player, capable of being an exceptionally good attacking and defensive left-back.' For all his qualities, both as an attacking outlet and fearsome defender, Knowles did have his weaknesses, as Chivers recalls: 'One thing he lacked – he wasn't a very good header of the ball. We could put up with that because big Mike England was around...'

Knowles' commitment to the Tottenham cause was evinced by more than just his eagerness to supplement attacks. He was a ferocious tackler, 'the type of player who would put fear into some of the wingers' according to Chivers, in *Nice One Cyril*. Indeed, Bill Nicholson recalls that when he first joined the club no less a warrior than Dave Mackay was seen to hurry out of his way in pre-season training: "I thought to myself if he can be another Mackay that's great."

With his bone-shuddering determination and his irrepressible urge to join an attack – not to mention his loveable persona – it is understandable that the White Hart Lane faithful took Knowles to their hearts. Nevertheless, that he earned such iconic status remains mightily impressive. For a start, Tottenham folk could be notoriously impatient with new arrivals, particularly in the wake of the disbanding of the Double-winners, with Terry Venables and Alan Mullery in particular suffering for the unenviable – but hardly blameworthy – tasks of having to follow in the footsteps of Blanchflower and Mackay. For Knowles, emulating his predecessor Ron Henry was no mean feat. Moreover, the Tottenham team in which he played contained such luminaries as Jennings, England, Peters, Gilzean and Chivers; as such, Spurs supporters could hardly be said to be lacking in choice of potential hero-fodder.

However, on the back of a TV commercial for *Wonderloaf* bread in 1973, the chorus of "Nice one Cyril, Nice one son, Nice one Cyril, Let's have another one," could be heard to reverberate regularly around White Hart Lane. Terrace chants are one thing, but this went further, taking root and developing a life of its own. The ode was given full studio treatment, and released as a single by a beat combo going by the name of The Cockerel Chorus, reaching a respectable high of number 14 in the UK charts (at a time when Slade's *Cum On Feel The Noize* was number one). That a song about a single player should prove so popular, and that the player in question should be a full back rather than one of the club's star strikers, speaks volumes of Knowles' popularity. It also adds another chapter to the curious musical history of Tottenham Hotspur. Alongside FA Cup victories, style of play, audacious foreign signings and super strikers, it seems that a musical imprint of the era plays a dubious yet integral role in the club archives. 'Nice One Cyril' sits alongside 'Ossie's Dream' and 'Diamond Lights' in a most peculiar catalogue of recordings, following on from more traditional stadium refrains as 'McNamara's Band' and 'Glory Glory Hallelujah'.

While it hardly ranks as a blot on the escutcheon of those involved, the Spurs that Knowles joined in 1964 never did emulate the successes of their illustrious predecessors. In fact, statistics viewed through the infallible lens of hindsight indicate that the team could be considered to have gradually declined until the departure of Nicholson. Be that as it may, they proceeded to garner silverware with a regularity mightily impressive for a team supposedly on the wane. Knowles was a member of the team that beat Chelsea in the 1967 FA Cup final, Norwich in the 1971 League Cup final, Wolves in the 1972 UEFA Cup final and Aston Villa in the 1973 League Cup final. The team may have lacked the consistency to challenge for the League title, but let it not be forgotten that their efforts comfortably surpassed those of many Spurs sides of later years.

The 1975/76 season was Knowles' last as a footballer, a persistent knee injury limiting him to just 12 appearances, the last of which was at home to Everton shortly before Christmas. He nevertheless ticked off one final landmark that campaign, in surpassing a quite astonishing 500 games for the club. His testimonial that October against Arsenal, a 2-2 draw in which he scored, was the very least the club could bestow upon him for such loyal and downright entertaining service.

Knowles' bright and bubbly persona was as evident on the pitch as off it, yet as a young man he had had to endure the death of his six-year-old son in a desperately sad car accident. Tragically, Knowles himself was to die young, succumbing to a brain tumour at the age of just 47, in 1991. Two memorial matches were held for him that year (between Spurs' 1971 League Cup winners and Arsenal's 1971 Double-winners; and between the Spurs teams of 1981 and 1991), appropriately played to a packed White Hart Lane, which resounded once more to the reverent, but mournful strains of 'Nice one Cyril'. It is a further tribute to the man that every player approached to play in these games willingly agreed.

Knowles had been unfortunate not to win more than his four England caps, picked up from 1967 to 1968, as he was forced to settle for a place behind Everton's World Cup-winning Ray Wilson and Leeds' Terry Cooper in the pecking-order for left-back. However, his status as one of – if not *the* – finest left-backs in Tottenham's history was cemented by 12 seasons at Spurs, comprising 507 appearances and 17 goals, and years after his death his popularity at White Hart Lane remains undimmed.

ALAN GILZEAN

'GILLY'

1964-1974

SPURS CAREER

Games	439
Goals	133
Caps	22

MAGIC MOMENT

Leading the line, both in the air and on the ground, to help set up Spurs' victory in the 1967 FA Cup final

THE venue was White Hart Lane; the opponents Birmingham City; the occasion the an FA Cup quarter-final replay – but it was a scenario so familiar as to be expected each week by legions of Spurs supporters from 1964 through to 1974. When a lofted cross was delivered from the wing towards the unmistakeable balding figure of Alan Gilzean, one almost felt sympathy for opposition defenders, so inevitably doomed to failure were their attempts to challenge. Rather than jumping for the header, the Birmingham players might as well have waved white flags; for in the air Alan Gilzean reigned supreme. From the inch-perfect cross of John Robertson, Gilzean delivered with his head a perfect amalgam of precision and power, almost lovingly directing the ball to nestle in the Birmingham net. Spurs ran rampant that evening in a 6-0 victory, and were on their way to Wembley, where 'Gilly' would collect his first winners' medal with the club. He would repeat the feat in the 2-1 semi-final victory over Nottingham Forest at Hillsborough, this time outjumping Forest's Bob McKinlay to guide his header perfectly into the path of Jimmy Greaves to score Spurs' first goal. However, that scenario, of a Gilzean leap and achingly elegant header, was one to be replicated countless times, across the country and beyond. Gilzean hung up his boots after 10 years at White Hart Lane, having earned membership into the elite '100 Club' of players who had reached a century of goals for Spurs.

Indeed Alan Gilzean was not just a goalscorer, for although his 133 goals in 429 appearances place him within the top ten scorers in Tottenham's history, his role in the team was as a creator as much as scorer of goals, and in particular, through the quite extraordinary talent he possessed in heading the ball.

Gilzean was brought to White Hart Lane for £72,500 in December 1964, from a Dundee side that had won the Scottish title and then reached the semi-final of the European Cup, eventually losing to AC Milan. He had proved his pedigree with two hat-tricks in this European run, his CV also including the goal which beat Milan in the semi-final First Leg. Although his transfer to Spurs was completed in December 1964, his first appearance at White Hart Lane had actually been the previous month, when, in a performance that offered a hint of glories to come, he had scored twice in the memorial match for another Scottish Spurs legend, John White.

With his distinctive appearance – greying, balding head and hunched gait – he looked anything but an athlete. In the words of one long-time fan, Alan Granville, "Gilly never looked like a footballer, more like an Oxford Don". However, the Book of Gilzean was not one to be judged by its cover, for beneath that seemingly mundane exterior lurked a supremely gifted footballer, who coated bundles of natural ability with an elegance and finesse that made spectators drool.

Amongst the glowing tributes sprinkled on Gilzean by Terry Venables, in *The Greatest Ever Spurs Team*, are 'artist' and 'craftsman', fitting accolades for a man with the rare ability to turn football into an art-form. In an era in which such unrefined attributes as blood, thunder, thud and blunder were gaining credence within the English game, Gilzean fought the good fight for football's aesthetic value, and effortlessly so, his wondrous control frequently warranting close scrutiny just to confirm that the ball was not indeed somehow stuck to his feet. In one aspect of the game in particular he earned the right to be spoken of in terms of most awestruck reverence, for his ability in heading the ball was absolutely unrivalled. It is for this unique gift that Gilzean is most fondly remembered by his adoring fans in N17, but even here some clarification is required, for his reputation was built not so much upon powerful, bullet headers as deft and delicate glancing flicks that were swiftly to become his trademark. As long-time fan Ian Stokes put it: "Gilly could do things with his head that other players couldn't do with their feet!"

It seems an opinion unanimously held by those who saw him in action. Journalist Hunter Davies opined of him in *The New Statesman*:

'His most distinctive skill was in the air, he could flick the ball on from corners and take free kicks so subtly that you half believed he hadn't touched it, yet he had changed its direction enough to land it in the corner of the net.'

Incongruous though it seemed, time and again the gleaming pate of the ungainly Gilzean would caress the ball with all the delicacy of a silk glove. This ability to glance the ball with such unerring accuracy from his forehead was married to the unteachable gift for reading what was happening around him on the pitch. A potent concoction, as a result of which he was able to thread short, headed passes in a manner that at times seemed to defy the very laws of physics, the eye of a needle no impediment to the astonishing heading ability of the languid Scot.

As well as the graceful headers into the paths of others, Gilzean was also able to act as a strong target-man in his own right. His strength in the the air was of particular value from corners, free kicks and, in the latter part of his Tottenham career, the long throw-ins of team-mate Martin Chivers, while goalkeeper Pat Jennings recalls, in *Match of my Life*: 'Alan was a super target-man. For me it was brilliant because I could always pick him out with clearances up field.'

Manager and team-mates made full use of this asset, frequently working it into the team's strategy, as Jennings recalls of the 1967 FA Cup final against Chelsea: 'During the opening period, our plan to utilize Alan Gilzean's aerial strength worked well and we gained the early initiative … Alan's flicks caused Chelsea all sorts of problems.'

Such was his influence that day, in helping Spurs to a 2-1 victory, that Geoffrey Green of *The Times* was moved to write: 'Holding the whole line together, too, and keeping it on the move, was the graceful, balanced Gilzean. Always master of [Chelsea defender] Hinton in the air, and often on the ground with subtle touches, Gilzean indeed glanced his passes in many directions like reflections from a mirror.'

Such was his talent that while Tottenham had built a reputation upon flowing football along the ground, the ability of Gilzean enabled the team to take the aerial route without sacrificing the aesthetic value so integral to their play. Fans brought up on the irresistible brand of football purveyed by the 'push-and-run' team of the 1950s and 'Super Spurs' team of the early '60s were still able to laud the style and skill which Gilzean brought to the game when needed in the air, with supporter Alan Granville recalling: "To fully appreciate how subtle he was with his head you needed to be halfway up the terraces looking down on the top of the players' heads."

It should be emphasised that while his heading ability conveyed upon him an almost unfair advantage, this was not to the detriment of Gilzean's play on *terra firma*. Even without his talent in the air, Gilzean was a player who oozed that style craved and demanded by generations of Tottenham fans. Every iota of grace and élan he exhibited in the air, he was able to match with his feet, deploying his phenomenal touch to make the ball do his bidding, either in killing it instantly as it arrived, or sending it on its way with perfect weight and timing to a team-mate.

However, as well his style of play, in the tradition of the game's very finest cult heroes, Gilzean's off-field persona also captured the imagination. While reluctant to court the attention of the press, he established over time a reputation as a booze-fuelled reveller of the highest order. The tales of his exploits are legendary – some related as the sworn truth by those who witnessed them, others having emanated mysteriously, lacking verification, but still passing into folklore. Moreover, by sidestepping the glare of the media he attained an off-field mystique, which served to enhance his hero status. Indeed, to this day he remains something of a recluse, famous for eschewing fame in his retirement.

In an age before nutritionists and dieticians, footballers were notoriously hardened drinkers – those of Spurs no exception – but few if any could live with Gilly. Any medical test during his career at Spurs would have done well to find traces of blood in his alcohol-stream, for here was a man who, on being questioned by manager Bill Nicholson about having been spotted leaving a nightclub at 2am, responded that the information was incorrect, and that he had in fact been *entering* the club. With his taste for the liquor and eye for the ladies, Gilly lived the dream, destroying defences by day, and owning the town by night.

He may not have had the boy-band looks of the modern game's pampered *prima donnas*, but Gilzean was never short of admirers amongst the fairer sex. Hunter Davies, who spent a season chronicling life at White Hart Lane in his book *The Glory Game*, recalls that the team's young man and eligible bachelor, Joe Kinnear, had gone for a night out with Gilly but been forced to abandon halfway through as he simply could not keep up. Martin Chivers recalls in his autobiography that Gilzean was once discovered by his team-mates asleep in his car in the car-park before training, after one particularly energetic night out, while on another occasion he curled up and slept in spare netting on the training pitch. A further tale, passed from one generation to the next, suggests that while his team-mates trained under the auspices of the famously austere Nicholson and his assistant, Eddie Baily, the unflappable Gilly would remove himself to the massage room and read the *Daily Mirror*. The veracity of the tale may be questionable, but it certainly fits the template.

Inevitably then, even Gilly's greatest fans would struggle to construct a compelling argument for him as the work-horse of the Tottenham team. His lackadaisical appearance, completed by a frequently morose demeanour ("He looked so miserable most games," recalls fan Steve Smith), accorded with his reputation as a man unashamedly loath to apply himself to the rigours of daily life, Hunter Davies writing of him: 'He was dead lazy – getting into his Jag to drive a hundred yards to the newsagent.'

And yet, astonishingly, in spite of this lifestyle he remained a fine athlete, of such exceptional fitness that he continued playing at the top level for Spurs until he was 36.

Nor was he any bit-part journeyman, simply making up the numbers, but a vital cog in a team that won silverware in the three consecutive years prior to his final season in the game. Supreme footballer; one of the club's highest ever goalscorers; a born ladies' man; his laid-back attitude translating into on-pitch insouciance; and capable of out-pacing even the hardest drinkers of his day whilst retaining his fitness – with good reason was Gilly so regularly serenaded by his adoring fans with choruses of "Gilzean, Gilzean – born is the King of White Hart Lane".

While his off-the-pitch antics fast became the stuff of legend, his talent on the pitch was fully utilised by Spurs over the course of a decade. With his abilities both in the air and on the ground complemented by his astute reading of the game, Gilzean boasted all the attributes to be the perfect foil for an adept striking partner. One can imagine the dismay with which Tottenham team-sheets were greeted by opposition defences on a weekly basis, for Spurs were blessed, during Gilzean's time at the Lane, to have in their ranks first Jimmy Greaves and then Martin Chivers, two men pre-eminent in the art of goalscoring, and therefore able to reap the rich harvest he sowed. As fan Terry Dignan summarised: "During his long tenure at the Lane Gilzean played up front alongside the great Jimmy Greaves for five years and then with Martin Chivers for a further four. Both would surely agree that Gilly was a terrific striking partner, rising on countless occasions to beat his marker in the air and flick the ball on to create a goalscoring opportunity."

Spurs have been fortunate over the years to provide the stage for a number of sublime striking partnerships, displaying an awareness and understanding that borders on the psychic. Crooks and Archibald; Sheringham and Klinsmann; even Berbatov and Keane – it is difficult to utter one name without the other swiftly springing to mind, such were the inextricable qualities of these pairings. The precursor to such fabled duos were, as they were reverently christened by White Hart Lane worshippers, 'The G Men' – Gilzean and Greaves. Gilzean had arrived at Spurs following the departure of Double-winning striker Bobby Smith, but the two were cut from decidedly different cloth. While Smith was something of a battering-ram in attack, Gilzean's approach to the game was far subtler. After joining in late 1964, Gilzean went straight into the team alongside Greaves, and the pair clicked immediately, combining as if they had played together all their lives. On his Tottenham debut, at home to Everton in December 1964, Gilzean had a hand in both of Greaves' goals in a 2-2 draw, and the G-Men never looked back. Greaves, the highest goalscorer in Tottenham's history, is not hesitant in attributing credit to Gilzean, recalling in his autobiography: 'I enjoyed a great understanding with Gilly. As striking partners it was almost as if we had been made for each other. We had an almost telepathic understanding right from his very first game.'

The appreciation of this partnership was echoed, and amplified, in the stands. Fan John Craig recalls: "Gilzean and Greaves were a wonderful combination, something I shall never forget."

However, despite the instant rapport struck between the two strikers, the fortunes of the Tottenham side Gilzean joined were decidedly less rosy than in previous years. Following the glories of the early 1960s, enforced changes in personnel inevitably had a detrimental effect, and as the team was rebuilt it was some time before they made another title challenge. The club's reputation in the Cup competitions, however, was repaired somewhat sooner, and Gilzean was to play an instrumental role alongside Greaves in Spurs' march to the 1967 FA Cup final. Spurs actually almost exited the competition at the first hurdle that season, progressing only through a predatory Gilzean strike to seal a 1-0 victory over Millwall in a Third Round replay. He followed this with a brace against Portsmouth in the Fourth Round, and was on target again in the quarter-final replay demolition of Birmingham, scoring, inevitably, with his head, but also creating goals for Greaves and Venables in a 6-0 win. He delivered a superlative performance in the final itself, pulling the team's attacking strings in the 2-1 win over Chelsea, to earn his first Winners' medal in England.

Greaves departed in 1970, but this was merely the cue for another great striking partnership to be forged on the White Hart Lane turf, for having been signed in 1968, Martin Chivers was now returning from a career-threatening injury to enjoy the fruits of Gilzean's labours. Gilzean and Chivers were to prove just as potent a partnership as the G-Men. They were, recalls long-time fan Jill Lewis, "A joy to behold." Chivers himself recollects in his autobiography:

'I had to anticipate Gilly's flick-ons, which he managed brilliantly off that shiny bonce ... He would never head the ball down but had such a deft touch to his flicks.'

With Gilzean's delicate touch wreaking havoc, Chivers thrived, by common consent progressing to become the best striker in Europe, and Tottenham duly profited accordingly. In the 1970/71 season Chivers amassed 29 goals, and, the year ending in '1', Spurs inevitably triumphed at Wembley, Gilzean featuring heavily in the their first ever League Cup triumph.

The following season, 1971/72, brought more success, this time in Europe, the head of Gilzean now tormenting defences across the continent. Iceland's' Keflavik, defeated 15-1 on aggregate in the opening Round, inevitably counted a Gilzean header amongst their wounds. A couple of Rounds further into the competition, and the backwards and sideways headers of Gilzean were carving open the defence of Rapid Bucharest, creating oals for Martins Chivers and Peters. Gilzean's value at set-pieces, by then such an established feature of Tottenham's game, evidently still retained an element of surprise on the continent, as reported by Brian James of *The Times*, following Spurs' quarter-final victory over UT Arad of Romania: 'Tottenham scored again with a set-piece goal quite famous in football, which yet caught Arad unprepared. Morgan's short corner, Gilzean's back header at the near post and [centre-back Mike] England's stabbing volley at the far post were the goal's well-rehearsed components.'

Spurs won the competition with a 3-2 aggregate victory in the final against Wolves, and having missed out on European success as a 25-year-old in his Dundee days, in 1963, 9 years later, Gilly had his first European medal. One suspects it may have been particularly sweet for him to have featured in the 3-2 aggregate vanquishing of AC Milan in the semi-final, having suffered defeat to the same opponents while plying his trade north of the border.

1973 was to be the year of another League Cup triumph, but not for the first time Spurs made hard work of the early Rounds, riding their luck and requiring two replays to dispose of Middlesbrough. Of one of the replays, Norman Fox of *The Times* wrote: 'Bill Nicholson, Tottenham Hotspur's manager, publicly admonished his team ... and only Gilzean deservedly escape Nicholson's and the crowd's fury ... Only Gilzean was positively and totally engaged in the anaemic affair at hand ... Because his colleagues were so unbelievably slack, Gilzean looked after their interests in defence, midfield and attack. In each area he was superb.'

Rumours of the old man's demise as a footballer, it seemed, were premature ('Even in the last minutes of extra time he was pounding the Middlesbrough goal,' added Fox), his performance that night serving to emphasise how much he brought to the team beyond goals. Having almost settled the tie with an impudently backheeled shot, he did eventually score the goal in a following replay which took Tottenham into the next Round. Spurs went on to win the competition, defeating Norwich 1-0 in the final, but the silverware, and the still-thriving partnership between Chivers and the evergreen Gilzean, could not disguise the fact that the Spurs of 1973 were a pale imitation of the team that had ruled the roost, the cockerel crowing proudly, a decade earlier. While their defence of the UEFA Cup ended in a creditable run to the semi-final – where eventual First Division champions Liverpool were to knock them out – they fell to eighth in the League, inadvertently reaffirming that their inconsistency had turned them into Cup specialists.

There were still some highlights in the League, including victory over the enemy. Gilzean scored in the 2-0 home win against Arsenal in October 1973, a week before his 35th birthday, displaying both his strength and impeccable technique to execute a delicately weighted lob over the goalkeeper, whilst being harassed by half the opposition defence. Noted Tom Freeman of *The Times* in his match report: 'One old player we will all be sorry to see leave is Gilzean, who looks a little greyer, balder and a little more like a statesman each year, but who, in his play, shows no signs of growing old.'

The strike against Arsenal was naturally lapped up by his adoring public, and it is likely that Gilly himself would have derived particular pleasure from scoring against Arsenal goalkeeper Bob Wilson, for there was no love lost between the pair. Typically so famously laid-back, it appeared that the only man who truly invoked his ire was Wilson. Gilzean, a proud Scot with 14 goals in 22 caps, was reportedly apoplectic that the Chesterfield-born goalkeeper, unable to earn England recognition ahead of Gordon Banks and Peter Shilton, opted to play for Scotland by virtue of a distant relative. This issue, so goes the story, was the reason for one particular tête-à-tête, in which, having spent the game making sure that Wilson felt the full force of his challenges, Gilzean then knocked the ball out of the goalkeeper's hands and tapped it into the net as the goalkeeper bounced it. An outraged Wilson protested, while Gilly presented himself a picture of innocence. Although the referee had seemingly missed the incident, he eventually disallowed the goal, but not before scenes of bedlam had broken out on the pitch and in the Paxton Road end of White Hart Lane.

However, Tottenham's slide continued, as in 1973/74 they finished only 11th in the League and failed to bring home silverware, losing the UEFA Cup final to Feyenoord. Gilzean's contribution was reduced, as he entered his 36th year, appearing in only 25 League games, compared to 35 the previous season, but as Spurs continued to demonstrate their prowess at least as a Cup side, the Scot continued to roll back the years. Wrote *The Times* of his two-goal contribution to the 5-1 defeat of Grasshoppers of Zurich, 'Gilzean ... showed he still possesses at least some of the old magic', while in the following Round, his role in a 4-1 win over Aberdeen was noted thus: 'For Spurs, Gilzean was his usual elegant self, though a bit short of pace these days.'

It was because of his myriad talents – his touch, technique, elegance and awareness – that he was able to expiate for any lack of pace in his advancing years, and continue playing for so long. His final season at Spurs was 1973/74, his departure heralding a further slump by the club, which finished 19th in its first season *sans* Gilzean, and were relegated two years later.

It was in keeping with his enigmatic character that despite his outrageous talent Gilzean did not actually have any particular love for the game once the final whistle blew. As Hunter Davies recalled, in an article for *The New Statesman*:

'Gilly seemed neither to enjoy the act of playing, nor talking about it. He was good at it, tried hard, but that was it. Once off the pitch, he forgot it. He thought the pleasure in playing had been ruined by the need to win at all costs, while the thought of staying in the game after retirement filled him with horror ... He told me, "When I've finished with playing, that's it. I couldn't stand the aggravation of being a manager, having fans, directors, press, everyone after you, no thanks."'

After leaving Spurs he briefly played in South Africa, managed in the lower leagues, and ran a haulage business in Enfield – but as had always been the case, he shied away from publicity, and his whereabouts now, fittingly, if frustratingly, is a mystery to most.

An enigmatic, maverick but sublimely talented performer with a booze-fuelled lifestyle, Alan Gilzean was the archetypal cult hero. Prior to kick-off in his testimonial against Red Star Belgrade in November 1974, one fan raced onto the pitch, and on reaching him, bent down to kiss his feet. In doing so that fan seemed to act for a whole generation of Spurs supporters, each of whom would want to thank him for the good times, but none of whom would consider themselves worthy to do any more than kiss the boots in which he once strode, as King of White Hart Lane.

MARTIN CHIVERS

1967-1976

SPURS CAREER

Games	367
Goals	174
Caps	24

MAGIC MOMENT

Scoring braces in the
1971 League Cup and
1972 UEFA Cup finals

'BIG CHIV'

IN the dying moments of the 1972 UEFA Cup final First Leg between Tottenham and Wolverhampton Wanderers, wearied limbs across the mud told the tale of an attritional battle, yet from this quagmire of sweat and toil there was to emerge a quite sensational finale. Martin Chivers had already made his mark in heading Tottenham in front, but Wolves had equalised and the beckoning finger of parity appeared irresistible as the clock ticked down towards 90. Then, three minutes from the end, Chivers collected the ball by the left touchline – closer to halfway than the Wolves goal – and, suddenly imbued with a most exhilarating spirit of daring, put his head down and ran.

Pity the unfortunates of the Black Country, for having matched Tottenham stride for stride throughout the game there could be no legislating for the spontaneous and irresistible charge of the sort about to be unleashed. Chivers, belying the energy-sapping effects of the Molineux pitch and a season elongated by Cup runs, drove forward like a bull sighting the red rag. Such was the determination in his eyes, one suspects he could have kept running until doomsday, but as a gap appeared ahead of him, Chivers, dispensed with subtlety, drew back his right leg and from 30 yards let fly. The ball flew past Wolves keeper Phil Parkes like an Exocet and straight into the Tottenham Hotspur annals, bulging the net in front of the massed ranks of Spurs fans gathered behind the goal.

Within the pantheon of the club's greatest ever goals, Chivers' strike against Wolves rightfully holds pride of place amongst the elite, the big man's effort that night on a par with those later, timeless classics offered by Villa and Gascoigne. For timing, occasion, impudence and, above all else, sheer quality, Chivers' second goal in the 1972 UEFA Cup final First Leg is one of the most memorable in the club's history.

Tottenham Hotspur have been blessed with pre-eminent centre-forwards throughout their long history, on their own providing a *Who's Who* of the game's greatest goalscorers. Amongst the mesmeric dribblers, long-serving captains and thunderous hardmen, the fans have always been particularly appreciative of a finisher at the pinnacle of his trade, and it is an opinion so widely held it is virtually tantamount to fact that, for a couple of years in the early 1970s, Martin Chivers was the best centre-forward in Europe. Indeed, the chorus acclaiming him boasts some illustrious personnel. 'Chivers was the top man in Europe at the time,' opined Steve Perryman in Jeremy Novick's *Winning Their Spurs*; 'He had two years when he was absolutely magnificent ... world class,' asserted Terry Venables in *The Greatest Ever Spurs Team*; 'Martin Chivers had two terrific seasons where he couldn't do anything wrong,' recalls team-mate Ralph Coates, in *Winning Their Spurs*. Fans too, were fully aware of quite how brightly Chivers' star shone at the Lane, long-time supporter Gary Wright recalling: "For a while he was probably the best center-forward in the world, leading the line and scoring for fun."

Martin Harcourt Chivers had been an all-round sportsman as a schoolboy, representing his school in national level athletics championships (the high-jump his event of choice) and turning down an offer to sign for Hampshire County Cricket Club, before joining CPC Sports, the nursery team of Southampton FC. He became a professional in September 1962 and made his first-team debut just four days later, setting up the only goal of the game against Charlton Athletic. Within a year he was a first-team regular, helping his team win promotion, and consequently making his White Hart Lane bow – as a Southampton player – in November 1966.

Judging by his words in his autobiography *Big Chiv*, that first encounter with the White Hart Lane turf made quite an impression: 'It was a magnificent, unique stadium and I always remember how imposing The Shelf was on the that day. It was the best atmosphere I had ever experienced at that point in my career.'

Interestingly, the seeds of a move to Spurs were sown by the man Chivers was eventually to replace as Tottenham's goal-getter-in-chief, no less a luminary than Jimmy Greaves. The notion had been casually mooted after the pair had played together for a Football League Select XI against Ireland, in the autumn of 1967. If the Tottenham hierarchy were at that point undecided, the very next League game of the season would help substantiate the case for Chivers' signature, as he scored against Spurs at the Dell. The £125,000 deal was completed in January 1968, a move which saw Frank Saul, scorer in Spurs' 1967 FA Cup Final victory, move in the other direction.

Chivers marked his Spurs debut with a goal, and quite one to behold – collecting the ball on halfway, steaming forward and pulling the trigger from outside the area, in a 2-0 victory over Sheffield Wednesday. He also created one for Greaves that day, and was to add a further half dozen League goals that season, plus four in the FA Cup. However, while he ultimately became the cream of Europe, lauded at the Lane practically as a deity with a cockerel on his shirt, in common with a number of the club's other favourite sons, those cheers in his name had been jeers not so long before. As long-time fan Alan Granville put it: "After a slow beginning (he was slaughtered when he first played for us), he became a fantastic player and scorer of remarkable goals." His performances early in his White Hart Lane career could loosely be grouped under the category 'Unspectacular', offering precious little suggestion of the glories to follow. Chivers' cause was hardly aided by the fact that when he started out, the affections of the Tottenham faithful still lay with the twin striking delights of 'The G-Men', Greaves and Gilzean.

However, a more critical issue was to arise early in the following season, 1968/69. The threat of injuries hovers unforgivingly and indiscriminately over the career of any professional footballer. Amongst the heroes of White Hart Lane they have both brought down the final curtain in a Tottenham career – as illustrated so unhappily by Mr Gascoigne – and proved a stimulus to recovery and the return of an even stronger man, as evinced by the astonishing rehabilitation of Dave Mackay from a twice-broken leg. Merrily, Chivers fell ultimately into the latter category; but when he collapsed to the White Hart Lane turf on 21 September 1968, his knee-cap having completely crumpled, the prognosis appeared frighteningly serious. While Bill Nicholson told him in hospital the following day, following an operation, that he would be out for at least six months, privately the club was already investigating insurance cover against what they saw as Chivers' likely retirement. Fast-forward a couple of years however, and Lazarus himself was standing back in awe at the spectacular manner of his recovery.

Chivers' long period of recuperation finally began to pay dividends in 1969/70 pre-season training, as he began kicking a ball again. That season he returned to the first team, albeit with understandable caution. Although a return of 11 goals from 35 League

Spurs players celebrate Sandy Brown's first goal in the 1901 FA Cup final at the Kennington Oval. He scored twice in a 2-2 draw. Sheffield United's gargantuan goalkeeper William 'Fatty' Foulke can be seen retrieving the ball from the back of the net.

Tottenham Hotspur's 1901 FA Cup-winning team: (back row, l-r) Harry Erentz, George Clawley, Sandy Tait; (middle row, l-r) John Cameron, Tom Morris, Ted Hughes, Jack Jones, Jack Kirwan; (front row, l-r) Tom Smith, Sandy Brown, David Copeland. Brown scored the third goal as Spurs defeated Sheffield United 3-1 at Burnden Park in the replay. It proved to be his last action for the club as he returned to Portsmouth in mysterious circumstances just days later.

A rare photograph of Bill Nicholson in his playing days. Bill played at right-half in Arthur Rowe's legendary 1951 League title-winning 'push and run' side.

Captain Danny Blanchflower (left) and centre-forward Bobby Smith parade the FA Cup, the second leg of the historic 1960/61 double, around Wembley.

Welsh wing wizard Cliff Jones (second from left) celebrates scoring his first goal of a 17-minute hat-trick and Spurs' third goal in the 8-1 thrashing of Górnik Zabrze in the European Cup preliminary round in September 1961.

Jimmy Greaves rises to poach Spurs' second and equalising goal against Manchester United in January 1962 in typical predatory fashion. Greaves scored a phenomenal 266 goals in 379 games for Tottenham.

Danny Blanchflower sends Burnley goalkeeper Adam Blacklaw the wrong way to score his team's third goal from the penalty spot in the 1962 FA Cup final.

Spurs' heroes arrive at Tottenham Town Hall to the tumultuous welcome of a huge crowd, massed to greet them after their 1962 FA Cup final triumph.

Left to right: Bill Brown, Jimmy Greaves, Danny Blanchflower, Dave Mackay, John White, Cliff Jones and Terry Medwin show off the FA Cup to Spurs fans after retaining the trophy thanks to the 3-1 victory over Burnley.

Jimmy Greaves (right) and Terry Dyson show off the European Cup Winners' Cup upon their return to England, after thrashing Atlético Madrid 5-1 in the final in Rotterdam.

Manager Bill Nicholson, affectionately known as Bill Nick, won almost half of his games in charge during Spurs' halcyon period under his leadership from 1958 to 1974.

Scottish striker Alan Gilzean scoring the first goal in Spurs' 4-2 victory over Chelsea at White Hart Lane in December 1965. Gilzean netted 133 goals in 439 games for the club.

Perhaps the most famous football photograph ever. Captain fantastic Dave Mackay sorts out upstart Billy Bremner of Leeds United on the opening day of the 1966/67 season.

Manager Bill Nicholson (second left) makes his point to (l-r) Frank Saul, Joe Kinnear, Terry Venables and Pat Jennings five days before the 1967 FA Cup final.

Big Martin Chivers scores the third goal of the 3-0 win UEFA Cup Third Round over Rapid Bucharest as goalkeeper Raducanu Nucula and defender Alexander Boc look on. Spurs won 5-0 on aggregate on the way to defeating Wolves 3-2 on aggregate in the final.

Spurs players celebrate Steve Perryman's (no. 8) second goal of the night which clinched a 2-1 victory over AC Milan in the UEFA Cup semi-final first leg in April 1972.

A plethora of cult heroes shoulder captain Alan Mullery as he shows off the UEFA Cup after a 1-1 second leg draw gives Spurs their second European trophy. Supporting Mullery are (l-r) Ralph Coates, Alan Gilzean, Mike England, Martin Peters, Pat Jennings, Joe Kinnear, Cyril Knowles and Martin Chivers.

The keeper with the shovel-sized hands, Pat Jennings, dives to save Tommy Smith's penalty to make his second stop from the spot of the game at Anfield in March 1973.

Cyril Knowles (right) and Martin Peters parade the League Cup on their lap of honour after the 1-0 victory over Norwich in the 1973 final.

Manager Keith Burkinshaw welcomes two of the most glamorous signings in Spurs' history to the Lane: World Cup-winning Argentineans Ricardo Villa (left) and Osvaldo Ardiles.

Ardiles proved to be one of the most-loved Spurs players ever. Here he wins undying affection by scoring against Arsenal, Spurs' winning goal in the 1-0 Fourth Round League Cup victory in November 1980.

Spurs' 1981 FA Cup-winning team, featuring cult heroes Perryman (crouching second from left), Hoddle (back row centre, holding cup) and Ardiles (crouching second from right).

No-one has played more games for Spurs than Mr Consistency Steve Perryman – an incredible 854 matches.

The most majestic creative midfielder ever to grace White Hart Lane, Glenn Hoddle takes on Nottingham Forest's Steve Hodge.

Graham Roberts was the ultimate do-or-die defender and captain who would put himself through anything for Spurs.

Roberts' greatest moment was his display in the second leg of the 1984 UEFA Cup final. He powered Spurs forward and scored this vital late equalising goal against Anderlecht, then netted one of the spot-kicks as Tottenham won a dramatic contest 4–3 on penalties.

The unmistakable jinking gait of wonder winger Chris Waddle, here taking on Coventry's Greg Downs in the 1987 FA Cup final. Waddle made Clive Allen's opening goal in only the second minute, but Spurs lost an incredible final 3-2 after extra-time.

Clive Allen notches another of his incredible haul of 49 goals in the 1986/87 season, this time, satisfyingly, against Arsenal in the League Cup semi-final first leg at Highbury.

Allen scored a remarkable 84 goals in 135 games in three years at Spurs.

Clive Allen gets vocal support from rock gods Chas and Dave during the recording of one of the team's many famous FA Cup singles.

The iconic Paul Gascoigne free kick flies past David Seaman into the Wembley net to give Spurs a 1-0 lead in the 1991 FA Cup semi-final.

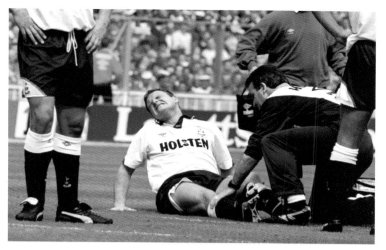

Gazza pays for his challenge on Nottingham Forest's Gary Charles in the final with a ruptured cruciate ligament in his right knee.

Captain Gary Mabbutt parades the FA Cup after the 2-1 victory over Nottingham Forest in 1991.

Paul Gascoigne shows off the FA Cup in his own inimitable style.

Gary Mabbutt organises his defence as he did throughout his Spurs career over 16 years and 611 games.

Jürgen Klinsmann celebrates scoring one of his 38 goals in 68 games over his two seasons at White Hart Lane.

Klinsmann shows off his 1995 Footballer of the Year award.

David Ginola shows off his no.14 shirt and his six pack on joining the club in July 1997 for £2.5 million. He would prove well worth it.

Ginola in full flight – the last of the true individual geniuses who have graced White Hart Lane over the years.

games was creditable, and appreciated as such by the fans, his visible appearance was not that of man on the cusp of greatness, betraying instead only a lack of confidence.

That 1969/70 season heralded a critical moment in Chivers' Tottenham career, as Martin Peters arrived at White Hart Lane in January, as part of the deal that saw Jimmy Greaves move to West Ham. Chivers and Peters quickly developed a highly effective on-pitch understanding, principally from open play, but also from set-pieces. Although Peters' wife famously claimed, in Hunter Davies' legendary tome *The Glory Game*, that her man never received the credit he was due for Chivers' metamorphosis into the continent's leading striker, seasoned observers are quick to extol Peters' virtues when singing Chivers' praises. In fact Chivers himself, in *Big Chiv*, credits Peters as being 'The major influence' in the continued upward curve of his career.

While the presence of Peters playing behind him helped to catalyse Chivers' elevation to the game's highest echelons, his partnership in attack with Alan Gilzean was what captured the imagination, the pair quickly evolving into one of the great strike partnerships of the time. Somebody up there evidently liked Chivers, for with Peters behind him and Gilzean alongside him the pieces began to fall perfectly into place, and following the travails of his early years he now began to thrive. He was ever-present in Tottenham's 42-game Division One campaign in 1970/71, his 21 goals helping to fire the team to third place (a feat they had not achieved since 1968, and would not replicate for a further 14 years). The several thousand-strong jury sat in the stands of White Hart Lane had by this time also reached a positive verdict, for when Chivers ran out onto the pitch it was to cries of adulation, as fan Julian Clarke recalls: "My first visit to White Hart Lane was in 1971, when we beat Manchester City 2-0 and Chivers scored both. 'Chivers for England' was the cry and boy did we love him." Chivers' rehabilitation, both in terms of his recovery from injury and the winning of the hearts and minds of fans, was confirmed when he was named the club's Supporters' Player of the Season. Full international recognition quite rightly followed, and he marked his Wembley bow as an England player most appropriately with a goal in a 3-0 victory over Greece, in April 1971.

When God created the original, archetypal centre-forward, He named that mould 'Martin Chivers'. A hulking figure, powerful in the air yet possessed of quick feet and a quite startling burst of pace, Chivers ticked every box. Spurs' specialist weight-trainer Bill Watson deemed Chivers the strongest of the squad, while sprint tests established him as fastest over a half-pitch sprint. In fact, his only physical imperfection seemed to be his front teeth, which had rotted and fallen out in his youth, as part of a hereditary condition. As Steve Perryman recalls in *Match of my Life*, such was Chivers' talent that his team-mates considered that they could simply feed him the ball on halfway, and watch him sprint away, dribble round the opposition and score.

However, crucially and quite sensationally, the only men who seemed incapable of bringing themselves to acknowledge Chivers' talents were manager Bill Nicholson and his trusty lieutenant Eddie Baily. Nicholson had bought Big Chiv as a replacement for Bobby Smith, the bruising centre-forward in the legendary Double-winning team of 1961, but while there may have been physical similarities, Chivers has recalled that he and Smith were very different types: "I could never be a Bobby Smith because I did not have that aggression in me." In an era of rudimentary physical tactics, Chivers eschewed such an approach, preferring to nick the ball delicately off an opponent's foot rather than agriculturally plough right through him. The adage would have it that football is a game for gentlemen played by hooligans, but Nicholson it seems was driven to distraction in his attempts to nurture the hooligan in his overly gentlemanly striker. Their relationship deteriorated to such an extent that a stand-off ensued between forward and manager, lasting several years and eliciting moods veering between exasperation and rage in the two men.

Adamant that Chivers was not utilising his physical presence, Nicholson's criticism also incorporated the observation that his star striker simply did not work hard enough, either on the pitch or in training. On this front however, Chivers drops his protests, his retort amounting to a philosophical shrug and a *mea culpa*, unashamedly writing: 'Bill and Eddie would expect people to run round the track and throw up at the end of it. I have never once done that. Maybe I didn't push myself to the absolute limit but I think I gave more than enough.'

Never men to bestow praise particularly liberally at the best of times, Nicholson and Baily would relentlessly criticise Chivers' performances, considering the stick rather than carrot as the most suitable tool with which to instil some aggression into him. Come hell or high water, Chivers, it seems, could be guaranteed a verbal lashing. One given to understatement might venture that such treatment irked him somewhat, particularly so when his efforts proved match-winning, as was often the case. One of the most famous of the pair's confrontations was after Spurs' 0-0 draw with Nantes, in the early stages of the 1971/72 UEFA Cup, a competition which Spurs would go on to win. On this occasion, observers report, Chivers lit the blue-touch paper, inciting Nicholson with the sarcastic comment "Poor, poor team," seemingly as if to expose his manager's pre-match complacency. The wrath of Nicholson and Baily duly followed, heated language reportedly turning the air purple, *ad hoc* missiles flying across the dressing room and shattered crockery decorating the floor. Nicholson later revealed that if anything, the presence of *Glory Game* writer Hunter Davies in the dressing-room served to stifle his rage; one can only speculate as to quite what levels his apoplexy would otherwise have reached.

If Chivers was the instigator on this occasion, on another he seemed more sinned against than sinner, returning to the dressing room after a blistering two-goal salvo in the first half of a League game against Stoke, in October 1970, only to receive a barrage of criticism from Nicholson for the quite heinous crime of not having scored a first-half hat-trick. When Alan Mullery fairly reasonably pointed out that some praise for Chivers' goals might not go amiss (his second in particular had been vintage Chivers), all hell broke loose, Mullery and Nicholson almost coming to blows.

Such were the dynamics of the relationship between the club's greatest ever manager, and their headline-grabbing striker. The combination of Chivers' occasionally aloof and introspective nature and his brittle self-confidence did not sit well with a management team determined to arouse the beast in him by whatever means necessary. In hindsight one can smile at the level of exasperation Nicholson must have felt in one day instructing his towering centre-backs, Mike England and Peter Collins, to adopt towards

Chivers in training an approach of such physicality it bordered on assault, in an attempt to incite his aggression. The exercise may be deemed a success, for England and Chivers ended the session in a fist-fight.

The captivating tale of this relationship has a happy epilogue, for after their retirements Chivers and Nicholson mended their bridges, becoming close friends until the latter's death in 2004. However, when Nicholson stepped down as manager, 20 years earlier, Chivers admits that he was one of the few who shed no tears. Indeed, it has been suggested that the disputes with Chivers were the primary reason for Nicholson's resignation; but scorn has been poured on this notion by many close to the Tottenham inner sanctum, not least the two protagonists themselves.

Infuriating he may have been to the management, but Chivers had established himself as a favourite of the White Hart Lane supporters, adapting comfortably to the role of headline-grabbing hero as Spurs reached four Cup finals in as many seasons in the early 1970s. While lacking the consistency of their predecessors of ten years to challenge for the title, the team boasted sufficient star quality to triumph in the Cup competitions, blazing a trail for so many Spurs teams since. The first addition to the White Hart Lane trophy cabinet was the 1971 League Cup, and with six goals on the road to Wembley it is reasonable to assert that Big Chiv was one of the principal cast-members in this production. In the final itself, lowly opponents Aston Villa, of the Third Division, produced a spirited performance that had threatened an upset, but with 12 minutes remaining Martin Chivers cleared his throat, strode forth and took centre stage. First he pounced in predatory style to capitalise when Villa keeper John Dunn failed to hold a shot; then he burst through the heart of the Villa defence in trademark style to score a spectacular second, and seal Tottenham's 2-0 win.

1971/72 brought Chivers a remarkable 43 goals in all competitions, including 7 as Spurs reached the League Cup semi-final, and 6 en route to the UEFA Cup final against Wolves, in which he was to play such a central role. Following his late virtuoso goal to give Spurs a 2-1 first leg lead to bring back to White Hart Lane, Chivers even drew praise from arch critic Eddie Baily. To quote from *The Glory Game*:

'Eddie Baily was the first to sprint on to the pitch, embracing Chivers as the whistle went. In the dressing-room he said that if Martin liked he would lie down on the floor and let him walk all over him. "What can I say? I can't say nuffink, can I? You've knocked me out, Martin. I'm out for the count. I'm on the floor for the count of three, and you're saying 4-5-6-7-OUT! Martin, what can I say?"'

Chivers would have done well to savour such praise for its rarity. Normal service would swiftly be resumed.

The following season, 1972/73, brought a further eight UEFA Cup goals, including one memorable strike against Victoria Setubal of Portugal at the quarter-final stage, as reported by Brian James of *The Times*: 'Martin Chivers took his moment. A free kick 35 yards out was driven beyond the Setubal wall and rose into the net with massive unconcern: the crowd grew silent, Chivers merely shrugged...'

Spurs were knocked out by eventual League champions Liverpool at the semi-final stage, but collected silverware on the domestic front, with victory again in the League

Cup. The final belonged to Ralph Coates, scorer of the only goal and perpetrator of one Wembley's most famous (and exuberant) celebrations, but Chivers was again instrumental. His famous long throw set up the goal, while he also contributed four goals on the road to Wembley, including the winning goal in the semi-final, as he reinforced his status as nemesis of Wolves by scoring with six minutes remaining of extra-time. Big Chiv had also made the crucial contribution in the defeat of the mighty Liverpool at the quarter-final stage, with two goals in the second leg giving Spurs a 4-2 aggregate victory, as reported by Geoffrey Green of *The Times*:

'In the second minute Chivers, who moved throughout the game as fluidly as a great white phantom, nearly scored after out accelerating Liverpool's defence. And in the sixth minute he took the first goal … Peters touched the free kick and Chivers' shot rocketed through the gap … Later a fine through pass put Chivers in possession and a slip by Lloyd gave him the room to turn and score from 18 yards with a marvellous low shot.'

A second winners' medal in the competition was particularly apt for Chivers, whose 23 goals for Spurs in 33 League Cup ties remains a club record. That second League Cup final victory meant another European tour in 1973/74, but only after England had been eliminated from the World Cup at the qualifying stage, Chivers amongst those in the team that lost at Wembley to Poland, in what proved to be his 24th and final cap. Perhaps spurred by this disappointment, he continued to assert himself on the European stage at club level, with six goals in Tottenham's progress to the 1974 UEFA Cup final, including a brace at home to the highly rated Dinamo Tibilisi: 'Chivers and company came thundering in on headers. Chivers in fact was a lion this night, utterly unrecognisable from the man Sir Alf Ramsey had dismissed,' as reported by John Hennesy of *The Times*.

However, for all his aerial prowess, upper-body strength, ability to run with the ball, ferocious long-range shooting and reliable long throw-in, Chivers continued to exasperate his managers, who, rather than bending over backwards to accommodate him, seemed instead to obsess over his combination of skulking aloofness and outrageous talent. Following the years of disagreement with Nicholson, the next Spurs manager, Terry Neill, also had his misgivings about the hirsute striker (Chivers having by then taken the fantastic step of cultivating that ultimate symbol of bloody-minded male obstinacy – a beard). The beard remained for over a decade, but Chivers was needed for just one more game that season, the crucial final fixture against Leeds, which Spurs needed to win to ensure top-flight survival. His contribution that day was described thus by Geoff Green in *The Times*:

'As for Tottenham, they had Chivers back, now bearded and at last showing some drive and initiative, especially in the second half when at times he moved like a steam engine to unsettle the middle of the Leeds defence.'

Inevitably the big man was on the scoresheet as Spurs won 4-2 and maintained their top-flight status. Matters at White Hart Lane were, however, coming to a head for Chivers. The club was lacking quality, and the man himself considered that the alteration in style (long straight balls from deep, rather than crosses at an angle from the wing, on the instruction of manager and long-time Arsenal man Neill) left him little natural opportunity to pose a threat on goal. With Neill evidently not fancying him in attack, his transfer request was eventually granted, and in 1976 he joined Swiss outfit Sevette Geneva for £80,000.

Thus ended the Tottenham career of Martin Chivers. While his introspective and often sullen personality may have had successive managers seething with increasing levels of apoplexy, he will be best remembered by fans as the great hero of the early 1970s, the finest centre-forward in Europe who each week graced the turf of White Hart Lane. Inducted into the club's Hall of Fame in 2007, he now dons suit and tie of a Saturday afternoon in his role as Tottenham match-day host, but for thousands of fans, the abiding memory of Big Chiv is that of a man in lilywhite jersey and cockerel, bulging nets across the country and beyond.

STEVE PERRYMAN

'STEVIE P'

1969-1986

SPURS CAREER

Games	**854**
Goals	**39**
Caps	**1**

MAGIC MOMENT

Scoring two memorable long-range goals in the 1972 UEFA Cup semi-final First Leg against AC Milan

IT is the evening of Thursday 14 May, 1981. Steve Perryman leads his Tottenham team up the 39 steps of Wembley, at the end of the 100th FA Cup final. He receives the trophy, but seemingly too embarrassed to bask in the personal glory of holding it aloft, shuffles along to shake the hands of more dignitaries. Eventually he turns to the massed ranks of the Tottenham faithful, smiles that unmistakeable, boyish shy smile and raises the FA Cup, to a roar of approval. As he does so one young fan with no such sense of bashfulness vaults onto the platform to bestow his personal congratulations.

Rewind four years however – to Saturday 7 May 1977, to be precise – and the significance of Perryman lifting the FA Cup is underlined. For that afternoon, one of the darkest in Tottenham history, Spurs crashed to a 5-0 defeat at Manchester City, confirming the ignominy of relegation to the second tier of English football. Focus, naturally, turned to the future of club captain Perryman, particularly as League champions Liverpool had come sniffing at his door. Perryman's reaction? "This club went down on my watch, and I'm getting them back up." That he did, and the eventual FA Cup triumph completed a quite remarkable renaissance. Spurs went on to enjoy something of a golden period, and having rolled up his sleeves and dug in through the bad times, Perryman was deservedly able to enjoy it.

With 854 appearances in lilywhite to his name, Steve Perryman simply is Mr Tottenham Hotspur. *854 games* – it is a mind-boggling statistic, and one which gains further sheen with each passing day, particularly given the current trend of player loyalty to lucre first and fans second. Such devout service transcends any salary packet or personal ambitions, instead representing genuine affection for the club. Spanning 17 seasons as a professional, Perryman's career at White Hart Lane explains straightforwardly why he is held in such high regard and affection by supporters. Perryman is a true Spurs man, regarded by fans as one of their own. The fans suffered the agony of defeat, and sat through the humiliation of relegation with no option to leave for pastures new. Perryman had that option, to jump a ship that was most evidently sinking, but remained true to the club. His loyalty, through the thick and thin of almost two full decades, supremely qualifies him to rank amongst the club greats as a Spurs cult hero. Even today, in his current role as Director of Football at Exeter City, he tells fans that Exeter is *their* club, but Tottenham remains his.

Perryman grew up in Middlesex, the youngest of three brothers. While a talented all-round sportsman as a schoolboy, he pursued his primary passion for football, sagely rejecting the advice of one of his brothers that he opt for West Ham United and instead joining Tottenham as a 15-year-old apprentice in July 1967. West Ham had been one of a number of London clubs courting him, Chelsea being another, with all manner of perks being offered by scouts eager for his signature, as was almost *de rigeur* at the time. As he recalls in *Match of my Life*, 'My mum used to have packets of biscuits sent to her, I was invited to play golf ... one scout even came round and offered to cut our lawn!'

However, while such enticements might have appealed to more superficial characters, Perryman was already displaying the maturity that belied his years and was to become his trademark, his head instead turned towards N17 by the straight-talking approach of Bill Nicholson. This is hardly surprising, for Perryman himself is cut from such cloth – as former team-mate Martin Chivers noted of him in *Big Chiv*, 'Reputations did not impress him.' Of working-class roots, he was a hard but honest man, who would train fiendishly but hold his own when it came to team drinking sessions. His hard-working attitude – not to mention his appearance in 1969 with the same suedehead haircut sported on the terraces – quickly led to him earning the reputation amongst fans as 'one of us'.

Perryman turned professional in January 1969, and made his first-team debut that September, brought into the side by manager Bill Nicholson for a game away to Sunderland, after Spurs had lost 5-0 the previous week. His debut that day included one heart-in-mouth moment, as he has recalled on club website *Tottenhamhotspur.com*: 'I gave an awful backpass to Pat Jennings and I think Dennis Tueart ran onto it and Pat ended up deflecting his shot onto the post and out for a corner.'

Had Tueart scored, Perryman's career and Tottenham's history might have run a decidedly different course, but Jennings' intervention meant that the mistake did not prove costly. While Spurs lost, Perryman's overall performance went down well – the 'only satisfaction from the match', according to the club programme the following week – and he played a further 27 games that season, adding to appearances that same campaign in the club's youth, reserve and 'A' team, as well as England Under 23s.

Perryman was blessed with natural ability – notably an eye for a pass which compensated for any perceived lack of pace – but it was his industry and energy that earned him his spell in the first-team. As he puts it in *Match of my Life*, Tottenham at the time had 'Too many chiefs and not enough Indians', and the indefatigable Perryman was seen as the sort of hard worker who could complement the likes of Jimmy Greaves and Martin Chivers ahead of him, glamorous international players adored by the fans but not necessarily model professionals when it came to the hard yards.

Perryman's attitude to training is the stuff of legend, mirroring as well as explaining his on-pitch work-rate. In *The Glory Game*, his seminal work charting a season at Spurs, Hunter Davies describes the efforts of the 19-year-old Perryman at a weights training session thus:

'Steve Perryman, the youngest first-team player, had his eyes fixed almost manically, pummelling himself to greater effort. Some of the older players, like Mullery, though working no less hard than Perryman, from time to time exchanged looks with each other, putting on the groans.'

It is a scene easy to envisage for anyone who has watched Perryman in action on the playing field, and hardly surprising that the man himself recalls, on *Tottenhamhotspur.com*:

'Every afternoon by the time I got home I went straight into the front room, put some music on and fell asleep within a couple of minutes. It was a habit I got into because it was so physically demanding.'

The man just would not stop running for the Tottenham cause, always encouraging – or chiding, when appropriate – his team-mates to perform similarly. A supremely honest and whole-hearted worker, one suspects he would not have been able to sleep at night for guilt if he did not finish each game ready to drop from exhaustion. Indeed, such was

Perryman's work-rate that when Ralph Coates scored the late winning goal for the club, in the 1973 League Cup final against Norwich, and famously went haring around the Wembley pitch in celebration, the only man able to keep up with him was Perryman.

'That non-stop approach didn't do me any good in the long-term, because I got a reputation as a runner and a tackler and that wasn't really what my game was about,' he recalls in *Match of My Life*, yet having established himself thus, Perryman had little option but to continue offering the same qualities to a Spurs team which needed them.

It was a curious period, both for Spurs and the English game. Tottenham were becoming increasingly reliant upon the transfer market, with only two homegrown players featuring in the '67 Cup-winning team (namely Joe Kinnear and Frank Saul), and halfway through Perryman's first season as a professional, Spurs' greatest ever goalscorer, Jimmy Greaves, was sold.

Meanwhile the style of football in England was evolving. The push-and-run Spurs team of 1951, and slick Double-winners of the following decade, were no longer the blueprint, with England winning the World Cup in 1966 through the 'Wingless Wonders' formation, which placed more emphasis on midfield graft. The departure of legendary hard-man Dave Mackay from White Hart Lane in 1968 did indeed leave Tottenham a few Indians short amongst the midfield chiefs.

As a home-grown, industrious, midfield busy-body, Steve Perryman was therefore able to tick a number of boxes, and even though still a teenager, cemented his place in the team. He claims that this personal success owes much to good fortune, and the talents of those around him, remarking in Jeremy Novick's *Winning Their Spurs*: 'My first two seasons, things had gone extremely well in a weird sort of way. I would just clear balls from the edge of the box, put Jimmy Greaves in for the goal, he'd beat five players and I'd be acclaimed for the pass, and all it was was a clearance.'

While Greaves' class is beyond debate, it is safe to conclude that Perryman is rather glossing over his achievements here, exuding that same humility which prevented him from waving around the FA Cup like a maniac the moment it was presented to him in 1981. At the age of just 20, Perryman was made captain of Tottenham Hotspur for the first time. Even Jimmy Greaves, for all his talents, cannot be credited for engineering that.

Disciplined and supremely hard-working even as a youth player, Perryman was an obvious choice as captain, despite his tender years. He gave everything for the Tottenham cause – expecting the same of those around him – and thereby won the respect of his team-mates, as well as the adoration of the fans. Terry Venables has said of his leadership, in *The Greatest Ever Spurs Team*: 'He had a terrific influence as a player, perhaps even more so as a captain and as a personality', while Ricky Villa, when asked about Perryman, simply smiles and says, "We haven't had a great captain since Steve."

Perryman's influence as a leader extended beyond the pitch. When Keith Burkinshaw (manager from 1976 until 1984) introduced renowned sports psychologist John Syer into the sanctum of the Tottenham changing room, the players only acquiesced once Perryman had given the move his blessing. In fact, when the idea of singing musical classic 'Ossie's Dream' was proposed, prior to the 1981 FA Cup final, Perryman was again instrumental in its production, liaising between his team-mates and the musical parties to make it happen. He has noted that such was his authority, and to such an extent did he command respect, that even to this day when the players reconvene it is not unusual for them to call him 'Skip'.

Burkinshaw recalls of his relationship with Perryman: 'Steve and me were as close as any manager and captain in the game.' Perryman had already been installed as captain when Burkinshaw arrived at the Lane, and in one of the most straightforward, yet important, decisions of his tenure as manager, Burkinshaw retained the status quo. The revelation by Burkinshaw that he would allow Perryman to make on-field tactical changes, and take the blame himself if they didn't work (although, he notes, 'Steve didn't do it very often') has echoes of the wonderful dynamic that had existed between manager and captain of the previous great Spurs side, Bill Nicholson and Danny Blanchflower in the Double-winning team. Like Blanchflower, Perryman was a renowned thinker of the game, and Burkinshaw recalls that Perryman would ring him and talk for two hours the day after a game. Perryman himself has said that he considered that one of the most important things he and his team-mates did was go out after a match to talk about football, discussing the minutiae of the game they had just played. Cliff Jones, winger in that Double-winning side, has said of Blanchflower that he bridged the gap between the boardroom and the dressing room, and such leadership and responsibility came just as naturally to Perryman.

It is worth noting that the relationship between Perryman was not always serene, with the pair falling out over contract talks in 1983, a feud that lasted for a year, and was indicative of Burkinshaw's growing disillusionment with the increasing role of money in the game and at the club (a disillusionment which ultimately led to his departure in 1984, as Spurs moved to become a public limited company).

Long before he took on the permanent captaincy, Perryman's commitment to the Tottenham cause had become as well-established a part of the fabric of the club as the cockerel atop the clock at the entrance to White Hart Lane stadium. A UEFA Cup tie in 1971 against Rapid Bucharest saw him play on after sustaining a dislocated shoulder. A North London derby – never a bad occasion in which to turn in a lion-hearted performance – in October 1974 saw him sustain more impressive battle-scars, following a low attempted header which earned his face a full-blooded clout from the boot of Arsenal's Liam Brady. Many would describe it as brave, some, perhaps, as churlish, but all can rest assured that there was little possibility of Perryman shirking the challenge. He had already scored the opening goal that day, and was described by the *Daily Mirror*'s Harry Miller as 'a non-stop bundle of midfield energy', finishing the game with a black eye, which left him nursing double vision for several hours and wearing an eye-patch for several days.

However, the whole-hearted commitment in his game was complemented by a silky touch and exceptional footballing brain. Amidst all the medals and trophies, his proudest moment in a Spurs shirt came in the 1972 UEFA Cup semi-final against AC Milan. Spurs fell behind to an early goal, a nightmare scenario given the Italians' well-earned reputation for being able to guard with their lives such European leads. Nevertheless, Spurs turned the tie around, with Perryman coming to the fore as an unlikely hero, to enjoy a rare day in the limelight. First he drove home sweetly from just outside the area to bring parity, then he produced an even better effort, belting the ball through a crowded penalty area and into the net after Milan had failed to clear a corner. Norman Fox of *The Times* gushed, 'Perryman's first goal had been splendid and invaluable, his second was even better. This time he was all of 20 yards out when he spotted a rare corridor of space and sent his shot tearing thought without Cudicini [Milan goalkeeper, and father of later Spurs keeper Carlo] moving off his studs.'

Perryman has admitted that Bill Nicholson's typical drill to a player receiving the ball in such situations, from a half-cleared corner, was to avoid any risk of conceding possession and vulnerability to the counter-attack, by playing the ball back out wide whence it had come. It renders all the more incongruous the spectacular strikes unleashed by Perryman, an essentially defensive-minded player, while two such goals in a single game were a thing unheard of. However, Perryman's immediate reaction to his second wonder-goal is telling, as he notes in *Winning Their Spurs*: 'I was thinking more of what my defensive responsibilities were. I never used to congratulate people when they scored goals because I was always worried about conceding one from kick-off.'

Nevertheless, the goal gave him a brief insight into the glamorous world of the headline-grabbing superstar footballer (a world, one suspects, in which he would have felt thoroughly uncomfortable), as the crowd sang his name and, when the team arrived in Milan for the return leg, the Italian press incessantly sought him for interviews.

Perryman assumed the captaincy full time in March 1975, following the departure of Martin Peters, but by this point it was clear that all was not well on board the good ship Tottenham. Cup triumphs in successive seasons from 1971 to 1973, and a further Cup final in 1974, were not crowning glories in successful campaigns, but rather were masking the fact that the team was some way off challenging again for the title. The 1973 League Cup triumph was described by then captain Martin Peters, in *Match of my Life*, as 'A high point in a disappointing season', while 1974 brought the club's first ever Cup final defeat – over two legs in the UEFA Cup, a tie marred by crowd violence. Throughout this period the team were gradually slipping down the First Division table, to mid-table obscurity and worse. The team's troubles were epitomised by the messy departure of the long-serving Bill Nicholson at the start of the 1974/75 season, and the appointment as his replacement, of Terry Neill – a man whose long association with Arsenal had only recently ended (and who was later to return to Highbury even before the dust had settled on his departure from White Hart Lane). Almost as an act of apologetic recognition of their descent into the mire, the team tumbled down the table that season, only avoiding relegation with a final-day victory at home to Leeds, and finishing in 19th. Two seasons later however, there was to be no such late reprieve, and the penultimate game brought relegation, with the 5-0 defeat to Manchester City.

Perryman's diagnosis of the problems of the time is typically trenchant: 'The fact was that we just didn't replace in good enough style.' A tale he tells in *Winning Their Spurs* is particularly illuminating: 'Terry [Neill] told me once, "If you want a centre-half, you make a list of ten, and you make the phone calls until you get one and it might have to be the tenth." Well, I'm not sure that was Bill Nick's ethics.'

Where Blanchflower, Mackay, Jones and Greaves had once trod, followed by Chivers, Gilzean, Peters and England, Spurs were no longer attracting star names and star quality. A dark period in the club's history, without a doubt; yet one from which Perryman himself identified a silver lining, for he describes the club's relegation as a "breath of fresh air." His reasoning is that after seasons of under-achievement masked by Cup runs and survival, relegation finally released the growing pressure on the players and management, and gave a natural clean slate and starting-point from which to begin the rebuilding process. A long-term plan was put into place by Keith Burkinshaw, a plan which was eventually to come to fruition with the trophy successes of the early 1980s, and which saw the club come within a whisker of the ultimate prize in English football.

A long-term plan it may have been at Tottenham, but the 'breath of fresh air' of which Perryman speaks was noticeable immediately. With their relegation confirmed in 1977, Spurs went into the final game of the season with a more relaxed attitude, and promptly dealt Leicester City a convincing 2-0 defeat at White Hart Lane. The club then embarked upon an end-of-season tour of Scandinavia where, buoyed by the shoots of recovery evidenced by the Leicester victory, the rebuilding process began in earnest with the adoption of a free-flowing style which, in truth, the club never ought to have abandoned.

That end-of-season tour makes for an interesting parallel with the Tottenham of a generation earlier. At the end of the 1959/60 season Bill Nicholson took his Spurs team on a tour of Russia, where flying winger Cliff Jones has recalled that the signs that the team could achieve the much-vaunted League and Cup Double first became evident. Almost 20 years on another end-of-season tour appeared to lay down a marker for the team.

Other factors also helped, not least the decision of Perryman to remain with the club, rather than take one of the opportunities offered to remain in the top-flight by transferring elsewhere. A move to Coventry City almost materialised, and League champions Liverpool were reportedly also an interested party, but it is a mark of the professional pride and club loyalty of Perryman that he remained at the Lane to see the job through. Astonishingly by today's standards, in which successive top-flight defeats can see pressure heaped upon a manager, the Tottenham board in 1977 elected to retain the services of Keith Burkinshaw, and he was able to set about hauling the club back into the top-flight. Although goalkeeper Pat Jennings was allowed to leave – for Arsenal, of all places – Tottenham played confidently in the then-Second Division, winning automatic promotion at the first attempt.

Not for the first – or last – time, Perryman took one for the team, moving from midfield into central defence. He was later to find a new niche at right-back, again sacrificing his ability for the good of the club, and it is a widely-held view that his career total of just a single England cap was the price he paid for his versatility, for his reputation grew as jack of all trades rather than master of one. Playing in the Second Division however, centre-back was a role he grew to relish, revelling in the extra time on the ball afforded to him. The refreshing liberation brought to Perryman's game by relegation reflected the general mood of the club, which found itself on an upward curve, in contrast to the troubles of previous seasons.

Promotion was followed just weeks later by the astonishing capture of a pair of Argentine superstars, as the pieces began to fall into place. A lad called Hoddle, another product of the youth system, had emerged in midfield, while in the summer of 1980 striking duo Garth Crooks and Steve Archibald were brought to the club, developing an instant on-pitch rapport. Such purchases received the approval of Perryman, who, a Tottenham fan as much as a player, appreciated the importance of big-name signings at White Hart Lane, remarking in Phil Soar's *Tottenham Hotspur The Official Illustrated History*, 'It brings an air of excitement to the club.' Although a club renowned for its flair attackers and glamorous transfer policy, the reliable, loyal servants have always retained a place in the fans' affections, and Perryman's presence throughout the rebuilding was as important an element as the big-money arrivals. Defensive steel was added in the form of Graham Roberts, Paul Miller and Chris Hughton, and with a balanced team and growing optimism around the camp, the good times duly rolled.

The FA Cup has been a particularly important competition for Tottenham, regular triumphs in one of the world's oldest and most revered club competitions helping to establish them as one of the great teams of English football. In this respect it was therefore fitting that the rebuilding process at the club, which had begun immediately after their relegation was confirmed, should finally bring tangible reward with an FA Cup triumph. Fitting also that a club with such a fine heritage in England, and in the FA Cup in particular, should win the trophy in its hundredth year of contest.

As is well known to fans, it is also a peculiar quirk of the club's history to claim a trophy in a year ending in 1. Spurs' first silverware had been the 1901 FA Cup; they followed this with a further FA Cup triumph in 1921; then won the League for the first time in 1951; won the League and Cup Double in 1961; and brought home more silverware in 1971, with the League Cup. From the nadir of relegation in 1977, it was therefore apt to the point of inevitability that they should announce themselves once again as worthy of a seat at the top table of English football with the FA Cup in 1981. Hindsight may be 20-20, but the fact that 1981 was also the Chinese Year of the Cockerel ought to serve as yet a further rebuke to those who laid a wager on any other team to win the 1981 FA Cup.

Of course, factors on the field played their part, with Spurs giving early indications that they were a renewed force by becoming early-season League-leaders. Tottenham were eventually to finish in 10th, their highest position since their return to the top-flight, while FA Cup victories against QPR, Hull and Coventry set up a home quarter-final against Exeter City, from the former Third Division. Ironically now the team of whom he is Director of Football, Perryman has recalled that it was on being drawn against Exeter for the quarter-final that Spurs began to believe that glory beckoned, recalling in *Tottenham Hotspur: The Official Illustrated History*: 'We knew then that we could win the Cup.'

Exeter were duly despatched, setting up a semi-final with Wolves. Denied victory at the first attempt by a dubious refereeing decision, Spurs produced a spectacular performance in the replay, winning 3-0 in a game held at Highbury. The enemy's stadium was appropriated that evening by Spurs fans, and evidently unused to such a din, it seemed to shake to its very foundations as a Tottenham masterclass sent supporters into delirium.

After all the hype and crescendo towards the 100th FA Cup final, the game itself was a slightly turgid affair, ending in a 1-1 draw after extra-time. The replay however, proved to be one of the most famous games in the club's history, Ricky Villa achieving immortality with his mesmeric winner. His very involvement in the game has itself passed into the realm of the legendary, for one Steve Perryman had argued against his inclusion, after his dismal showing in the first game had ended with his substitution and very public, tearful exit. It prompted an urgent discussion between Perryman and manager Burkinshaw in the dressing room immediately after the game, with the skipper claiming his selection for the replay would be a mistake.

Back in May 1981, the disagreement between Perryman and Burkinshaw in the Wembley dressing-room after the 1-1 Cup final draw with City was hardly comparable to those fiery rows of a few years hence, but would prove to have just as dramatic repercussions, as Ricky Villa played his starring role in the replay. Spurs won 3-2, and Steve Perryman followed where Jack Jones, Arthur Grimsdell, Danny Blanchflower (twice) and Dave Mackay had gone before, and lifted the FA Cup for Spurs.

The triumph was a fantastic reward for the fans, who had had to endure recent miseries, and went a long way to restoring the reputation of the club that had been tarnished by several barren years and relegation. In particular, however, it was a triumph for manager Burkinshaw and captain Perryman, who had been such loyal and instrumental figures in the recovery of the club.

The following season, 1981/82, Perryman featured in a team he now labels as the best Spurs side in which he ever played ("No question") in his 17 seasons. While the team collected more silverware, retaining the FA Cup, the achievement barely did justice to the Herculean efforts of a four-pronged challenge for glory, adding a European Cup Winners' Cup campaign to the three domestic competitions. The inevitable fixture pile-up put paid to the club's League campaign as they ran out of steam, recording just 3 wins in their final 12 First Division games, to finish fourth – creditable in retrospect, and their best finish in over a decade, but an anti-climax at the time.

Meanwhile Spurs progressed to the semi-finals of the Cup Winner's Cup, and the finals of both the League and FA Cups. One statistic in particular is instructive to those in any doubt as to how the club has garnered something of a reputation as being Cup specialists, for the eventual League Cup final loss to Liverpool in March 1982 was their first defeat in an astonishing 26 successive Cup-ties. That League Cup final defeat was indicative of the finale to Spurs' season, as they let slip a one-goal lead in the dying minutes, then succumbed in extra-time, eventually going down 3-1.

FA Cup victory nevertheless lent some cheer to the club's centenary season, and by then the club's record-holder for appearances, it was fitting that 100 years from the formation of Tottenham Hotspur FC, Steve Perryman lifted the FA Cup again. Victory in a replay over Second Division QPR meant that Perryman emulated Blanchflower by captaining Spurs to consecutive FA Cup victories. The 1981/82 season also brought Perryman personal accolades, as he was voted the Football Writers' Association Footballer of the Year, and won his sole England cap, as a substitute against Iceland in Reykjavik.

The following season did not bring any further silverware, but nevertheless saw Spurs continue to cement their position as one of the luminaries of the English game, with another fourth-placed finish, before picking up a further trophy in 1984 with the dramatic victory over Anderlecht on penalties in the Second Leg of the UEFA Cup final. Perryman missed the occasion, having been cautioned in the First Leg, but, 12 years after receiving his first European winners' medal, he received another that night, as well as an MBE at the end of that season.

It had been a wonderful era for Spurs, laden with trophies and exorcising the demons of the previous decade. Perryman had been endured the rough as well as the smooth, and no player was more deserving of an opportunity to lift English football's greatest prize; but, to his immense frustration, the League title always eluded Spurs. Despite playing some sparkling football and maturing as a team, the record-books will have it that Tottenham simply did not have the consistency to maintain a challenge throughout an entire League season. When Keith Burkinshaw left at the end of the 1984 season, some of the magic left with him. New manager Peter Shreeve was promoted from within the club's coaching staff, but the dazzling Spurs side of the early part of the decade was beginning to disband, with the departures of Crooks and Archibald following that of Burkinshaw. Finally, in March 1986, Perryman himself played his last game for the club, in the 2-1 FA Cup defeat to Everton.

The end when it came was messier than would have been ideal. Perryman has made no secret of the fact that he believed he could have continued to help at Spurs in a coaching role, thereby maintaining continuity from the Burkinshaw era; but it was not to be. He did briefly re-join the club as assistant to Ossie Ardiles in the early 1990s, when boardroom turmoil left the management team on a hiding to nothing; and he took charge of the club for one game in November 1994, but only in an interim capacity, in a defeat to Blackburn.

If every player to tread the White Hart Lane turf had Perryman's commitment to the badge, one can barely imagine what a frighteningly good team Tottenham would be. If anything, the decades which have passed since his final appearance for Spurs have magnified the size of his contribution to the club, for 17 continuous years of service is virtually unheard of in the current era, such fierce commitment more typical of supporters. A relatively unsung hero he may have been, but beneath the glamour of those headline-grabbing Spurs teams of the '70s and '80s, Steve Perryman earned the unswerving respect and admiration of team-mates and fans alike.

GLENN HODDLE

1975-1987

SPURS CAREER

Games	490
Goals	110
Caps	53

MAGIC MOMENT

A goal against Watford in 1983, an extravagant flick past the defender and even more outrageous chip over the goalkeeper

'GOD'

DOES any single player better encapsulate the playing style of Tottenham Hotspur Football Club than Glenn Hoddle? If football is the beautiful game, Hoddle was one of its most fervent proponents, turning it into an art-form and making it a joy to behold. Exquisitely talented, he was able to create goals from nothing, score from all angles, deliver short or long passes with immaculate precision – and all with either foot. Glib though it seems to single out an isolated highlight from such a sparkling Tottenham career, it is telling that when the club produced arguably their greatest, purest, most perfect display of the 1980s, Hoddle was at its hub. On Wednesday 19 October 1983 Feyenoord came to the Lane, boasting Dutch maestro Johan Cruyff in their ranks – and were duly blown away, as an irresistible Spurs raced into a 4-0 half-time lead, with Hoddle pulling the strings. Steve Perryman has described that first half as "perfection", and does not hesitate in naming Hoddle as the architect of the performance. Hoddle himself regards it as his favourite Tottenham game, and Keith Burkinshaw said of his display that day, "I don't think I've ever seen him play better". Creating goals, pulling the strings and upstaging Cruyff, in the famous floodlit atmosphere of a European night at the Lane – it was a definitive performance from one of the most talented players ever to wear the Tottenham lilywhite.

He had a hand in all four Tottenham goals in the first half, turning to gold everything he touched. Britain's tabloid newspapers have occasionally been known to dabble in hyperbole, but there was no exaggeration from the *Daily Mirror's* Harry Miller when he wrote the following day of 'Glenn Hoddle at his dazzling, devastating best … For 45 minutes of a match that was a marvellous advert for open, attacking football, Hoddle's mastery of the midfield had threatened to leave Feyenoord in tatters.'

How satisfying for Tottenham to dish out a lesson to a team that itself took pride in playing football as the beautiful game; and oh how satisfying for Hoddle to upstage one of the game's all-time great footballers. Prior to the game Cruyff had been outspoken about his confidence of bettering Hoddle; afterwards the Dutchman admitted he had heard much about the young Englishman, but had not realised quite how good he was until he played against him. Hoddle's reward for his greatest performance in a Spurs shirt was to receive the shirt of the greatest Dutch player of all time.

Hoddle grew up a Spurs fan, his family hailing from Hayes in Middlesex, and later moving to Harlow in Essex. Not an eyelid will be batted at the news that, as a schoolboy, he regularly played against children four years older than him. Nor will the slightest degree of surprise be registered at the news that his talents were recognised at an early age by scouts. Indeed, former Spurs striker Martin Chivers, has recalled, in *Big Chiv*, that the process of identifying the teenage Hoddle amongst the throng of hopeful trainees ranked amongst the decidedly less difficult tasks he undertook in his capacity as club scout: 'He was like an elephant in a haystack, as opposed to a needle'. Hoddle signed schoolboy forms for the club aged 16, in January 1974, but was blooded in the reserve and youth teams before entering the first-team fold. Even back then, before reaching the first-team, word had spread amongst the fans of the skinny lad in the reserves with sublime passing and control, and anticipation grew for the arrival on a bigger stage of a young man who seemed born to play the Tottenham way.

Hoddle was handed his debut by Terry Neil, who oversaw the beginning of an era on 30 August 1974 when he brought on the future hero as a substitute in a 2-2 home draw with Norwich. Recalls Spurs fan Dick Carpenter:

"It was a potboiler against Norwich in 1975 and he came on as sub at half-time. With his first touch he 'drifted' past his marker, took it on a few more yards, looked up, sighted the goal and clipped the ball from 25 yards. It shaved the outside of the post, leaving the keeper standing. I suddenly found myself staring at the bloke next to me, both of us gawping like idiots, pointing at the pitch and mumbling incoherences at each other. I sensed the buzz of a collective 'f**kin' hell' rise off the terraces and linger a moment in the chilly White Hart Lane afternoon. It was a 2-2 draw in the end, but nobody was talking about the result – only about this new kid."

While his talent was immediately obvious, Neill wisely opted not to place too great a burden upon 'this new kid', and waited several months before giving him another taste of the action, handing Hoddle his first start on 21 February 1976, against Stoke. He proved well worth the wait, scoring past Peter Shilton with the sort of spectacular long-range effort that would prove so typical throughout his career. The goal came following an unsightly melee in the penalty area, in which players from each team had failed to bring the ball under control or even keep it on the turf. One almost wanted to weep at the ugliness of it all, yet from this ungainly mess the ball fell to Hoddle, who struck a pure, first-time, left-footed volley which soared into the net. The shimmering technique of his shot stood in stark contrast to the bedlam which had immediately preceded it – but there, in a microcosm, was Hoddle, his graceful elegance shining forth above the messy, scrappy nature of the English game.

However, the goal almost proved to be the last of his Spurs career, as, unhappy with Neill, he considered a move to pastures new. It is indicative of the incongruity of Terry Neill managing Spurs that he came within a whisker of driving out one of the club's most famous sons. Mercifully, crucial intervention came from Steve Perryman, who – as the man with more appearances for Spurs than anyone else in history – stood as the polar opposite of Neill in terms of knowing what was best for the club. Perryman talked Hoddle out of the unthinkable, and instead, in one of the most welcome trade-offs in Tottenham history, it was Neill rather than Hoddle who left White Hart Lane that summer.

Keith Burkinshaw succeeded Neill as manager, overseeing relegation in his first season but immediate promotion in his second, Spurs bouncing straight back up as they adopted an adventurous, attacking style in the old Division Two. There were goals aplenty, at both ends of the pitch, as the team scored 83 times in 42 League games, while conceding 49, and within such an open, free-flowing side, Hoddle began to find his niche. The Tottenham renaissance did not end at promotion, as the club continued to progress once back in the top tier. Hoddle found like-minded artistes introduced alongside him as Messrs Ardiles and Villa were sensationally brought to the club, and the team's playing style altered accordingly. The use of width offered by overlapping full backs was replaced by an approach that made greater use of the creative talents in midfield.

Although mischievous media types would have us believe that there was a rivalry between Ardiles and Hoddle for the playground crown of the best player, the little

Argentine has been effusive in his praise of the Englishman of whom he had never heard when he arrived. "Maradona without pace," is his verdict on Hoddle, which probably ranks as the most complimentary criticism ever dealt a footballer in the history of the game. Ardiles' compatriot and Tottenham team-mate Ricky Villa has recalled saying of Hoddle, "Why have Spurs bought us? They don't need us – they already have Hoddle", while Ardiles identified Hoddle as the "third South American" in the Tottenham team, high praise indeed from a World Cup-winner.

In describing what it was like to play with Hoddle, Ardiles called it a pleasure – 'we were on the same wavelength' recalls the Argentine, in his autobiography *Ossie's Dream* – and mentions that the pair talked a lot about the game, particularly in those early days. Hoddle flourished alongside the Argentine, as was sublimely demonstrated in a League Cup match with Manchester United, at the start of the 1979/80 season. Receiving a pass with his back to goal on the edge of the area, Hoddle knocked the ball inside to Ardiles and spun away from his marker. Ardiles delicately chipped the ball back, first time, for Hoddle to run onto and spectacularly volley into the top corner. It was the sort of goal that has purists drooling, an amalgam of grace, technique and power. Hoddle himself ranks it as the best in his career – and as once noted by a commentator, a sentiment with which the man himself concurs, "Glenn Hoddle is not a great goalscorer, but he is a scorer of great goals."

Never a truer word. A DVD of Hoddle's every goal would be a greatest hits selection for any other player. As well as the volley against United fans particularly remember the impudent turn and backspun chip against Watford; and the equally brazen strike against Oxford, when he beat two defenders on halfway, raced to the area, and produced an extravagant dummy bought so whole-heartedly by the goalkeeper that he dived full-length to his left, while Hoddle walked the other side of him and rolled the ball into the empty net.

Back to 1979/80, a landmark year in Hoddle's career. He went on to become PFA Young Player of the Year that season, also making his England debut, and marking the occasion with a goal as spectacular as it was audacious, improvising – nay, *inventing* – a new technique, as he powerfully placed into the top corner a long-range side-footed half-volley. By this time had become a firm fans' favourite. "Hoddle Hoddle, Hoddle, Hoddle – born is the King of White Hart Lane" was sung to the tune of Christmas carol 'The First Noel', but heard all year round at White Hart Lane. As if to emphasise the fact that here was the quintessential Tottenham player, the embodiment of the club's traditional style, the fans bestowed upon him the greatest epithet imaginable – God. Hoddle has laughed off the nickname – remarking on *FourFourTwo.com*, 'It was just a term of endearment' – but the fact that he does not feel uncomfortable with the weight of expectation that comes with the ascription as a footballing deity speaks volumes about his blistering self-confidence. He has variously been described as arrogant, but many of those who are or have been closest to him describe his attitude instead as belief in his own astonishing ability. 'It's not arrogance, it's confidence,' is the verdict of Chris Waddle, in Mel Stein's *Chris Waddle: The Authorised Biography*, but whatever the verdict, it was crucial to Hoddle's game, as he complemented his ability to produce the extraordinary with a confidence to effect it. Whether pinging 40-yard passes, scoring audacious goals, or shamelessly belting out dubious melodies on *Top of the Pops*, Hoddle was blessed with the confidence to express himself. Even when asked about his permanently untucked shirt, on *FourFourTwo.com*, he replied, 'When I got in to the side at 17 I kept my shirt tucked in, I thought it would have been a bit bold to let it out, because it can be a sign of confidence. Later on, it just never felt right to have it tucked in …'

As well as the presence of players like Ardiles and Villa alongside him, and Perryman often behind him, Hoddle also benefited from the purchases in the summer of 1980 of strikers Garth Crooks and Steve Archibald. Hoddle relished having quick strikers ahead of him making darting runs, and described the pair, in his autobiography *Spurred to Success*, as 'The perfect front men to capitalise upon my 40-yard service … In the end I could find them with my eyes shut.'

In 1981 he collected his first winners' medal. Fittingly, for a player who typified the romantic notion of the beautiful game, it was in the most romantic competition of them all, the centenary FA Cup. Prior to the final, Hoddle was to make his mark in the run to Wembley – bamboozling opposing keeper Paul Bradshaw to score with a free kick in the semi-final; then wrongly being penalised for something of a collector's item – a tackle inside his own area – to concede the equalising penalty; before, in the replay, threading a typically inch-perfect pass for Crooks to race onto and score, as Spurs won 3-0 and booked their place in the final. For manager Keith Burkinshaw the achievement of reaching the FA Cup final was the culmination of a five-year project that had begun in 1976, when he had taken over a Tottenham team on the slide, and sought to invigorate it. That five-year cycle coincided with Hoddle's emergence in the team, and after the initial disappointment of relegation, as Hoddle had sought to establish himself in the side, the fortunes of player, manager and team had neatly aligned.

And so to Wembley, for the first time in his club career. With ten minutes of the FA Cup final remaining, Tottenham were 1-0 down to Manchester City, when Hoddle, Perryman and Ardiles stood over a free kick on the edge of the City area. Hoddle took it, and as his shot curled toward the goalkeeper's left it was flicked on by the head of City's Tommy Hutchison, and landed in the corner of the net to the goalkeeper's right. Even Hoddle's most ardent fan would struggle to attribute the goal to him. Call it divine intervention …

If that first game was a disappointment, the replay was a classic, with Hoddle rising to the occasion on the greatest stage in the club game. Typically Ricky Villa is the name on most lips when minds are cast back to the match, but when Keith Burkinshaw was asked who was the most influential man on the pitch that night, he had no hesitation in naming Tottenham's number 10. "Not Villa. Not Perryman. Not Ossie. Glenn worked harder than anyone," he said, adding, almost in disbelief, "I've never seen him defend like he did that day." Villa gave Spurs an early lead; Steve Mackenzie equalised for City, with a sublime volley, unfortunately overlooked latterly, despite being worthy of Hoddle himself. With the scores level Hoddle's influence was growing, and a trademark free kick flew past the goalkeeper but rebounded off the post, before City took a second half lead. Then as a Tottenham corner was half-cleared, the massed ranks of City defenders raced to close down Hoddle, but rather than panic he deftly chipped the ball into the path of the Spurs striking pair, beating the offside trap, and Crooks was able to slide the ball home. Villa grabbed the headlines with his winner, but after several years in the wilderness Spurs were most definitely back, and Hoddle was the man pulling the strings.

It was the first of a smattering of trophies, as Tottenham played football that was at times irresistible, but, equally, effective. They had steel at the back in Roberts and Miller, South American skill from the Argentineans in midfield, the lethal prowess of Crooks and Archibald in attack, with Perryman providing leadership – but it was the genius of Glenn Hoddle that elevated that team from a decent side to a trophy-winning one. The following season was the club's centenary year, and might have seen them win several trophies. They lost a domestic Cup final for the first time that March, when a flighted ball from Hoddle was converted by Archibald for an early lead, only for opponents Liverpool to equalise late on and win in extra-time. The club also reached the semi-finals of European Cup Winners' Cup, Hoddle's bow in European club competition including a typical curling effort from just outside the area in the quarter-final tie against Eintracht Frankfurt. However, Spurs were beaten by Barcelona in the semi-final, while a fixture pile-up late in the season put paid to their Championship challenge.

The season would nevertheless finish on a high for Hoddle. In the final League game of the campaign, against a Liverpool side that had by then been crowned champions, he scored a goal which was special even by his own high standards, receiving possession, just outside the centre circle, moving forward ten yards, and letting fly with a dipping, swerving right-foot shot. It was, as with just about every other goal he scored, a contender for goal of the season.

There then followed the FA Cup, and as holders against Second Division QPR, Spurs were well-fancied. For the second year in succession, Hoddle found the net in the Cup final with the benefit of a heavy deflection, his shot – inevitably, from outside the area – flicking the legs of defender Tony Currie before flying in. However, an energy-sapping season had taken its toll, and a late equaliser from QPR meant the game was level after 90 minutes, and another replay beckoned. This time the glory of a Cup-winning goal was to be, indubitably, Glenn Hoddle's, confidently converting an early penalty. In the year of the cockerel, and the club's centenary year, arguably the most gifted player in its history had scored the winning goal in the final of its favourite competition.

Hoddle scored 8 goals in 53 appearances for his country, but it is a truth fairly universally acknowledged that he should have had many, many more. Michel Platini asserted that he would have won 150 caps if he were French, and that the national team would have been built around him. England's, by contrast, was built around Bryan Robson – a fine player in his own right, but one whose energetic and combative style was the polar opposite of Hoddle's. In these two players could be witnessed the conflict in English football at the time. Rather than mould the team around Hoddle's flair, the England team had Robson as its captain. The Tottenham man, by contrast, was considered a liability, particularly in international football, where there is rarely the safety net of a game the following Saturday, to expiate for a disappointing showing the preceding week. Although he was a regular in the England team of Bobby Robson in the season prior to the 1986

World Cup, for much of his international career Hoddle was considered a luxury, and England did not have time for luxury players.

If the English style involved long balls and flying tackles on muddy pitches, Tottenham rebelled against it, providing a more suitable home for Hoddle's talents than the national team. England considered Hoddle a luxury; Tottenham built successive teams around him. Danny Blanchflower, Tottenham through-and-through, identified in his own inimitable style this mistake of the English national team when he opined: "It's the bad players who are a luxury."

If he was never quite given the opportunity to shine on the national stage as he ought to have done, the more expansive style of European club football did at least provide Hoddle a worthy stage for his talents. 'They were very special nights at Tottenham,' he recalls, in Jeremy Novick's *Winning Their Spurs*. 'There was a difference there for the supporters, the atmosphere seems electric'. Hoddle's role in the glorious 1984 UEFA Cup triumph was to be limited, as an achilles injury deprived him of the chance to star in the final. While he admits that this, naturally enough, took some of the gloss of the victory, his role in reaching the final cannot be understated, not least in that Second Round tie against Feyenoord.

The win over Feyenoord was Hoddle's definitive game, but not just because of the bravura first half performance in which was established the 4-0 lead. In the second half, Spurs' defensive sloppiness saw them concede two away goals, to leave them with an unnecessarily fragile 4-2 lead to take into the second leg in Rotterdam. That defensive frailty has been as much a hallmark of modern Spurs teams as the quality they ooze going forward. And just as the rampant, exquisite attacking play was Hoddle all over, so the weakness in defence was another of his trademarks, albeit less celebrated.

Not without good reason was another of his nicknames 'Glenda', for Hoddle was famously reluctant to roll up his sleeves and go flying in to tackles. "If we were practising defending in training, he would say he had a problem with his achilles, or he had a tight calf," grins Burkinshaw at the recollection. While some criticised this attitude, and his England career almost certainly suffered for it, romantics adopted a different view. He retains to this day the unstinting worship of Tottenham fans, while the late Brian Clough not only exonerated Hoddle for his reluctance to defend, but praised his "moral bravery" in adopting this approach. Hoddle himself has pointedly rejected any criticism of his style, remarking in a 2003 interview with *Observer Sport Monthly*: 'People talk about character, but what is character? Is it tearing around at 100 miles an hour? If I thought defending was that important I could improve my game by 50 per cent. But it isn't.'

Instead, business up the other end of the pitch was Hoddle's real delight. Walking off the pitch at half-time in the game against Feyenoord he recalls feeling exhilarated, unsurprisingly so for a man who has had made no secret of the fact that his preference is to create goals rather than score them. Indeed, he even has a favourite 'assist', the outrageous long pass with the outside of his left foot, that set Garth Crooks on the way to score in the replayed FA Cup semi-final vs Wolves at Highbury, in 1981.

After Keith Burkinshaw's departure in 1984 the Tottenham team underwent changes, but there was to be one last hurrah for Hoddle before he wound down his contract and sought pastures new overseas. In the 1986/87 season David Pleat placed him at the centre of a five-man midfield, inviting him at the start of the season to 'play in the Platini role', named after the French midfielder regarded in the 1980s as one of the greatest passers in world football, and the inspiration behind France's victory in the 1984 European Championships. Having already drawn comparisons to Cruyff, it is indicative of the exalted company Hoddle kept in the world game that he was deemed the only player in the English game equipped to play the 'Platini role'. By this point Hoddle had been joined at Spurs by close friend Chris Waddle, while Ossie Ardiles was still keeping things ticking over, as Tottenham purred under the guidance of another manager who embraced the traditional Tottenham style. The team rolled back the years, another attacking, free-flowing outfit that was easy on the eye. Spurs finished a highly creditable third in the League, offering a realistic challenge to the dominant Merseyside duopoly of the day, and reached the League Cup semi-final, before Hoddle's last match dawned, and a chance to return to the scene of some of his greatest moments, as Spurs played Coventry City in the FA Cup final. The stage seemed set, and fate seemed to decree, that in the competition with which the club, *his* club, had such an affinity, Hoddle was to bow out in style once more, with a winning performance in the FA Cup final.

There was to be no fairytale ending however. Hoddle turned in a strangely muted performance, and Spurs suffered a shock 3-2 defeat in extra-time. It was Hoddle's 490th and final game for Spurs; that summer he moved to Monaco for £1 million. He was well aware that his game was particularly well-suited to the continental style; and with English clubs having been banned from European competition from 1985 there was no other means of playing abroad. Naturally, he flourished in France, helping Monaco to the French title in his first season at the club, under the tutelage of a certain Arsene Wenger.

After spells as player-manager of Swindon Town and Chelsea, and manager of Southampton and England, Hoddle returned to Spurs as manager, in 2001. However, despite remaining fiercely loyal to the club's ideals, and taking them to Wembley in the 2003 League Cup final, the move did not produce hoped-for results, and a parting of the ways occurred early in the 2003/04 season. The spell as manager hardly blots his escutcheon, as a poll by the club's official website later saw him voted the greatest player in Tottenham Hotspur history. It is a point that evokes earnest debate, and is impossible to decide conclusively, but the man's talents are certainly beyond doubt, nor is there any debate that he was the most gifted English player of his generation.

OSVALDO ARDILES

'OSSIE'

1978-1988

SPURS CAREER

Games	311
Goals	25
Caps	63

MAGIC MOMENT

Setting up the opening goal of Spurs' victory in the 1981 FA Cup final replay

SOME players just seem born to play the Tottenham way, and the Tottenham way seems meant for them. Ossie Ardiles had not even heard of Tottenham when Keith Burkinshaw flew to Buenos Aires to court him in the summer of 1978 – indeed, he never quite wrapped his tongue around the name – yet the Spurs philosophy could not possibly have accorded more with his own style of play if he had penned it himself.

Ardiles' arrival coincided with the club's emergence from the darkness of relegation to the glory of Cup successes in the 1980s. It was a gradual process, but Ardiles was central to it, and one game in the 1978/79 season marked a significant moment in the club's renaissance, whilst also summing up the qualities of the little Argentine genius. It was a Fifth Round FA Cup tie against Manchester United, who at the time were turning into something of a knock-out nemesis for Spurs, and who had sneaked a late equaliser to force a replay at Old Trafford. The game was already notable for the curious sight of Glenn Hoddle going in goal, after injury to regular goalkeeper Milija Aleksic, but then, in the final seconds of extra-time, Ardiles struck. Ricky Villa had jinked down the left-hand edge of the penalty area towards the byline, where just about everybody in the stadium expected a cross. Ossie however was on his compatriot's wavelength, and peeled off towards the edge of the area. Villa duly pulled the ball back to him, and Ossie took one touch, steadied himself, then powerfully curled the ball past two onrushing defenders, beyond the despairing dive of goalkeeper Gary Bailey and into the top corner of the net. It was a goal of precise technique, awareness and balance, epitomising the qualities Ardiles brought to the Spurs midfield and the English game at large, and delivered with an impeccable sense of timing for good measure. While Spurs were to exit the FA Cup that season at the quarter-final stage, the hard-earned result – over two matches, down to ten men and without the outfield contribution of Hoddle – injected into the club a genuine sense of belief that, following their promotion back to the top flight, they were once again ready to compete with the big guns. It was fitting that Ardiles should cement this turnaround, so central had he been to the club's revival.

There were of course numerous other endearing traits about the little man – his humble charm, inimitable accent and natural *joie de vivre* – but above all else, and as demonstrated in that goal against Manchester United, he encapsulated the fine playing tradition of the club. Here was a man who took Danny Blanchflower's immortal words on how the game should be played – the Tottenham way, of doing it in style – and lived, breathed and played by that maxim. A man who would play a 15-yard pass along the ground even if his life depended on a long-ball. Naturally, Spurs fans loved him for it.

As with so many of Spurs' great cult heroes, the very signing of Ardiles was the stuff of fantasy. Ardiles was at the very pinnacle of the game, having just realised the dream of every schoolboy – and, indeed, grown man – by winning the game's greatest prize, the World Cup, in front of his home crowd. By contrast, Spurs had only just won promotion back into the top flight of English football, after the ignominy of relegation in 1977. Yet when these two unlikely worlds collided it eventually proved a match made in footballing heaven, played out on the turf of White Hart Lane.

At the time, foreign players in England were very much the exception rather than the norm – and foreign players who ranked amongst the world's best, a thing unheard of.

However, barely a month after he had starred in Argentina's 3-1 win in the World Cup final against Holland, Ardiles was on his way up the High Road to White Hart Lane. As was typical of the time, and remains the case to this day, Argentina's greatest players eyed moves to Europe. It was a logical progression, to sample a different way of life, gain greater exposure and earn more money, but moves to Italy or Spain represented the more typical route. Nevertheless, Spurs boss Keith Burkinshaw was alerted to the availability of Ardiles by then Sheffield United manager Harry Haslam, who had himself been made aware of the situation by his Argentinean coach but was unable to afford the mooted £300,000 fee. Burkinshaw recalls the day when Haslam rang Spurs to alert him, and the call was taken by the great Bill Nicholson, at that time working at Spurs in his capacity as scout: "Bill told me it was Harry Haslam on the phone, asking if I wanted to sign Ossie Ardiles. I said 'Bill, you're a straight-talking man – but now you're taking the piss'".

Burkinshaw, like many others in England, had watched Ardiles in action at the hub of his national team during the World Cup, and was well aware of the talents of the man. A rapid sequence of events unfolded, with Burkinshaw swiftly gaining board approval for the move and jumping on a plane to Buenos Aires, coming face to face with Ardiles within 24 hours. It quickly became clear that the transfer was mutually agreeable – but then came an unexpected twist.

In Tottenham folklore the name of Ossie Ardiles simply cannot be mentioned without another name springing immediately to mind. It was a pattern established on that hot afternoon in the Sheraton hotel in Buenos Aires, with Burkinshaw there at its inception. Precisely who mentioned it is unclear – Ardiles himself has denied that it was his idea – but as the minutiae was established in the deal to bring him to North London, the name of Ricardo Villa was also suggested to Burkinshaw, and White Hart Lane prepared to welcome another famous son.

As Burkinshaw recalls, prior to flying out to Argentina, he had heard on the grapevine that interest in Villa was actually being expressed by Arsenal: "In the end though, the Arsenal directors decided not to buy him," says Burkinshaw, a mischievous twinkle in his eye. "They didn't want to bring foreign players to their club you see ..."

Burkinshaw had recalled seeing Villa come on as a substitute on a couple of occasions in the World Cup, a strapping man who looked capable of handling himself. While in Argentina Burkinshaw phoned his chairman Sidney Wale, and minutes later the nod was given, the papers signed. Both Ardiles and Villa were on their way to London for a combined £700,000. As Wale recalled at the time, quoted in Phil Soar's *Tottenham Hotspur The Official Illustrated History*, 'It was a big gamble to take, we were putting our heads on the chopping block, but looking back on it now, it was the best decision I ever made'.

A gamble without doubt, but, as it would later transpire, a momentous coup. For the media it was manna from heaven, and they naturally went into overdrive. As the *Daily Mail* put it, 'If Spurs had bought Batman and Robin they could scarcely have created greater curiosity'. Spurs' history is littered with such extravagant signings, which capture the imagination of the public. In particular the outlandish signings of Ardiles and Villa blazed a trail, which was to be echoed almost two decades later with an equally brazen transfer swoop in North London when Spurs signed another international superstar, Jürgen Klinsmann. At this time, by coincidence, the Spurs manager was none other than Osvaldo Ardiles.

That Ardiles, rather than Villa, makes the final list of *Spurs' Cult Heroes* is essentially due to the longevity and consistency of the former. Ardiles would go on to make over 300 appearances in lilywhite, during a ten-year White Hart Lane career, compared to 179 by Villa in five years. Villa plays an important role in the Ardiles story – the careers of both being almost inextricably linked in the minds of many Spurs fans – and for contributing one of the most glittering moments in the club's history, through his famous Cup final goal, his Tottenham career merits due deference, but his broader contribution was unmistakeably fitful, genius frequently co-habiting with the distinctly disappointing. Ardiles by contrast immediately settled into the English game and the Tottenham way, quickly becoming a vital component in Keith Burkinshaw's team, and a fans' favourite from the outset.

The differing career paths of the pair were highlighted almost immediately, by the manners in which they initially adapted to arrival at White Hart Lane, back in 1978. The move from Argentina to Essex was, naturally enough, a culture shock for the pair, but particularly so for Villa, who identified language as the principal difficulty. Ardiles for his part already knew some English, although he quipped of the instructions he received from Burkinshaw in those early days, in *Tottenham Hotspur The Official Illustrated History*: 'It is the same in both countries. The only difference is that in Argentina I understood them.' Ardiles immersed himself in English culture. This task was made easier, he recalls, by the fact that the English were so passionate about the game. As he recalls in his autobiography *Ossie's Dream*: 'Immediately I arrived in England I absolutely adored, I loved, the football culture. It was football, football, football from the beginning to the end.'

He also embraced the dressing room banter – even though much of it passed him by in the early days – with his sunny optimism and quirky nature making him a popular dressing room figure. The adaptation to a new culture inevitably brought the occasional social faux pas – notably when Ardiles, Villa and their wives attended in casual wear a social function at which Princess Margaret was present, and black-tie was *de rigeur*. His whole-hearted adaptation to English culture also involved indulging in such national delicacies as fish and chips, and Sunday roast ('overcooked' is his verdict on the English style of preparing roast beef). However, he was not one to match the beer-drinking exploits of his team-mates, and Keith Burkinshaw has recalled that he and Villa were model professionals, looking after their bodies and never presenting any disciplinary problems.

Off the pitch, the club went to great lengths to help the pair acclimatise in London – buying them homes next door to each other and a short distance from Spurs' Chigwell training ground, and hiring an English teacher. The pair have also paid tribute to their team-mates, for going out of their way to make the new arrivals feel at home. John Pratt and Terry Naylor are named by both Argentines as particularly gregarious characters in the new, strange environment of the Spurs dressing room, and Ardiles also doffs his cap in the direction of Steve Perryman, for taking the pair under his wing and helping them to bed in.

If anything, Villa faced a greater struggle to adapt, again highlighting why cult hero status is more naturally conferred upon his compatriot. With no knowledge of the language, Villa found that, despite the best efforts of the club, he was often at a loose end beyond the training ground, with no newspapers, television or, most pertinently, people with whom to converse. However, having his compatriot there alongside him was a massive benefit. The pair had already roomed together at the World Cup, and as new neighbours in their brave new world they became even closer, a bond that has remained to this day. They are godparents to each other's children, and Ossie even escorted Ricky's wife into hospital when she was in labour with her first child, due to Ricky's leg injury leaving him practically immobile. As Ossie puts it in his autobiography, 'We never took two cars to training, it was always "Yours or mine?"'

Spurs fans, as curious as they were excited by the signings of two World Cup-winners, also gave the pair a warm welcome, heralding their home debuts with ticker-tape receptions, to recreate the extraordinary scenes many had witnessed on TV from the Argentina World Cup in 1978. The memories of Martin Cloake, long-time fan and established football writer, capture the mood of incredulous delight that heady summer: "Suddenly we've signed these blokes that I saw on the TV, in the best football competition in the world, for the team that had *won* the best football competition in the world ..."

The acclimatisation process Ardiles and Villa underwent off the pitch was equally pronounced on it, with doubts expressed in various quarters on the players' arrival as to how they would cope with the robust English style, not to mention the climate. Manager Keith Burkinshaw was not the only one who had originally feared that Ardiles would find it more difficult to adapt, in light of his diminutive frame, whereas the brief glimpses of Villa during the 1978 World Cup had included some bruising substitute contributions. Villa's bulkier frame, complemented by his hirsute appearance, suggested that he would fare better in the hurly-burly of the English league. Another concern was the English clime – freezing, rainswept pitches in England's bleak mid-winter sharing few similarities with Argentina, where games were simply abandoned if the elements proved particularly forceful.

In suitably fairytale fashion, the fixture-list threw up a mouth-watering debut for the Argentinians, as newly-promoted Spurs were pitched against League champions Nottingham Forest, and Villa marked the occasion with a goal, rounding Peter Shilton before flicking into the net, the equaliser in a 1-1 draw. Norman Fox of *The Times* wrote of the pair's efforts:

'They form an unlikely brotherhood. Ardiles is surprisingly small for such an indomitable worker. He is the one they said would be lost in the stampede of the British game. A lawyer's son and himself studying for the same profession, he thinks ahead and will escape many a blustering tackle like a cat through a closing door ... It was Villa, the larger one, thought to be bought as company for Ardiles as if they were children's pets, who scored Tottenham's equalizing goal and proved a challenge to the champions' defence. His strength is his jaunty ability to fend off any number of tackles ... Both Villa and Ardiles can look after themselves although no doubt some misguided oaf will catch them both before long.'

An impressive start, but just days later the pair's ticker-taped home debut finished in a 4-1 defeat to Aston Villa, and a fortnight later Spurs were thrashed 7-0 at Anfield. The media did not waste the opportunity to declare that the Latin pair were not cut out for the

English style – although such stories were of little consequence to Ardiles and Villa at the time, as neither understood what the press were saying. Nevertheless, such a baptism of fire was indicative of the task faced by the pair as they adjusted to the English game. As Ardiles put it, in *Ossie's Dream*: 'I basically spent the first few months, the first year even, watching the ball speed through the air'.

Team-mate at the time Paul Miller recalls, in Martin Cloake and Adam Powley's *The Boys From White Hart Lane*, that Tottenham fought fire with fire against less-refined opposition, deliberately bypassing the midfield and countering opponents' long-ball approach with a direct approach of their own, in order to stretch the game and ultimately create space:

'I remember Ossie coming in at half-time and saying we weren't giving any balls. We'd say, "But it's 0-0, and we'll get time to play second half", and we did, and we'd win games.'

Ardiles' small, wiry frame proved deceptive, and, in some contrast to his compatriot it must be noted, he quickly adapted to his new environs, winning legions of fans in the process. His impeccable control, low centre of gravity and innate awareness of incoming tackles allowed him to dance around heavy challenges, giving some indication of how he earned the nickname in Argentina of '*piton*' – python – and dispelling fears that he would struggle against the more agricultural opponents of the English League. Suggestions that windswept, rainy, muddy and frozen pitches might also be anathema to Ardiles were proved wrong in similarly emphatic style, as the little midfielder demonstrated himself to be a man for all seasons, recalling in *The Boys From White Hart Lane*: 'I loved it! I would fly around the mud – I never got stuck.'

Making the most of his exquisite balance, technique and reading of the game, he became one of the premier midfielders in England. A footballer in the finest tradition of Tottenham's playing style he was a master at retaining possession and keeping the Spurs team moving with short, intelligent passing and constant motion.

'He never stopped moving,' recalls Keith Burkinshaw. 'In his first two or three years at Tottenham he was probably the best midfield player in England.'

His short, intelligent passing quickly made him a vital cog in the machinery at Spurs, moving the ball and retaining possession, and in his Latin American philosophy of the beautiful game he quickly found kindred spirits in Glenn Hoddle and Steve Perryman. With the Argentineans in their ranks adapting to the English style, Tottenham themselves sought to infuse Latin American flair into their own game. The expansive style which had won them promotion in the previous season, using the full-width of the pitch through wingers and over-lapping full backs, was gently superseded by a shorter, slicker game, making better use of the creativity of Ardiles, Villa and Hoddle in central areas.

The 1978/79 season was one of consolidation for Spurs, as they established themselves back in the top flight with a respectable 11th-placed finish. The following campaign saw them end up three places lower, but it was also to bring that stirring FA Cup tie against Manchester United that was to prove memorable to Ossie, and something of a turning-point for Burkinshaw's team.

From that point on, everyone connected with the club – players, management staff and supporters – was renewed with belief that the club really could compete for the country's highest honours. Compete they did the following season, culminating with the centenary FA Cup final, one of the most famous nights in Tottenham Hotspur history. The omens that season were good, as the club first ended their developing quarter-final jinx, beating Exeter, before a drawn semi-final against Wolves at Hillsborough meant a replay at Highbury of all places. Spurs fans turned the ground into a home venue that night, and a magnificent goal from Villa was the icing on the cake. Receiving a Garth Crooks pass on the right, Villa jinked infield past two defenders before unleashing a swerving 30-yard left-footed effort into the top corner, as Tottenham cruised through 3-1. Spurs were on their way to Wembley once more – and the club needed a Cup final anthem. Cue Chas'n'Dave.

The now defunct cockney band were well known to the Spurs players, as regular attendees at games as well as social events and functions. The idea of a Cup final song was put to captain Steve Perryman and heartily backed by the players, summing up the strong spirit of a squad which still meets up today for reunion events. Ossie, however, was unaware of his starring role in the song until once inside the recording studio. He adamantly refused to sing his memorable solo line, only eventually relenting after having been plied with drink. As a Spanish speaker arriving in England, it had made sense to Ossie to pronounce 'Tottenham' as a three-syllabled 'Tott-ing-ham', given that in England, unlike Argentina, the letter 'h' was always articulated. Naturally, his team-mates derived great amusement from it, and the lyric was penned accordingly. As it happened however, by 1981, Ardiles had rectified the error, and set about pronouncing the lyric merely as 'Tottenham', to the consternation of Chas'n'Dave, who saw to it that in the recording studio at least Ossie would play a blinder 'in the cup for Tottingham'.

The song 'Ossie's Dream' was just one element of a huge media circus in the build-up to the Cup final, with much of the attention centring on the Argentineans. Appearances on *Top of the Pops* and *Blue Peter* famously followed, as the song reached number five in the national charts, while a surfeit of interviews included a live link-up to Argentina on the day of the final, for Ossie and Ricky to chat to their families. They were the first Argentines to appear in the FA Cup final, on the occasion of its 100th contest, and the match was being screened for the first time in their homeland. Inevitably, the pressure told on the day itself, and they, along with their team-mates, turned in underwhelming performances in an anti-climactic 1-1 draw. For Villa in particular, the game was a bitterly disappointing occasion.

There seemed no middle-ground for the big man – when he was good he was very good, and when he was bad... The 1981 FA Cup final illustrates this Jekyll-and-Hyde side to his game. Villa had not played well in the first game, and, substituted in the latter stages, cut a memorably disconsolate figure as he trudged straight towards the dressing room; four days later in the replay, he galloped away in triumph after scoring the greatest goal in FA Cup final history. Keith Burkinshaw deserves at least some credit for effecting the transformation. As he recalls of that first match, "Ricky was in tears in the dressing room afterwards. Steve Perryman came to me after the game and told me not to pick Ricky for the replay. I told him I'd think about it. A couple of minutes later I went up to Ricky and I told him he'd be playing again."

Perryman disagreed, but the gamble paid off. After just six minutes Villa had opened the scoring for Spurs – with Ardiles instrumental in the build-up. Ossie collected a short throw-in on the left, chipped the ball over an onrushing defender, and skipped past two more before shooting goalwards. The ball fell to Steve Archibald, whose shot was parried by the goalkeeper, presenting Villa with an open net, and he duly slammed home to begin the process of exorcising those demons of the first match.

Famously, however, his night was to become even better, as with 15 minutes remaining, and the sides locked at 2-2, he set off on the run that would write his name indelibly in FA Cup final history. The memory of that goal is etched into the minds of all Spurs fans to this day, one of the defining and iconic moments in the long proud history of the club. The mazy dribble, *that* dummy, Garth Crooks' right foot urging him to shoot, and the sheer unrestrained passion of his celebratory gallop – one of the great definitive moments in sport.

Everyone who saw it takes away with them their own unique memories – from Villa himself – 'For me, scoring in the Cup Final for Spurs was better than winning the World Cup' – to the families back home in Argentina; to Crooks, who, ten yards behind Villa on the pitch, had unconsciously mimed a shot with his own right foot; to BBC commentator John Motson who famously yelped an incredulous "And *still* Ricky Villa"; to the fans in the stadium. Recalls one such fan, Geoff Howe:

"I remember being in the upper stand at Wembley behind the goal where Villa scored. The upper standing terraces at Wembley in those days were very steep with each step about three or four foot deep and what seemed to be about two foot high. Each time Villa dropped his shoulder the crowd surged forward and it was necessary to jump off the step where you started and keep your balance as the surge went on. By the time the ball hit the back of the net it seemed we had all moved down so far that we were almost pitch side. More than 25 years later I can still remember that sensation more clearly than any other experience watching Spurs."

Tottenham's incredible FA Cup pedigree has been forged over more than a century, but within that time few have contributed more than did Villa in that famous ten-second burst. While, as a slightly isolated incident within his Tottenham career it is perhaps not sufficient alone to merit his inclusion amongst the final list of 20 *Spurs' Cult Heroes*, few would argue or complain about its addition to any tome celebrating the great history of the club.

The celebrations which followed that victory have also become the stuff of legend, with Ossie's antics now as infamous as Villa's goal was famous. As Glenn Hoddle recalled, in an interview for *ChannelBee.com*:

'We had all been drinking champagne out of the cup. Little Ossie, who couldn't hold his drink at the best of times, had been glugging this champagne back. Ossie has stood there stark naked, holding the cup. He's jumped in the bath, and thrown the cup up in the air. We've all jumped on him and held him up, because we've thought "He's going to drown here" – because he couldn't stand up. The cup has landed in the bath, and as we've picked it up – a hundred years, it's the centenary cup – there's an almighty dent around the edge of the FA Cup, because where's he thrown it up it's hit the ceiling … Where we were saving him one minute we're now trying to drown him!'

Photo opportunities that night for the players and their families with the FA Cup included the proviso – put your hand on it to hide the dent …

The FA Cup win was not just a triumphant end to the 1980/81 season, it was also the start of a glorious era for Spurs. As Ossie has recalled, in *Hotspur* magazine: 'The 1981 FA Cup success was my greatest achievement in a Spurs shirt, because of everything it represented. I believe there was a little revolution at Spurs at the time. Coming back from Division Two people were starting to believe in the team again. We had to win something, so the 1981 FA Cup was the crowning glory.'

The Argentineans had reached the end of their identical contracts, but remained at Spurs. Villa signed a one-year extension, while Ossie abandoned his original plan of leaving, and in an indication of how his love affair with Spurs had blossomed, signed on for another three years. The team went on to challenge on four fronts in the following season, as Burkinshaw's side gained balance and began to mature. Ossie recalls the time as the best of his Tottenham career.

However, within a few short months matters were to take a turn for the worse for the Argentineans, as in spring 1982 the Falklands conflict began. It meant that the country of their birth and their adopted homeland were at war. Argentina had invaded the Falkland Islands on 2 April, and when Spurs took on Leicester in the FA Cup semi-final the following day, Ardiles' every touch was booed by Leicester fans. Tottenham fans for their part offered Ardiles their unwavering support, with one banner at Villa Park that day reading: 'Argentina, You Keep The Falklands And We'll Keep Ardiles'. However, Ossie felt that the situation had become untenable for him, and when he left to join Argentina's pre-World Cup squad, as had been previously arranged, it was to be his last appearance in the lilywhite of Tottenham for some time. After the World Cup, rather than return to Spurs he asked to leave. Keith Burkinshaw allowed him only to depart on loan, and he spent the beginning of the following season at Paris St Germain.

By contrast, Ricky Villa remained in England, but politics was to prevail over football, as Burkinshaw and Villa between them decided it expedient that he was omitted from the Cup final team, rather than face the possibility of the Royal Box having to make a presentation to an Argentinean. Villa watched the game at home to avoid the media scrutiny, and after one more season at White Hart Lane was lured by the promise of sunnier climes to Miami, and the North American Soccer League.

Ardiles returned to White Hart Lane in early 1983, after an unsettled spell in Paris. However, in just his second game back a seemingly innocuous challenge against Manchester City resulted in a broken leg – what was to prove the first of a series of injuries. He made a crucial cameo appearance as a late substitute in the 1984 UEFA Cup final – his snapshot ricocheting off the crossbar allowing allowing Graham Roberts to poke home, to take the game against Anderlecht into extra-time, before Spurs prevailed on penalties. Frustratingly, as had been the case on that night, injuries prevented him from consistent contributions and appearances. Keith Burkinshaw's successor as manager in summer 1984, Peter Shreeve, had indicated his intention to build a team around Ardiles and fellow midfield maestro Glenn Hoddle, but the continued injury jinx meant that such best-laid plans went awry. At the end of the 1985/86 season Ardiles anticipated that his testimonial at White Hart Lane, against Internazionale, was to be a valedictory affair. As such, he pulled out the stops and called in a favour from an old friend and international colleague. Thus it transpired, that on one famous evening at White Hart Lane, Diego Armando Maradona donned the lilywhite shirt and cockerel badge, and, to choruses from the stands of "Sign him, sign him", became a Spurs player.

The day after his testimonial, Ardiles had a double hernia operation – but incredibly, thereafter, was passed fit to play again. By this time David Pleat had taken charge of Spurs. A new one-year contract was agreed, and Ardiles was able to indulge in something of a bonus season at the end of his Tottenham career. Pleat switched to a 4-5-1 formation, and Ardiles enjoyed an Indian summer, regularly featuring as the deepest member of a classy midfield alongside Hoddle and Waddle amongst others, supplying ammunition for the prolific Clive Allen. Ossie rates it as the second-best Tottenham team in which he played, bettered only by the quadruple-chasers of 1981/82. Spurs finished third in the League, reached the semi-finals of the League Cup, and set themselves up for one final tilt at Wembley glory, in the FA Cup final against Coventry City. It was to end in disappointment however, as Ardiles was substituted and Spurs lost to an own-goal in extra-time.

The following season, after the early departure of David Pleat, Ossie briefly became part of the interim management team at Spurs, but the arrival of Terry Venables as new manager ultimately brought down the curtain on his playing career at White Hart Lane, and he went on loan to Blackburn in the latter stages of the 1986/87 season, before moving to Queen's Park Rangers.

The epilogue to Ossie Ardiles' love affair with Tottenham was his return to manage the club, in June 1993, as under-fire chairman Alan Sugar sought to appease fans with a populist appointment. After a promising start to the season, injury to key striker Teddy Sheringham sparked off a poor run of results, and Spurs only narrowly avoided relegation. The summer of 1994 brought the astonishing news of the acquisition of Jürgen Klinsmann following the USA World Cup, an extravagant and incredible transfer that evoked memories of the similarly spectacular arrival of Ardiles himself, alongside Ricky Villa, after the 1978 World Cup.

Ardiles was as enthralled as the fans. In the press conference at which Klinsmann was unveiled, with all the giddy excitement of a schoolboy unwrapping his presents on Christmas morning, he commented, "I am very, very excited about our ability to score goals ... Don't ask me about defence." They proved prophetic words, as the romantic notion of the beautiful game presented by Ardiles came replete with scant regard for defence. Tottenham began the season away to Sheffield Wednesday with an astonishing 5–0–5 formation, and although they scored freely, they conceded just as frequently, if not more so. Such an approach was doomed to failure. After a run of just 3 wins in 12, including defeat to Notts County in the League Cup, Ardiles was sacked in October of that season, remarking as he left, with typical dignity and humour, "I did it my way". The Ardiles way had, during his playing-days at least, been very much the Tottenham way.

Language, culture, aggression, climate – Ardiles met all these challenges head-on, immersed himself in the English style – and the Tottenham way – and duly reaped the benefits. As both a footballer in the classic Spurs mould, and a man who lived life with a charming smile on his face, it is little wonder that he remains one of the most popular and iconic figures in the club's history.

GRAHAM ROBERTS

1980-1986

SPURS CAREER

Games	287
Goals	36
Caps	6

MAGIC MOMENT

Lifting the 1984 UEFA Cup
as Spurs captain

'ROBBO'

UEFA Cup-winning captain and double FA Cup winner – yet nothing epitomises the Tottenham career of Graham Roberts quite like the challenge he dished out on New Year's Day 1986, that sent an Arsenal player hurtling into the stands. The venue was a Highbury pitch so cold that some parts of it were frozen over; the recipient of the challenge was Charlie Nicholas, a show-boating glamour-boy who was the darling of the red half of North London. As a Spurs corner was cleared to the flank, Nicholas reached the ball first, but 'Robbo' was in quick pursuit, and ploughed into the Arsenal man, sending him hurtling through the air, over a metal railing and into an aghast Highbury crowd. Over two decades later, when appearing on the White Hart Lane pitch for a half-time presentation, Robbo was greeted once more by the joyous refrain which had reverberated around the ground so many times in 1986, spawned by that memorable challenge: "Who put Charlie in the crowd? Robbo! Robbo!"

It may came as a surprise to the uninitiated, but for all the tradition of aesthetically pleasing football, Tottenham fans have a special place in their hearts for a hardman. Diving head-first where angels feared to tread, and regularly shedding blood for the cause, Robbo was a man willing to run through brick walls for the Tottenham badge. He did not just adopt this approach, he positively thrived upon it, bringing to the pitch the same passion for the club that fans felt in the stands – and they loved him for it (particularly when Arsenal players were on the receiving end!).

While revelling in the instant justice so frequently meted out by Robbo, fans also appreciated the importance of the role he played within a team which oozed flair in more advanced positions. The tenacity he brought to the team was reminiscent of the great Dave Mackay in the '60s – and it is little coincidence that the '80s side in which Robbo snarled and growled made the first realistic title challenge of any Tottenham team since the Double-winners of 1961, of which Mackay was such an integral part. As Mackay had provided a solid platform for the attacking flair of Jones, Dyson, Medwin, Smith and Allen, so Roberts' defensive steel complemented the creative qualities of Hoddle, Ardiles, Villa, Archibald and Crooks, in Keith Burkinshaw's entertainers of the early '80s. It is telling that in over 20 years since Robbo left the Lane Spurs failed to field another player of his ilk – and failed to match the trophy-winning exploits of that era.

Roberts signed for Spurs in the summer of 1980. Hollywood has always done a notoriously bad job of depicting football, but the tale of Graham Roberts' emergence as a Spurs cult hero really does seem sufficiently unlikely to be something from the silver screen. The tale of a non-league journeyman signing for one of the country's biggest clubs, slotting in alongside World Cup winners, winning the FA Cup in his first season and going on to captain the side to European glory sounds like a particularly far-fetched *Roy of the Rovers* strip, yet it forms the nutshell version of Roberts' Tottenham career.

When starting out, the glamour of Wembley finals and European glory would have seemed a million miles away. Rejected by Southampton, and denied a promised contract at Portsmouth by an untimely injury, he seemed set for a solid but unspectacular career on the non-league milkround, having plied his trade with Dorchester and then Weymouth. While at the latter he was scouted and sweet-talked by one Ron Atkinson into a move to West Bromwich Albion, before the sort of bizarre incident that would have a Hollywood producer raising an eyebrow in incredulity. The legendary Bill Nicholson, Tottenham's greatest ever manager, struck up a conversation with a stranger on a train platform, following an aborted scouting journey to Swindon, and was advised by this mysterious character to head over to Weymouth in order to cast an eye over a young talent by the name of Roberts. Nicholson did so, the wheels were set in motion and Roberts received news of Tottenham's interest while he was actually in Ron Atkinson's office discussing a move to West Brom. Unlikely though it sounds, it is a true story, as Roberts wound up at Spurs due to the combination of the greatest manager in Spurs' history and an unidentified stranger (to this day Roberts has no clue as to the identity of the man to whom he owes his extraordinary career-change).

Roberts gave himself 24 hours to decide between the two clubs, accepting an invitation from Spurs to partake in a training session. Famously however, he found the occasion painfully indicative of the gulf in class between non-league and First Division, recalling in his aptly-named autobiography *Hard as Nails*: 'I never got a kick of the ball – I'd lost about a stone in weight just running around chasing shadows.'

Having rendered himself unable even to speak in response to the polite queries of the other players as to his health, Roberts feared the worst, but the offer from Spurs remained on the table, and Roberts opted for them above West Brom (to the chagrin of Ron Atkinson). However, the tale took yet another surreal turn, as Keith Burkinshaw revealed to his new charge that he had no idea what position he played. Burkinshaw quite openly admitted that he knew nothing about Roberts, but was signing him on the recommendation of Bill Nicholson, which, alone, he considered quite sufficient. To round off the bizarre episode, Roberts found that on transferring from non-league to First Division he would actually earn less at Spurs than at Weymouth, as the move would mean he also gave up his second job at a ship-building firm.

Thus, Graham Roberts became one of Spurs' signings that summer, along with big-money arrivals Garth Crooks and Steve Archibald. While any Premiership manager attempting to buy a non-league player in the modern era would probably be carted off to the nearest psychiatric ward, such a philosophy was not unheard of at that time. Two summers previously Tony Galvin had been signed by Spurs from Goole Town, while the likes of Stuart Pearce and Cyrille Regis went on to tread similar paths from non-league to top-flight. Be that as it may, Roberts could have been forgiven for feeling a mite overawed on wandering into the White Hart Lane dressing room. Hefty wads of cash had been flung around that summer on high-profile forwards Crooks and Archibald, while the company he found himself keeping also included Glenn Hoddle, as well as World Cup winners Ardiles and Villa.

Roberts made his debut as a late substitute in a 3-2 win at home to Stoke in October, before being handed his first start in a suitably low-key fixture – away at Anfield to reigning Champions and First Division leaders Liverpool. There is an amusing inevitability about the fact that Robbo was only called into the squad because his robust style had inflicted injury upon a team-mate, albeit accidentally. A tussle between Roberts and Terry Yorath in Spurs' indoor training pitch the day before the game had led to Yorath injuring his hand on the walls of the arena, and within 24 hours Roberts was lining up at Anfield. Although

Spurs lost 2-1, Roberts made a positive first impression, as reported by Gerald Sindstadt in *The Times*:

'When [Liverpool forward Terry] McDermott promptly lobbed the ball back towards goal, Roberts dashed in to make a last-second interception. It was not the only time that Roberts, who was signed from Weymouth last May, made a good impression in his first full game in the first division.'

It was a sufficiently impressive debut, in the unfamiliar position of full back, to earn Roberts a run of games in the team. A couple of months later an injury-crisis at the Lane signalled a turning point in his Tottenham career as he was switched to centre-back, to form a brutally effective partnership alongside the similarly uncompromising Paul Miller. One suspects that in the 21st century era of whistle-happy referees, protected attackers, histrionics and outlawed tackles, football's authorities would take a dim view of the forthright approach purveyed by Messrs Roberts and Miller, but in the early-1980s they regularly dined on 3pm meals of raw legs and spilled blood.

Tottenham's inconsistent League form saw them finish mid-table, but the fairytale story was to continue for Roberts with a glorious FA Cup run. The atmosphere within the White Hart Lane camp that season was buoyant, and still fondly remembered by the players to this day. It may have been a polyglot mixture of World Cup winners and non-league veterans, Londoners and South Americans, hard men and flair-players, but the squad knitted together, with Roberts very much to the fore, both on the pitch as a defensive enforcer, and off it, as a willing participant in team-bonding drinking sessions. The successful cup run reflected a fantastic camaraderie and team spirit, perhaps epitomised by the timeless musical classic that is 'Ossie's Dream'.

The FA Cup final against Manchester City was to provide another of the many iconic moments in Robbo's Tottenham career, the memory of him sweating blood for the club another illustration of precisely why he is held in such affection by fans. A clash of heads with City's Kevin Reeves initially had the claret flowing down the Roberts visage, but more was to follow when he lined up a header, only for team-mate Chris Hughton to launch a full-blooded swipe at the ball with his boot. Roberts insists that he called for the ball, but frankly such was this man's appetite for the ugly that one wonders if he was simply unsatisfied with his previous injury, and demanded a more prominent battle-scar. He certainly received one. Knocked unconscious and minus two and a half teeth, Roberts eventually staggered into the dressing room at half-time a bloodied mess, with exposed nerve endings in his teeth leaving him in agony. Manager Keith Burkinshaw had intended to substitute him, on medical advice, but Robbo was not about change the habit of a lifetime and shirk a challenge. Instead, he locked himself in the toilet to prevent Burkinshaw from finding him, and stuffed some paracetomol down his gullet, before emerging, seemingly in fine fettle, to take to the field again for the second half.

The game finished in a draw, but five days later Spurs returned to Wembley for the replay, where Ricky Villa's wonder goal sealed a famous 3-2 victory in extra-time. While Villa's name has gone down in history, even Robbo's own legion of worshippers might be surprised to know that this goal marked another one of his crucial contributions to Tottenham history. Roberts has never been shy to point out that he set the wheels in motion for the Villa goal, by winning a block tackle on the edge of his own area, before spraying a 40-yard pass to Tony Galvin on the left flank. Galvin played the ball infield to Villa, and the rest is history.

Naturally, there followed a mammoth, alcohol-fuelled celebration, and amidst the merriment Roberts completely forgot about a hospital appointment, scheduled for 8.30 the following morning, to fix his teeth. With traces of blood barely detectable in his alcohol-stream he underwent the procedure several hours later than planned. Staff at the Epping-based hospital perhaps wisely opted for a local rather than general anaesthetic, but nevertheless the cumulative effect of the previous night's various excesses combined to knock him flat out for the rest of the day. He awoke later that night, FA Cup winners' medal still in his pocket, and obliged hospital staff with a tour of the wards, dishing out autographs and posing for photos with patients, before returning home 24 hours after it had all begun.

It had been a whirlwind year for Roberts, fast-tracked from non-league everyman to FA Cup winner, and fast earning cult hero status for his die-hard attitude. However, that season was to prove just the beginning, as Spurs began their centenary 1981/82 season realistically mounting a challenge for glory on four fronts – the League, FA Cup, League Cup and European Cup Winners' Cup. There were echoes of the efforts of the Double-winners of 20 years earlier, as a mammoth fixture list ultimately took its toll, the team playing over 70 games that season, including a stretch of 11 in 23 days at the tail-end of the season. The European Cup Winners' Cup campaign – Robbo's first taste of European action – included a glorious 6-1 aggregate thrashing of an Ajax team that was to go on and became one of the strongest forces in European club football that decade. Ultimately the European run came to an end at the Nou Camp, where a 1-0 Barcelona victory on the night earned them a 2-1 win on aggregate. Robbo had scored Tottenham's First-Leg goal in that tie, but was left startled and disgusted in equal measure by the approach adopted by Barca in that tie. While Roberts played by the hard-but-fair mantra, he views the Catalans' tactics that night as a 'dirty-tricks' campaign, that included elbows to the ribs, studs to the Achilles and flying Catalan spittle. For a player as hardened and thick-skinned as Roberts to label the first leg as the "dirtiest and most violent" in which he had ever been involved is quite some description. The lessons learned were taken on board as part of the players' European schooling, for future campaigns – and to good effect, as it would later transpire – but defeat at the semi-final stage proved a hammer-blow to the team's quest for glory that season. A run of just three wins in their final dozen League fixtures saw them finish fourth in the First Division; but the manic quadruple-pronged quest for honours meant that there were still two Wembley dates for the club to contest – the domestic Cup finals.

First up was the League Cup final against a Liverpool team who were to become League champions later that season, but the game was to bring massive disappointment for Spurs in general and Robbo in particular. By this time he was playing in midfield, after having missing several games through injury and returning to the team to find Paul Price the favoured centre-back. However, having played in every previous round of the League Cup Robbo was dropped for the final, to make way in midfield for Ricky Villa, who was himself returning from injury. Robbo's career had been defined by such setbacks, right from his days as an apprentice rejected by Lawrie McMenemy at Southampton, but he nevertheless admits the decision devastated him. No grudge is held against Keith Burkinshaw, whose honesty Robbo respected, but, not even included on the substitutes' bench for the occasion, he understandably felt removed from the team for that game.

Spurs took the lead through Steve Archibald, but conceded a late equaliser, and wilted in extra-time, the endeavours of a mammoth season beginning to take their toll. It was to prove the club's first defeat in a Wembley Cup final, and one of the great hypotheticals is whether Roberts' presence would have altered the result. Winger Tony Galvin had begun the game strongly, prompting a thunderous challenge from Liverpool's own hard man, ex-Spur Graeme Souness. Galvin limped his way through the rest of the game, and without their own midfield enforcer on hand to bring parity in the realm of bone-crunching challenges, Spurs were edged out.

Robbo was back in the Spurs team for their second Wembley date, in the FA Cup final against QPR, and playing in midfield he was to have a significant impact on both the drawn final and the replay five days later. In the first game Glenn Hoddle played a one-two with Robbo before hitting a shot which deflected into the net to give Tottenham the lead with just ten minutes remaining, but they were to be denied by a late equaliser. Within six minutes of the replay Robbo had played an instrumental role in a Spurs goal, in a manner perhaps more easily identifiable than his assist for the Ricky Villa goal 12 months earlier. Winning the ball on halfway he then embarked on an audacious solo run, which took him past no fewer than five Rangers players and into the penalty area, threatening to culminate in a goal to emulate that of Villa's the previous year. However, a desperate, ill-timed lunge from QPR's Tony Currie was to deny Robbo one of the all-time great Cup final goals, and resulted instead in a penalty, which Hoddle duly converted to give Spurs a 1-0 win. Such moments as his Cup final dribble help to dispel the myth that Robbo was simply an unrefined, agricultural defender. He actually began his non-league career as a striker, and having featured regularly for Spurs in midfield, was a vastly more accomplished ball-player than his 'hard as nails' reputation perhaps suggests. Further evidence of his ball-playing prowess came with a hat-trick at the Lane against his boyhood team, and then League-leaders, Southampton, in March 1982, with all three goals coming from open play.

If Roberts' role in the '82 Cup final was important, his contribution in the 1984 UEFA Cup final was absolutely crucial, in possibly the defining game of his Spurs career. The European run illuminated what was otherwise a slightly flat season, with a Fourth Round FA Cup exit, Third Round League Cup exit and eighth place finish in the League. However, a stylish win over a Feyenoord team boasting Johan Cruyff – and a young Ruud Gullit – set the club on their way. Victories against Bayern Munich and Austria Vienna followed, before Roberts put in a typically tenacious shift in the 1-0 semi-final Second Leg victory over Hajduk Split, which earned Tottenham a place in the final on the away goals rule. The opponents in the final were reigning holders Anderlecht, at whose ground Spurs grabbed an away goal, drawing 1-1. However, the result had come at a price, a caution for inspirational captain Steve Perryman ruling him out of the Second Leg. While obviously a massive blow for the team, it was a bittersweet moment for Robbo, who was given the honour of captaining the side in a European final.

True to form he played a captain's innings, leading by example and holding together a team that was deprived, through injuries, of Hoddle and Crooks, as well as Perryman. Anderlecht took the lead after an hour, and appeared to be clinging on until the dying stages, but on that night of all nights, Roberts was not to be denied, grabbing the game by the scruff of the neck and refusing to relinquish his grasp until Tottenham were back on level terms. In a frantic late goal-mouth melee, a close-range effort from substitute Ardiles rattled the woodwork, and the ball fell to Roberts from close range. Displaying remarkable composure in the midst of the bedlam, Roberts kept his head, calling upon the striking skills of the early days of his career. He controlled the ball on his chest, and took a touch while holding off a challenge, before slamming the ball home. As fan Dick Carpenter recalls, it was a goal scored "by sheer force of will". A finale such as that, in a European final, in front of home support, was the stuff of dreams, and White Hart Lane erupted.

Robbo has described it as the best moment of his career, the sort which makes the hairs stand up on the back of his neck even recalling it today – but as the game was therefore forced into extra-time he hardly had a moment to enjoy it. With the extra 30 minutes failing to produce a goal, the game went to penalties. That he, as captain, duly shouldered the responsibility of taking the first spot-kick is treated by Robbo as too obvious a point to merit debate. He duly despatched his effort, as did Mark Falco, Gary Stevens and Steve Archibald, and although Danny Thomas had his saved, young goalkeeper Tony Parks kept out two Anderlecht efforts to win the Cup for Spurs. It was one of the greatest nights in Tottenham Hotspur history, and Graham Roberts had been the heartbeat of the team. He and manager Keith Burkinshaw were in no doubt however that Steve Perryman ought to be the man to collect the cup, but as Roberts recalls in *Hard as Nails*, Perryman refused, paying tribute to the efforts of the stand-in skipper with the words: 'You did more than anybody else on the pitch to win us the cup, so I'll just watch if you don't mind'.

To receive such a glowing tribute from a man of the stature of Perryman is exalted praise indeed, and with this blessing, and the sound of 50,000 delirious Tottenham fans ringing in his ears, Roberts lifted the UEFA Cup. The celebrations continued long into the night, many fans recalling that several hours after the game a fresh roar was heard from outside the ground, as revellers on the Tottenham High Road were treated to the sight of Robbo leaning out of the window just above the old fixtures sign, holding the UEFA Cup and making as if to throw it towards the fans. The Tottenham team of the 1980s had some history of damaging their silverware through the exuberance of their celebrations, as detailed elsewhere in this book, but on this occasion it seemed that wiser counsels prevailed, and Robbo instead showered the fans with champagne.

In terms of silverware, the UEFA Cup triumph was to prove the zenith of Robbo's Tottenham career, although in the minds of many fans, the true highlight was to follow later, at Highbury on 1 January 1986, when Charlie Nicholas was sent flying through the chilly North London air. For his troubles, Robbo's momentum had sent him sprawling into the Arsenal dugout. The Arsenal physio asked him if he was ok, to which Robbo replied "Fine thanks". "Well you're not now," responded the physio, and dealt him a right hook to the nose, sparking a full-on brawl involving both benches. While Robbo admits the challenge on Nicholas worthy of a red card (it earned him a yellow), and expresses relief that the striker was not injured, the incident has gained immortality amongst Spurs fans.

Robbo certainly knew how to endear himself to the Highbury faithful on those derby away days, having given them a two-fingered salute the previous year after a 2-1 Spurs victory – although he has since protested that this was merely a helpful reminder to the statisticians in the crowd of the number of points Spurs would gain for the victory. How thoughtful…

They were memorable times, yet it always rankled with Robbo that the dashing Spurs team of the early- and mid-80s failed to win the League title. The disappointment of the 1981/82 League campaign was followed by another near miss in 1984/85, with the title virtually hinging on a crunch encounter with League-leaders Everton, at White Hart Lane on the night of Wednesday 3 April. Two goals for the visitors proved enough although Roberts almost salvaged a point, scoring with a long range effort and nearly repeating the feat minutes later, only for Everton goalkeepr Neville Southall to tip the ball to safety, and the title beyond Tottenham's reach. The club finished third, and that was to prove as good as it got for Robbo, to his immense disappointment.

Roberts ultimately transferred to Glasgow Rangers in December 1986, having failed to see eye to eye with then-manager David Pleat. Indeed, he has since insisted that he would have preferred not to leave Tottenham, and this genuine affection for the club is mirrored in the reaction of fans towards him to this day. A member of a most unique breed, Robbo's unswerving willingness to fight tooth and nail for the Tottenham cause earned him huge popularity on the White Hart Lane terraces. Rarely has the epithet 'cult hero' been more deserved.

GARY MABBUTT

1982-1998

SPURS CAREER

Games	611
Goals	38
Caps	16

MAGIC MOMENT

Becoming the sixth man to captain Spurs to FA Cup victory, in 1991

'MABBSY'

THE image of Gary Mabbutt, one of football's all-time good-guys, beaming from ear to ear and hoisting aloft the FA Cup in 1991 will live long in the memory of all Spurs fans. For the club it was a momentous occasion, after a season of off-field developments bordering on the traumatic – and epitomised by a first half of the Cup final in which every conceivable misfortune seemed to have befallen the team. However, for Mabbutt more than most, the victory was a moment to savour, signalling the exultant culmination of a four-year process of exorcism, after he had been so desperately unlucky in scoring the own-goal which lost Spurs that same trophy in the final in 1987.

Even beyond White Hart Lane, where he had long held hero status, few would have begrudged Mabbutt his moment of glory, because for all his talents as a footballer, much of the affection and admiration held for him within the football community at large was for the exemplary manner in which he always conducted himself. A respected upholder of the spirit of the game and regularly heralded as a role model for children in his playing days, Mabbutt made a habit of conquering adversity. He pursued his career in football despite diagnosis as a diabetic at just 17 years of age, going on to become an England international, and later overcoming career-threatening injuries with minimal fuss and hours of hard work. His loyalty to Spurs is another defining feature of his career, a remarkable and increasingly rare feat in the modern era. Having spent 4 years at Bristol Rovers he then spent an astonishing 16 at White Hart Lane, despite the attentions of numerous top-quality suitors, as well as the comings and goings of a slew of managers. This calming presence, while turmoil repeatedly reigned around him in the dugout, boardroom and often on the pitch, constitutes the other crucial factor making Mabbutt such a hero amongst Spurs folk. As the club lurched through an interminable stream of crises and repeatedly tore up hymn sheets to begin again from scratch, Mabbutt stood firm, exactly the sort of figure needed by the club as captain, to retain the team identity and provide a steadying influence, holding everything together amidst the bedlam.

The Mabbutts were a family of impressive football pedigree. In joining Bristol Rovers in 1977 Gary followed in the footsteps of his father Ray, while his brother Kevin holds the distinction of being one of a very select band to have scored a hat-trick against Manchester United at Old Trafford, the feat having been achieved during his days at Bristol City, and placing him alongside the likes of Tottenham's own Martin Peters, and Brazilian former World Player of the Year, Ronaldo.

Gary made 147 appearances for Rovers, but it was while there, at the tender age of 17, that he discovered he had diabetes. He clearly recalls experiencing the symptoms – lethargy, thirst – without realising their cause. Eventually, after an unusually poor performance in a defeat against Leicester, and having struggled to keep up with his teammates in training, he was sent to the club doctor, and diagnosed immediately. Understandably, the news came as a shock to a young man still at a nascent stage in his career, leaving him fearing for his future in the game. These fears were hardly assuaged when he made enquiries of the top four specialists in the country, to determine whether he would be able to continue playing professional football as a diabetic. He recalls: "The first three said it would be very difficult to continue in football, so my father went to the fourth specialist and he said 'If you really want to do it then give it a try'."

Lesser men may have crumbled; Mabbutt resolved not only to succeed, but vowed to become the first diabetic to play for England. As he recounts: "I had no thought whatsoever of giving it up. A professional footballer was what I wanted to be. Some people ask if it held me back, but if you look at the facts, before being diagnosed I was playing in the Third Division, but as a diabetic I played in the Premier League and for my country. It meant I had to be strict with myself, I wasn't able to go out drinking and partying."

This was no bolshy claim of an arrogant *prima donna* however, more an early indication of the lion-hearted determination that would typify his career for the next 20 years. Within five weeks he was back in the Rovers first-team, but the routine had changed, Mabbutt regularly having to test his blood sugar levels and inject himself with insulin. Not for the squeamish perhaps, but it was to become the habit of a lifetime, and even now he still requires four injections and up to eight blood tests per day.

Diabetes would prove to be not only a physical affliction, for a mooted transfer to Ipswich Town would later break down when the club's then manager, the late Bobby Robson, decided not to risk signing a diabetic. That gamble was instead taken by Keith Burkinshaw, in the summer of 1982, and for £105,000 Mabbutt became a Spurs player, albeit needing a letter from a specialist to confirm that he would be able to fulfil the three years of his contract. Robson, perhaps regretting one that had got away, would later, in his first game as England manager, select Mabbutt for his international debut, describing him as a "bionic man".

In keeping with a man who eschewed the trappings of fame that a career in professional football could bring, there was no particular fanfare surrounding his move to Tottenham. Instead, media focus that summer was directed towards the club's close-season, big-money buy, Alan Brazil, who arrived from Ipswich for quadruple the price of Mabbutt. However, Mabbutt was to slot straight into the Tottenham team, making his debut against Liverpool in the Charity Shield, and proceeding to make more League appearances than any outfield player at the club that season. It may prompt raised eyebrows amongst those who recall Mabbutt later making the central defensive berth his own for the best part of a decade, but he chipped in with ten League goals in that debut season, just one behind club leading scorer Steve Archibald. Such a healthy strike-rate proved an early testament to the man's versatility, for in those early days he typically featured in midfield, whilst also contributing at full back and centre-back, and occasionally even leading the line in attack.

The Tottenham side Mabbutt had joined in 1982 had mounted a determined, if rather incredible, assault on four fronts, competing strongly in the League, FA Cup, League Cup and European Cup Winners' Cup. The rigours of the season ultimately led them to fall agonisingly short on three of those fronts, with defeats in the European semi-final and League Cup final, alongside an eventual fourth-placed League finish, although some silverware was achieved in the form of the FA Cup. That Spurs side of the early 1980s were very much a force to be reckoned with, and Mabbutt's first years at the club were halcyon days. He joined a team that had grown up together, following promotion from the old Second Division, and evolved into regular hoarders of silverware, with successive FA

Cups to their name in the early '80s. Keith Burkinshaw had fashioned a team around the mercurial talents of Glenn Hoddle, Ossie Ardiles and Ricky Villa, while the likes of Steve Perryman and Graham Roberts provided solidity and steel at the back. Within two months of joining this team Mabbutt was called up for his England debut, against West Germany, while his industry as well as versatility helped him to establish himself as a vital cog in the Spurs machine in that period. Such a rosy state of affairs would stand in stark contrast to the majority of his Spurs career, in the following years, when false dawn followed false dawn and the club seemed perennially to stumble from one setback to another.

But Mabbutt did not have to wait long for his first medal in Spurs colours, as he featured in the UEFA Cup win of 1984. With two FA Cups, two top-four finishes and now a European trophy, the future appeared bright, but as was to happen so often during Mabbutt's time at the Lane, off-pitch troubles and a managerial change abruptly unsettled matters. Boardroom politics had prompted Keith Burkinshaw to announce before the end of the 1983/84 season that he would leave, after eight years at the helm, and coach Peter Shreeve was appointed to what was soon to become a poisoned chalice. Shreeve's first season was actually an extremely encouraging one, as Spurs launched a spirited challenge for the title, and finished a highly creditable third. However, flirtation with the relegation zone the following campaign was deemed unsatisfactory, as perhaps was the quiet, introverted public persona of Shreeve in an increasingly media-centric environment, and the summer of 1986 saw the wielding of the managerial axe, an instrument that was to gain regular use during the rest of Mabbutt's Tottenham career. The season had also brought about a mightily symbolic passing of the torch in the Tottenham ranks, for in March long-serving club captain Steve Perryman played his final game for the club, by which time Mabbutt had been moved into the centre-back position on a permanent basis by Shreeve.

Given the glut of extravagantly gifted ball-players vying for places in the Tottenham midfield, it is perhaps understandable that Mabbutt was eventually to find his home in the team in the centre of defence, although when pushed he professes to having most enjoyed the involvement offered by the central midfield position. Although only five foot nine inches, what he lacked in height he expiated for with an ability to leap for headers that verged on the prodigious, and ensured he was typically the equal of far bigger forwards, whilst on the ground he was a patron of the school of well-timed tackles.

Over the course of several seasons he was the choice of numerous managers as one half of a number of central defence partnerships, several of which showed genuine promise only to be curtailed by the abrupt departures of personnel. One such partnership, possibly the best of the lot, was that with Richard Gough. Signed from Dundee United in the summer of 1986, the Scot struck up an instant on-field rapport with Mabbutt, and the effectiveness of the combination was evidenced by the feats achieved by the club that season. Perhaps that should read 'so nearly achieved', for a fine season was to end frustratingly, without silverware, but instead with rueful memories of near misses and desperately bad luck. Spurs finished third in the First Division; were knocked out of the League Cup semi-final by Arsenal in the last minute of a replay, after the initial two-legged tie had finished level; and, finally, lost the FA Cup final in extra-time, with Gary Mabbutt famously to the fore.

It is rather fitting that a player universally regarded as one of the greatest servants of Tottenham Hotspur should be most memorably associated with the trophy so definitive of the history of the club. Spurs went into the game as overwhelming favourites, given their form that year, the prowess of Clive Allen in his 49-goal season and, of course, the famous pedigree of the club in the oldest cup competition in the world. Spurs had won all of their previous seven FA Cup finals, while opponents, lowly Coventry City, were making their Cup final bow. Bookmakers would have shut up shop and taken the afternoon off after just two minutes, when Allen headed Spurs in front. However, seven minutes later Coventry were level, and a classic Cup final was well and truly underway. Five minutes before half-time the Tottenham centre-backs came forward for a set piece, and when Glenn Hoddle's delivery enticed Coventry keeper Steve Ogrizovic off his line, the loose ball dropped in the general vicinity of Mabbutt and lion-maned Coventry captain Brian Kilcline. Via a combination of their legs the ball rolled into the unguarded net, and Spurs were ahead again. For all his versatility, Mabbutt's account of the goal betrays the fact that he is most decidedly *not* a natural born goalscorer. A true striker, a single-minded predator, in the mould of Greaves, Allen or Gary Lineker, would presumably have claimed the goal outright, refusing to countenance any talk of deflections and own-goals. Mabbutt is perhaps just too nice a guy to resort to demonstrate such an attitude: "We basically collided as the ball reached us, and as I looked up the ball bounced into the net. When we went off at half-time we were leading two-one, and my name was up in lights. Little did I know ..."

The annals have it as Mabbutt's goal, but if he was in the right place at the right time on that occasion, the footballing gods were to turn the tables in the cruellest possible manner later on. A second half Coventry equaliser had taken the game into extra-time, and seven minutes into the first period Mabbutt scored again, but this time past his own goalkeeper. Coventry's Lloyd McGrath went galloping down the right flank, and with Spurs left-back Mitchell Thomas out of position Mabbutt moved to block off the cross. McGrath fired in the ball, Mabbutt stuck out his leg and the ball looped off his knee, over goalkeeper Ray Clemence and into the net. This time there was no doubt – it was an own goal (although Mabbutt playfully argues, "Personally I feel it was more a of a deflection"), and it proved to be the winner. The adage suggests that nice guys finish last, and on 16 May 1987 the nicest guy in North London was at an all-time low. It had been a complete freak of a goal, and as Mabbutt wistfully recalls, "99 times out of 100 it wouldn't have gone in. I'd have stuck out my knee and it would have gone out for a corner, or I'd have stuck out my knee and knocked it back to Ray Clemence."

Instead of any of these 99 scenarios, Mabbutt had become only the second player in history to score for both teams in an FA Cup final – ironically, the first, Tommy Hutchison, had done so when playing against Spurs, in the 1981 final.

The aftermath of the final was to prove a critical time in Mabbutt's career. By this time he was being widely courted, with Arsenal, Manchester United, Liverpool, Atlético Madrid and Lyon amongst his suitors. While it is inconceivable that such a body-and-soul Tottenham man as Mabbutt should ever have been attracted by the first name on that list, he does admit that Liverpool's was an offer he considered. They had at the time just finished second in the League – only the second time in nine seasons that they had failed to win the title. The day after the Cup final their manager, Kenny Dalglish, rang Mabbutt to inform him that there were three names on the Anfield shopping list that summer – Peter Beardsley, John Barnes and Gary Mabbutt ("Maybe he saw the Cup final and was impressed by my goalscoring abilities," he deadpans). By that time he had spent half a decade at White Hart Lane, and at 25 it was a suitable point in his career at which to make a move. However, Spurs were tugging on his heartstrings, and seeing fans with banners proclaiming 'We don't blame you Gary' on the bus tour following the final had a big impact on his decision. As well as this, Spurs had produced a strong season of free-flowing football under David Pleat, and Mabbutt felt that the club was moving in the right direction: "I'd had five wonderful years at Spurs, and we'd just had a great season–finishing third and reaching the Cup final. I thought we'd move on and be challenging for the title."

Inevitably however, things would crumble, the manager would go, and Spurs would have to start again. Pleat left early in the 1987/88 season, following allegations about his private life, and by Christmas Terry Venables had been installed. It was to be a transitional season at the club – the first of many, truth be told – but a momentous one for Mabbutt, as he assumed the role for which he had seemingly been born, as captain of Tottenham Hotspur Football Club. The great, promising Spurs team of the mid-1980s was dismantled under Venables, some players sold, some opting to leave. Although a late surge in the 1989/90 season saw the club record a third-placed finish in the First Division, yet again the FA Cup was to provide the defining moments for the club in that period. By the 1990/91 season the club was once again beset by off-pitch turmoil, adding to the importance of a strong cup run – and what a cup run it was to prove.

Victories over Blackpool, Oxford, Portsmouth and Notts County set up an epic semi-final clash, the first ever to be staged at Wembley, against arch-rivals Arsenal. Spurs were very much the underdogs, in light not only of the boardroom problems, but, more prominently, the fact that Arsenal were comfortably on their way to the League title. Retuning to the scene of his nightmare of 1987, it was a proud Mabbutt who led his team out of the Wembley tunnel, alongside opposite number Tony Adams. Spurs fans barely need to be reminded that Paul Gascoigne's astonishing free kick gave Tottenham an early lead, and with fewer than ten minutes played that advantage had been doubled. A Paul Allen cross from the right prompted a most ungainly melee in the Arsenal penalty area, with Mabbutt feistily in the thick of it, culminating in a poacher's goal from Gary Lineker. Arsenal pulled one back before half-time, but in the second half Lineker scored again, following a neat exchange of passes with Mabbutt on halfway, and the day was Tottenham's.

Spurs were heading back to Wembley for the final, in a situation which almost seemed to touch the realms of fantasy. The club were desperately in need of on-pitch success to stave off boardroom collapse; the year ended in '1', as had been the case for so many of Spurs' previous glory days; and Gary Mabbutt would return to a Wembley FA Cup final, this time as captain, to banish the memories of 1987. In a first half so dramatic it was exhausting even to watch, Spurs lost the talismanic Gascoigne through injury; conceded a dubiously awarded goal; had a Lineker effort incorrectly judged offside; and then saw Lineker have a penalty saved. It appeared that more heartbreak might be on the cards for Mabbutt, but on this occasion even Lady Luck, so often a cruel mistress in his career, smiled upon the Tottenham skipper. A Paul Stewart goal had taken the game into extra-time, before which, while Venables set about instructing his players, Forest manager Brian Clough bizarrely left his team in the centre circle and opted instead to talk to a policeman.

As in 1987 the game was settled by a single goal in extra-time, and as in 1987 it was an own goal, but this time it put Spurs ahead. A Nayim corner was flicked on by Stewart, towards Mabbutt at the back post, and although he did not get his head to the ball, his pressure was enough – Forest defender Des Walker went where Mabbutt had gone four years earlier, and diverted the ball into his own net. Spurs had won the Cup, and this time Mabbutt climbed Wembley's 39 steps in triumph.

A new manager, an off-the-field dispute, a change in personnel, and Gary Mabbutt standing firm at the heart of the defence: the cycle would repeat itself in the following years with a monotony that was both galling and wearying in equal measure for Spurs fans of the time. The 1992/93 season produced one notable false dawn, when grizzled defender Neil Ruddock rejoined the club, and formed a partnership with Mabbutt that threatened finally to offer long-term stability in defence, and a platform for greater things. It was not to be however, as, in echoes of Richard Gough's Tottenham career, yet again off-the-field matters interfered, and Ruddock was sold to Liverpool after just one season.

Venables, Peter Shreeve and Doug Livermore each manned the helm as manager at Spurs in the early 90s, followed by Ossie Ardiles, espousing a romantic but ill-judged 5-0-5 formation, which Mabbutt was initially detailed to watch from the bench. Gerry Francis was next up, before Mabbutt finally finished his Spurs career under Christian Gross, at the end of the 1997/98 season. Looking back on this constant state of flux at White Hart Lane, Mabbutt muses, rather diplomatically, "It's always difficult when there's a lack of continuity. We found it hard to get a settled side and achieve any consistency, so we had very little success."

They are words which might as well have replaced 'Audere est Facere' as the club's motto during his career.

The FA Cup marked Mabbutt's most famous performances, and his permanence in a transient world at White Hart Lane was to become a defining feature of his career at Spurs, but Mabbutt is also, justifiably, lauded for his strength in adversity. His diabetes did not just necessitate injections, and dietary and fitness challenges, for there have also been a handful of occasions when his condition created life-threatening situations. Sometimes these incidents have occurred during training, when his blood-sugar level has gone awry, and he has gone into a hypoglycaemic coma in front of his team-mates. Indeed, he recalls, "The first time this happened there was a major panic, and the physios came rushing on. But after that, every time I fell over the other players would just say 'Get him some lucozade ...'"

Such situations were typically attended to promptly, and Mabbutt made a habit of keeping a glucose drink on the touchline, the only ostensible indication he ever gave of his condition. On one occasion, however, with no-one in attendance, Mabbutt came perilously close to a far more serious fate. As he detailed in his autobiography, *Against All Odds*, the incident happened in October 1986, on the day of a League Cup game against Barnsley. Mabbutt had been at home for his usual afternoon nap prior to the game, but just half an hour before kick-off that evening had still not turned up at White Hart Lane. After some frantic phone calls, a neighbour found him passed out in his bedroom, covered in blood. It transpired that he had attempted to give himself a blood test, but had been so 'low' that he had been unable to, and had instead repeatedly cut himself before going into a deep diabetic coma. He was rushed to hospital and awoke to find two intravenous drips in his arm. Yet despite this, as soon as the following day he was back on the training ground, and that weekend availed himself for the little matter of a trip to Anfield to face League champions Liverpool. It is a story as astonishing as it is frightening, and yet one receives the impression that this was the sort of incident with which Mabbutt dealt in typically phlegmatic fashion and without complaint, just another obstacle to be surmounted. Indeed, rather than complain about his situation, he has instead used his status as a leading professional footballer to raise awareness of diabetes and act as a role model to children in particular who are similarly afflicted.

As if the challenges posed by diabetes were not enough, the man has also had to deal with a number of career-threatening injuries during his time at White Hart Lane. In December 1993, a flailing elbow from Wimbledon's John Fashanu caught Mabbutt in the face, and it is no exaggeration to say the impact shattered his face. Mabbutt's right eye socket was broken in three places, and his cheekbone fractured in four places (to this day Mabbutt has no feeling on one side of his face) – yet referee Keith Hackett did not even award a free kick. He battled back from the injury, donning a *Phantom of the Opera*-style protective mask as he returned to top-flight action three months later, noting of his headgear, in an interview with the *Independent*: 'It was a bit strange. My head vibrated a bit.'

Two years later there was a further setback as, on the opening day of the of the 1996/97 season, at the age of 34, he broke his leg against Blackburn, an injury which kept him out of action for the entire season. Undeterred, he returned for the 1997/98 campaign, eventually making an emotional farewell appearance at White Hart Lane as a substitute on the final day of the season, against Southampton. As Peter Lansley of the *Independent* wrote, it was the end of an era, and fittingly recognised as such by the Tottenham faithful, who have a particular place in their hearts for long-serving and unstintingly loyal club servants:

'On a day of farewells at White Hart Lane ... club skipper Gary Mabbutt, after 16 years and 619 appearances, received the loudest and fondest cheer of the day by taking the armband for the final nine minutes.'

CLIVE ALLEN

1984-1988

SPURS CAREER

Games	135
Goals	84
Caps	5

MAGIC MOMENT

Hat-trick against Norwich in 1987 – his third of the season – when many present are adamant he only touched the ball three times in the whole game

'SUPER CLIVE'

Across from the wing, a dart to the near post, a Clive Allen flicked header into the net – it was a combination witnessed umpteen times by the Spurs faithful in the 1986/87 season; most memorably perhaps was on the grandest stage in the domestic game, the FA Cup final at Wembley, against Coventry City. The dignitaries were still taking their seats when Chris Waddle whipped in a teasing cross from the right flank, Coventry defender Trevor Peake blinked and missed the movement of the Tottenham number 7, and in a trice the ball was nestling in the net, while Allen wheeled away in familiar triumphant pose. Bathed in sunshine, on the immaculate Wembley turf and in a gleaming all-white strip, it was almost as if the gods – not satisfied with the previous 48 efforts – had wanted to create one definitive, picture-perfect goal to epitomise the extraordinary feats of Allen that season.

The top flight of English football is unlikely ever to see the like again. In that one astonishing campaign, Allen scored 49 goals in League and Cup competitions, a record for a Tottenham player in a single season. The feat is given some sense of context when juxtaposed with the figures of Spurs' next highest goalscorer in 1986/87, John Chedozie – who scored eight. Allen registered 33 goals in 39 League appearances (actually fewer than Jimmy Greaves' record of 37 League goals in a single season) but also notched up 12 in 9 League Cup appearances, a competition record for a single season, as well as 4 in 6 FA Cup appearances. When taken in isolation the total amassed by Allen that season seems scarcely believable, but to those who watched him score and score and score, week after week, his presence in front of goal soon carried with it a glorious inevitability.

The Allen family are of a proud and famous football heritage, with particularly strong links to Tottenham. Clive's father, Les, was an integral member of the club's legendary Double-winning team of 1960/61, scoring 22 League and 5 Cup goals in that campaign, in partnership with Bobby Smith. Thereafter, he competed with Smith to partner Jimmy Greaves, eventually leaving for QPR in the summer of 1965. If Clive felt any pressure in living up to the reputation of Allen Senior, he dealt with it in quite some style.

Another member of the Allen family to play for Spurs was Clive's cousin Paul, a midfielder signed from West Ham in 1985 for £400,000. In 1980 he had played in West Ham's FA Cup final defeat against Arsenal aged just 17 years and 256 days – at the time the youngest ever player to appear in the showpiece event – and he eventually made 370 appearances in a 9-year Tottenham career, winning the FA Cup with the club in 1991. Others of the Allen clan who made names for themselves in football included another cousin, Martin, whose playing career included spells at QPR and West Ham, before he moved into management; and younger brother Bradley, also once of QPR.

Although by no means the type to court controversy, Clive Allen's early career was headline-grabbing stuff. Having broken into the QPR first-team in 1978, scoring a hat-trick on his full debut, he was involved in an incident still spoken of with bemusement today. In an early game of the 1980/81 season he took a free kick against Coventry which flew into the net, crashed against the stanchion and flew straight back out again. After much consultation with his linesman, the referee decided against awarding the goal, in a game QPR eventually lost.

Allen's contribution to the trivia books continued in June 1981, when he signed for Arsenal – the £1.25 million for which he moved was, at the time, a record fee for a teenager. Bizarrely however, he moved again that summer, without having played a competitive game for Arsenal, transferring to Crystal Palace as part of the swap deal that saw Kenny Samson arrive at Highbury. His brief sojourn in the red and white of the enemy has been forgiven by fans, for Arsenal's loss was, ultimately, very much Tottenham's gain. Despite a hat-trick on debut, his career at Palace was something of a struggle, and a year later he returned to QPR.

At the end of the 1983/84 season, Clive Allen's form at QPR had earned him a call-up into Bobby Robson's England team for the tour of South America in the summer of 1984, and he made his debut as a substitute against Brazil in June at the Maracana – a game most memorable for a mazy solo goal from a young John Barnes. Three days later Allen made his first start for his country, in a 2-0 defeat to Uruguay, and earned his third cap shortly afterwards in a goalless draw against Chile. A decidedly hectic summer then saw him make the move that had virtually seemed his destiny, given his family ties, as he signed for Spurs for £700,000. Indeed, such was his familiarity with the club that he recalls, in *Match of my Life*, that on signing for Tottenham, manager Peter Shreeve had told him, 'I'm sure you know where the ground is Clive, I'll see you in the morning.'

Allen had actually already featured in Spurs colours once before, playing for London Schools against Coventry at White Hart Lane before his professional days, during a short spell spent training with the team, an occasion which was to serve as a hint of things to come as he duly registered a hat-trick. As a professional, his Tottenham career began in similarly rip-roaring fashion, with two goals on his League debut in a 4-1 win over Everton in August 1984. However, *in toto* his first two seasons in lilywhite were generally frustrating ones, marred by injuries and a subsequent inability to hold down a regular first-team place. Although few would have had any idea of quite what astonishing feats would soon be achieved, some signs of what was to come could be glimpsed at the end of the 1985/86 campaign. Despite having nothing for which to play in terms of honours, Spurs ended the season in rampant fashion, with 4 wins in 5 games, including a 14-goal blitz in their final 3 fixtures. Clive Allen featured prominently in these games, with two goals against QPR, a further brace against Aston Villa and a stylish volley in the final game of the season at home to Southampton. It was a confidence-boosting end to the campaign, and although the late-season flurry had come too late to force his way into the England reckoning for the following month's World Cup in Mexico, Allen went into the summer in high spirits.

Ahead of the new season there was a managerial change at White Hart Lane, as Peter Shreeve was replaced by David Pleat. Tottenham had scored an impressive 78 League goals under Shreeve during the previous campaign, adhering to their tradition as one of the game's principal entertainers by scoring four goals or more on ten separate occasions in Division One, yet that summer Shreeve paid the price for an ultimately inconsistent season – another, somewhat less glorious tradition of the club – in which the team had finished tenth in the League and made early exits in the Cups. Although Shreeve had signed Allen, the appointment of Pleat was to prove pivotal in the striker's imminent, record-breaking season. In particular, the decision to deploy a 4-5-1 formation away to Oxford United in late-November was a move upon which Allen was to thrive.

Prior to the start of the season much of the focus at White Hart Lane had been on the defence rather than attack, with the signing of Richard Gough from Dundee United a masterstroke, providing the sort of defensive colossus the club had been seeking for years. Gough formed a centre-back partnership with Gary Mabbutt, and as Allen himself noted, in *Hotspur* magazine, 'The defensive work really laid the foundations for us.'

Be that as it may, the headlines that season were to be written at the other end of the pitch – starting from day one, with a trip to Aston Villa. The season was just four minutes old when Allen opened his account. Latching on to a Tony Galvin cross from the right, Allen hardly made the sweetest contact – the ball came off the sole of his boot – but the net duly bulged, and Allen was up and running. As the first goal in what was to be such a mind-bogglingly prolific season, Allen has admitted wondering what might have happened had that first strike not taken its slightly fortuitous path to goal, noting in *Hotspur*: 'Confidence is such a big part of football … Certainly the fact that I had found the net did wonders for my confidence.'

If anything, it is rather appropriate that his first step towards his historic tally was achieved in such inelegant style, for Allen's success – and ultimately his cult hero status – derives from the ends rather than the means, from the goals recorded in the annals rather than any moments of wizardry etched in the mind's eye. Allen does not necessarily fit the historical mould of some of the classical White Hart Lane heroes. He was not a gifted ball-player comparable to his team-mate Glenn Hoddle, nor an entertainer of the ilk of a Gascoigne or Ginola. The club has a tradition for giving home to on-pitch artists, but the balletic sashaying could be left to the flair-blessed midfielders; Allen was more of a machine, and in this sense kept company instead with the club's elite band of supreme goalscorers.

As his first goal that season was a rather unsightly affair, there is an equal aptness to the fact that the effort with which he broke the Spurs record for goals in a season – his 44th, in the FA Cup semi-final against Watford – was another scrappy strike, a long-range effort which completely changed direction after cannoning off a defender. There was never any question of Allen conceding this to be an own goal, for that would have flown directly in the face of the classic striker's mentality. Like any born goalscorer, Allen was not concerned about how pretty his goals looked. If anything, an effete prettiness would have detracted from his primary talent. Allen was of the school of thought that goalscoring records were not broken by the game's aesthetes, but by the most ruthless.

Clive Allen's job was to put the ball in the net, by hook or by crook – or by penalties. A statistical note for the anorak-clad: Allen scored seven spot-kicks in 1986/87, although even without those he would still have broken the Spurs record for goals in one season. He did not care if the ball scraped off the studs of his distinctively small feet (he reportedly wore size six boots), as did his first of the season; or ballooned off the keeper, high into the night's sky and back to earth inside the net, as against West Ham en route to another hat-trick in the League Cup; or deflected massively off an opponent, as it did for his record-breaking 44th. He only cared that the ball ended up in the net, and in the course of that season he proved himself a master of that art. In a team brimming – nay, overflowing – full of aesthetes, Allen added a vital component, a lethal edge at the top of the team, to complement the silky skills elsewhere.

Back to the opening day of the season. Spurs' lead, and Allen's personal tally, was doubled on the half-hour, when striking partner Mark Falco flicked on a Glenn Hoddle cross, and Allen turned adroitly to strike the ball home. Curiously, Allen has professed to finding it difficult to remember the hat-trick goal itself. For the record, it was created by his cousin Paul, and finished straightforwardly after Clive had beaten the Villa offside trap, to give Tottenham a 3-0 opening day win.

Allen's voracious appetite for goals was whetted, yet nobody in their wildest dreams could have foreseen what was to come. By the end of October, indications were emerging that a freakishly efficient goalscorer was pounding the beat at the Lane, for Allen had scored 11 of Tottenham's 12 League goals to date in the campaign, prompting Pleat to sell the previously dependable target-man Mark Falco to Watford. Allen's tally at that point included both goals in a 2-0 victory against reigning champions and previously unbeaten Everton. The brace comprised a neat header and thunderous long-range drive – two very different types of strike, which, as a pair, neatly encapsulated the man's bloody-minded desire for goals. Irrespective of how he received the ball, or of the distance and the angle, Allen seemed to possess an almost mechanical instinct for goal. As long-term fan Chris Paterson observes, "His goals-to-shots ratio was exceptional, because so many of them were on target – and he was good in the air as well. He was the most clinical finisher the club has seen apart from Jimmy Greaves."

Pleat was similarly enthused by what he had seen, commenting after the Everton game, as reported in *The Times*: 'What can I say? He's amazing.' However, despite his apparent speechlessness, Pleat had evidently been devoting plenty of thought to his star striker, for shortly afterwards, on Saturday 23 November, he delivered his tactical masterstroke of switching to a 4-5-1 formation, with Allen as the lone front-man.

The move catalysed a marked improvement in Spurs' form, which until then had brought victories in fewer than half of their League games. For his part, Allen continued his white-hot vein of scoring form, thriving within a style that seemed tailored to his specific *modus operandi*, as the focal point of a Tottenham team seeping flair and brio from every pore. The creative masterminds of Hoddle, Chris Waddle and Ardiles pulled the strings behind him; while at various points in the season the attack-minded Hodge, Galvin and Claesen also featured amongst the five-man midfield which, although deployed by the French team which had won the 1984 European Championship, nevertheless bordered on the revolutionary in England.

The astonishing individual goal tally continued to mount, in the Cup competitions as well as the League, as Tottenham found themselves challenging on three fronts, reaching the semi-finals of both domestic Cups in March 1987. Indeed, Tottenham's route to the League Cup semi-final came via a 5-0 victory in the quarter-final replay at home to West Ham, possibly the team's most sparkling performance of the season, and a game in which the star striker plundered a hat-trick in the final ten minutes, bagging his second match-ball of the season. A couple of months later there followed his third hat-trick, in a

League game at home to Norwich. It is a game remembered with particular affection by Spurs fans as epitomising the bloody-minded desire to find the net that ranks Allen alongside the club's goalscoring legends, from Sandy Brown to Jimmy Greaves.

A cliché often attributed to the game's most natural goalscorers is that they can be anonymous for 89 minutes but still score. Observers recall that Allen, that day against Norwich, was worse than anonymous. He had been having a woeful game, and legend has it that when David Pleat arranged a substitution, Allen started walking towards the sidelines, only to see the number 11 raised, for his cousin Paul. Clive stayed on the pitch, and in the final ten minutes scored all three of his side's goals, having, in the opinion of many watching on with pleasant surprise, seemingly only touched the ball three times in the whole game.

Allen's phenomenal achievements were rightly lauded by all and sundry, as he was crowned Professional Footballers' Association Player of the Year – ahead of team-mate Hoddle – as well as Football Writers' Association Footballer of the Year, and called up by Bobby Robson into the England squad. However, the international nut proved a difficult one for Allen to crack, as Gary Lineker was the well-established incumbent in the role of principal England striker, having won the Golden Boot in the previous year's World Cup. If Allen were to feature it would have to be in partnership with – rather than in lieu of – Lineker, not a role that came naturally to a man whose unparalleled success all season had been reaped as a lone front-runner. As was noted in *The Times*, that February, 'So long as [Peter Beardsley] is setting them up for Lineker, Bobby Robson, the England manager, will resist the temptation to pick Clive Allen, a less unselfish player and a pure finisher.'

While ruthless in front of goal, Allen has a well-earned reputation for simply being too gentlemanly off the pitch to harbour any sort of grudge. Nevertheless, even this most mild-mannered and respectable character would have been forgiven for muttering a few choice oaths when, that April, having put the ball into the net in England colours against Turkey, he was denied what would have been his only international goal because Lineker of all people had strayed offside. Allen had been given his chance because of injury to Beardsley, but the record books showed that the game finished goalless. As Allen jested, in *Match of my Life*, 'I scored in that game but the goal was ruled out because Gary was in an offside position. I'll always hold that against him! Ha, ha!'

He gained international caps and Player of the Year awards, but for all his personal accolades and feats, winners' medals and team awards were to prove heart-breakingly elusive. Spurs faced Arsenal in the League Cup semi-final, and with that metronomic reliability Allen scored in both Legs, before the tie, level on aggregate at 2-2, went to a replay at White Hart Lane. Allen scored yet again, and in doing so became the leading goalscorer in the competition in a single campaign, with 12. Agonisingly, however, Arsenal came from behind to win in the dying seconds. Over the three games of football they had led for only one minute, but it proved sufficient to progress to the final and deny Spurs.

Having been very much part of a three-horse race for the title, Spurs' League campaign was also to falter. If anything the club was a victim of its own success, for as

Pleat noted prior to the FA Cup semi-final in mid-March, the club was about to play its 14th Cup match of the season – exactly half the number of League games they had played at that point. Ultimately, League form tailed away, a record of just 5 wins from the last 14 games of the season leaving them in third place come the final standings. It was a creditable effort, and one with which the club would be mightily pleased in the Champions League era, but with English clubs still banned from European competition it left just one chance of glory for the team, and one last chance of a winner's medal for Allen – the FA Cup final.

Allen's exploits had by this time attracted continental attention, with Real Madrid and Roma amongst the rumoured suitors. Despite the astonishing season he had enjoyed, Allen was under some pressure to perform in the showpiece final, with journalist Mihir Bose noting in *The Times* on the day of the game: 'Allen needs to prove to a world-wide audience that he can play football as well as score goals, for the two qualities are not indivisibly the same'.

Initially, it seemed as if the script had been written perfectly for Allen, as after just two minutes Chris Waddle danced down the right and delivered a cross for the striker to nod home at the near post. Number 49 of the campaign, and Spurs were well set to end the season on a high.

Fans will hardly need reminding of what followed, as the team were sunk by a Gary Mabbutt own goal in extra-time. It was the second time Allen had experienced Cup final heartbreak. While at QPR in his first spell, he had featured in the 1982 FA Cup final – ironically against Spurs. Although that game itself went to a replay, Allen's match fell apart after just two minutes when he received a hefty blow to the ankle, and after limping on was substituted shortly after half-time. Allen's disappointment was heightened when the injury forced him out of the replay, which QPR then lost. As he recalled in a *Daily Mail* interview:

'You don't get too many cracks at the FA Cup. If you are lucky you may get ten in your career and obviously once you are beaten, you are out and then you have to wait another year for another chance. I obviously played for QPR and had great disappointment in getting injured and losing to Spurs in 1982, while in 1987, when I was then playing for Spurs, we went into the game against Coventry as favourites and were expected to win. It was a boyhood dream to score in an FA Cup final, which I did to put us in front after two minutes, but we were ultimately on the losing team.'

Allen's achievements in 1986/87 proved to be something of a statistical anomaly. In terms of crude numbers, the magnificent 49-goal campaign was sandwiched in between several vastly less spectacular seasons. In his first term at the Lane, 1984/85, injuries limited him to 15 appearances, in which he scored a creditable 9 goals. The following campaign Allen did not appear until November, due to another string of injuries. It was a frustratingly underwhelming season for all concerned, Spurs underperforming and the fans' frustrations reflected by the fact that the 2-0 win against Birmingham, in April 1986, was watched by just 9,359 spectators, the club's lowest post-war attendance. Allen found himself in and out of the team and finished with 12 goals, including those 5 in the final 3 games of the season.

The period following 1986/87 proved similarly frustrating, and, in light of what had preceded it, vaguely perplexing, as Allen notched up 13 goals, before moving to Bordeaux at the end of the season. With Glenn Hoddle having departed after the 1987 Cup final, the team was immediately shorn of one of its primary creative outlets, while a homesick Richard Gough then returned to Scotland, before David Pleat's sudden departure, following allegations about his private life, in October 1987. The combination of off-field upheaval at the club, and fresh injuries with which he had to contend personally, meant that Allen was unable to replicate his feats of the previous season, while new manager Terry Venables brought in Paul Walsh and examined other striking options. There remained glimpses of his previous form, for to Clive Allen the skill of goalscoring was an innate ability. A magnificent chip against Oldham in the FA Cup, and a crisp drive in a League defeat against Arsenal were but two reminders of just how potent Allen could be in front of goal, but with his contract due to expire at the end of the season, in March 1988 he agreed on a £1 million move to France, to take place that summer.

Bordeaux was followed by Manchester City, Chelsea, West Ham, Millwall and Carlisle as Allen wound down his career, before returning to White Hart Lane in a coaching capacity. Despite – or perhaps because of – the accolades and achievements of the halcyon 1986/87 season, the nagging sense remains to this day that he never fulfilled his startling potential as a player, at either club or international level. Nevertheless, the extraordinary achievements of that campaign surpass those of any other player in the club's history.

CHRIS WADDLE

1985-1989

SPURS CAREER

Games	173
Goals	42
Caps	62

MAGIC MOMENT

Audacious first-time 35-yard chipped goal in the mud at Southampton, when in his prime, in the 1988/89 season

'THE WADDLER'

IN the spring of 1989 Chris Waddle was at the peak of his powers. With each passing week he seemed to surpass himself, reaching new heights of footballing genius and leaving spellbound fans talking of no-one else. He was to finish the campaign as Spurs' top scorer, attracting continental interest in the process, but rarely were his glittering array of talents better showcased than in a virtuoso performance at home to Aston Villa in early March. To report that he netted both goals that day, in a 2-0 victory, barely does him justice, for each goal was of a quality to be spoken of in awestruck tones for years – two in one game seeming almost to spoil the supporters. His first saw him embark on a trademark mazy dribble, from centre circle to penalty area, feinting extravagantly left and right, and adding the massed ranks of the Villa defence to the growing collection of dizzied challengers he had bested over the years. With the defenders sliding and stumbling around him, Waddle finished his one-man show emphatically, with a thumping shot into the top corner. In the second half, when presented with a bobbling ball at the corner of the penalty area he dispensed with all subtle trickery, instead unleashing a thunderous left-footed volley that rocketed in off the underside of the crossbar, a goal scored when few others would even have contemplated shooting. Recalls fan Alan Fisher of Waddle's performance that day: "In that home victory against Villa he was scintillating, they could not get near him and everything he tried came off. I recall that the crowd figure was low; the stay-aways missed a treat."

With his seemingly languid style, outrageous skill and, of course, that quite sensational mullet, Chris Waddle ticked virtually all the boxes of a classic cult hero. His trademark dip of the shoulder, and ability to beat players through extravagant body-swerves – often without even touching the ball – was married to an injection of pace from a standing-start, that made him a player the fans loved to see in action. He was the archetypal crowd-pleasing entertainer, possessing all those talents that spectators love most – mazy dribbling skills, pin-point crossing ability and an eye for goal. Augmenting these he had an irrepressible sense of mischief, seeming to delight as much as the crowd in the tormenting of opposing defenders simply as a cruel sport in its own right.

Adulation was duly heaped upon him from the White Hart Lane stands. Managers, however, did not necessarily view him in the same light, particularly at international level, where less frequent games meant he was afforded less room for error. Although he nailed down a regular spot in the England team that was to become so successful under Bobby Robson, he was, incredibly, jettisoned by Graham Taylor from a national team that, with the best will in the world, could hardly by deemed to be over-flowing with play-makers. It seems to have been a quirk of the English mentality from the 1970s onwards to have favoured those of a workmanlike breed over more naturally gifted flair players. Those who compensated for lack of natural ability with that most English of attributes – 'a good engine' – typically found their route to the national team more straightforward. Thus, Waddle was frequently overlooked for England duty, as a liability. As he himself has pointed out, in an interview with the *Daily Telegraph*, 'I was considered a luxury player until I went to France. I was never expected to defend at Marseilles.'

England fans as well as managers were inclined to criticise Waddle if he were deemed to be failing to deliver effective performances. At Spurs, however, he found a slightly more welcoming environment than at national level. While Tottenham fans can be notoriously fickle, and it is worth noting that they did indeed deal Waddle some criticism in his early days, despite a two-goal debut, generally the ethos of the club was – and is – vastly more conducive to players of the entertaining ilk of Christopher Roland Waddle. The famous Danny Blanchflower quote, that the game is about winning in style, rather than waiting for the opposition to die of boredom, created the perfect platform for Waddle, for he liked nothing more than to entertain on the football pitch. Waddle's thoughts on the matter, as given in an interview with the *Daily Telegraph* in 2001, could be considered a modern-day player's translation of the Blanchflower quote:

'I love entertaining people, being a showman. I loved the atmosphere on the terraces when I set off on a dribble. All fans want to see their teams win, but they love it even more when they're entertained as well. I like the thought of someone leaving the ground and going into work or the schoolyard on Monday morning and saying "Hey, you should have seen what Waddle did to this full back". People always remember Johan Cruyff's back-heel flick far more than any goal he ever scored. That's what football's about. Giving people something to smile about.'

As is the case with so many of Tottenham's favourite sons, his path to the top had been of the sort too fantastic to script. At the age of 19 he was still plying his trade in non-league football, with Tow Law Town. At the time he supplemented his wage with a job in a sausage factory – a job for which he had famously interviewed while wearing a cycle helmet, having been unable to remove the contraption on entering his future boss's office. In the summer of 1980 he moved to Newcastle in his native north-east, where team-mates were to include Kevin Keegan and Peter Beardsley, and he was to force his way into the England team. His time at Newcastle included a 3-1 defeat at White Hart Lane in December 1984. On that occasion Waddle turned in a performance that had Tottenham manager Peter Shreeve gushing, as reported in Mel Stein's *Chris Waddle The Authorised Biography*: 'Some of the things he did that day were world class. He always frightened me when he had the ball.'

He scored that day, wrong-footing Paul Miller with a body-feint and slamming the ball home, and his display was a significant contributory factor in the minds of the Tottenham top-brass to bring him to White Hart Lane. The wheels were set in motion in 1985, and with England team-mate Glenn Hoddle having used his powers of persuasion during international get-togethers, Waddle committed himself to North London, eventually moving that summer, for £590,000.

The Spurs side Waddle had joined were in fine fettle. Following the halcyon years of Keith Burkinshaw, Peter Shreeve had guided the club to a third-placed League finish in his first season in charge, although the ban on English teams following the Heysel disaster meant that there would be no UEFA Cup campaign to follow. Beginning his Tottenham career in attack rather than midfield, Waddle scored twice, both with his head, in an opening-day 4-0 thrashing of Watford, which was well-received by the White Hart Lane faithful, as reported by Malcolm Winton in *The Sunday Times*: '[The Watford defence] presented a couple of headed goals to a player, Chris Waddle, with the reputation of using his head for nothing more serious than thinking. Waddle, £600,000 from Newcastle, played well enough to generate chants of "Waddle we love you" from the East Stand.'

It could barely have been a better start, but frustration was to follow for Spurs and Waddle, with the sort of inconsistency that, in a microcosm, was to sum up the fortunes of both in the following months. Spurs' next four games brought just one point; the four games thereafter were all victories. Such patchy form continued throughout the season, as Spurs finished the season in tenth place, a showing that cost Shreeve his job, with Waddle alternating between roles on the left and in the centre.

There could be little doubt as to the man's talent, for he frequently embarked on mazy dribbles and delivered unerringly accurate passes; but just as often, it seemed, came a tendency to go gambolling off into cul-de-sacs. While fans would delight at the fact that White Hart Lane had another player of obvious unbounded natural ability, they were frequently left exasperated by those moments when he seemed to confuse even himself. Rather harshly, much of the criticism he had to bear derived simply from the fact that he perpetually bore the outward appearance of a man about to collapse from sheer exhaustion. The drooping shoulders gave him a languid look, as much in the first minute as the last, and even when running at full speed, leaving defenders trailing in his wake, he appeared strangely laboured. This ostensible appearance hardly endeared him to those who, as was fashionable in 1980s England, considered boundless energy and an indefatigable work-rate more than adequate substitutes for natural skill.

Peter Shreeve was replaced as Spurs boss by David Pleat in the summer of 1986, a significant change, as Pleat was to make a crucial tactical adjustment, switching Waddle to the right flank. Although naturally left-footed, Waddle quickly realised that he would need to expand his game beyond his favoured trick of cutting inside onto his left foot. The solution? Up to 20 minutes of work on his right foot every day in the gym after training. He notes, in *FourFourTwo.com*: '20 minutes a day for a couple of months is all it takes for a professional to improve his weaker foot. It makes me laugh that England are crying out for a left-footed player and the guys trying to get that role can't just practise for 20 minutes a day on their left.'

With two-footedness in his armoury Waddle was soon running riot, within a five-man midfield deployed by Pleat and comprising kindred spirits from the school of outrageous flair, including Messrs Hoddle and Ardiles. Such a formation would not have brought success without the appropriate personnel, but Waddle was a perfect component within it. A five-man midfield is often deployed with the aim of nullifying threats and grinding down opponents through sheer weight of numbers; but Tottenham's was a vehicle for creativity and expression, the extra number simply allowing for one further creative genius. Hoddle spraying the ball around; Ardiles intelligently keeping things ticking over; Waddle delving into his repertoire of tricks to dribble past opponents – the group overflowed with attacking talent. It met the exciting, pleasing-on-the eye tradition of the club and, with an in-form striker ahead of it, proved highly effective.

If Waddle's positional change was one contributory factor towards his improved consistency, another was the form and fitness of Clive Allen in attack. The previous season had been a fitful one for Allen, but in 1986/87 he barely missed a game, and deployed as the lone striker he thrived – as did Waddle, noting in *Chris Waddle The Authorised Biography*, 'If I was dribbling and running at pace I had to whip the ball into the centre because there was no time to control and place it. Clive would invariably gamble and get ahead of his man. It was a rare talent, and only Gary Lineker of the men I've played alongside could match Clive at it.'

After several near-misses at Newcastle Waddle had feared that the opportunity to compete for major honours would continue to pass him by, and indeed it was one of the main reasons for his move to Spurs. That 1986/87 season, however, his fears appeared certain to be allayed. After making the semi-final of the League Cup, Tottenham went one better by reaching the final of the FA Cup. Waddle had been in tears at the final whistle of the victorious semi-final against Watford, and come 16 May 1987 was to stamp his mark on the Cup final within seconds.

The game was only a minute old when he received the ball on the right in the Wembley sunshine. He duly dipped into his box of tricks, and with a typically extravagant body swerve feinted infield and then beat defender Greg Downs on the outside. To this day Downs is probably still spinning around wondering where the ball had gone; meanwhile Waddle whipped the cross – inevitably – to the near post, and there – inevitably – was the head of Clive Allen.

Delivered in the blink of an eye, it had been a classic Waddle moment. Seemingly so laboured and even lazy in his appearance, he had teased his opponent, offering him a good long sighting of the ball, suggesting that he would head sluggishly in one direction – and then with one perfectly executed dip of the shoulder, which even had the spectators in the crowd moving in the wrong direction, he had made room, before delivering a fiendish cross of pinpoint accuracy. One–nil Spurs, and glory beckoned.

It was not to be, however, as Waddle's cruelly unfortunate record in major competitions began to establish itself. A loser, famously, at the semi-final stage of a World Cup; on penalties again in the final of the European Cup a year later; followed by two domestic Cup final defeats in 1993 – the horrendous trend was to begin in 1987 as Spurs lost the FA Cup final to an extra-time own goal.

It was heartbreak for Waddle, and a first FA Cup final defeat for Spurs, but by now the winger had become a firm fans' favourite. It was not just the excitement he generated on his mazy dribbles, and the fact that, particularly with Allen in attack, there was typically a finishing-touch to the eye-catching build-up he contributed; it was the whole maverick style of the team, which Waddle exemplified. Waddle was not one to stick rigidly to formations. He was more of a free spirit, willing to break the mould and try the unexpected. His jinking runs would drag players out of position, and he had the capacity to disrupt game-plans. When Waddle received possession, an opposing full back in front of him, Spurs fans could expect the unexpected, and the full back in question a torrid time.

As well as this capacity to produce tricks from nowhere, Waddle's cult hero status was further cemented by his appearance, and the most famous mullet in English football. So short on top and at the sides that it resembled a crew-cut, at the back he cultivated a wavy mane that reached down to his shoulders. Truly a thing of awesome wonder, Waddle's mullet can trace its origins back to his Newcastle days, where it was born of superstition. Having had long hair and picked up an injury, Waddle tried a short style only to sustain another injury. He therefore opted for the short-on-top-long-at-the-back combination, went injury-free and the decision was made. Frequently, if most euphemistically, cited as the most 'memorable' haircut in English football, Waddle's mullet was so readily identifiable that it has become as memorable a feature of his playing career as his penalty miss in the World Cup semi-final. It is a matter of particular pride to Waddle that he once combined these elements to win a penalty shoot-out against former Marseille team-mate Rudi Völler, to claim the title of Mullet of the Year.

The extravagant, conspicuous hairstyle complemented his playing style. A decade later another showman was to delight Spurs fans with extravagant skills matched by long hair, but before David Ginola there was Chris Waddle. The look would have been quite a curiosity on a solid perfunctory full back, but it was perfectly suited to a dashing winger with the rare ability to bring the crowd to their feet, make them hold their breath in anticipation and then leave them cheering for more.

With his mullet and penchant for showmanship, Waddle was particularly popular with younger fans, who perhaps saw something of the rock star in him. Always ready to break from the norms of the coaching manual when he played, the haircut that had parents across North London tutting in disapproval simply endeared him to a whole generation of children, whose early memories of Spurs are of this rebellious-looking player mazily dribbling past one bewildered opponent after another.

Nor did the man's off-pitch infamies end at his fashion sense. In 1987 an unsuspecting music world had unleashed upon them a brand new pop combo, as Waddle and Hoddle were transformed into 'Glenn and Chris', and soft-rock classic, 'Diamond Lights', hit the shops. While a nation now cringes at the memory of Hoddle – sorry, *Glenn* – taking the falsetto notes, while Chris mumbled his way through the chorus, the song actually reached a creditable number 12 in the UK charts. Particularly memorable was a live – albeit lip-synched – appearance on BBC music show *Top of the Pops*, in which the pair donned what was at the time achingly cool '80s apparel (jackets with rolled up sleeves), with Hoddle giving it his all while Waddle (*sans* mullet) looked every inch the startled rabbit caught in headlights, swaying awkwardly to the music. Recalls Waddle, in *The Guardian*: 'I'm not joking when I say that standing on that stage was more nerve-wracking than taking that penalty in Turin. To actually stand in front of millions of people on TV, well it was absolutely petrifying.'

Waddle reminisces about the song in self-deprecatory style, and naturally he and Hoddle received incessant abuse from opposing fans thereafter, as chants of "Stick to making records" rung in their ears. Seemingly undeterred, however, Waddle unashamedly went on to make another song with a team-mate, recording 'We've Got A Feeling', complete with a quite baffling video, with Marseille colleague Basile Boli, during his time in France.

Such curiosities make for an intriguing character. Waddle actually rather eschewed the limelight, proving painfully shy when he arrived at the club, to the extent that he suffered early crises of confidence on the pitch, rarely feeling sufficiently comfortable to express himself. He far preferred family life in his quiet Hertfordshire home to the glamorous trappings of London. On the pitch, however, he was an entertainer, and as his confidence grew the performances improved. For Waddle simply giving the fans something about which to talk, and indeed to crow, was a reward in itself. While working to create and score goals, he derived ill-concealed glea from bamboozling opponents, noting in an interview with *The Telegraph*, 'I could never help but laugh when I nutmegged someone'. Indeed, his sense of mischief again comes to the fore when he relates that he often quipped to a beaten defender, "Don't worry about it mate, Maldini fell for it too."

Waddle, it seemed, did not just beat opponents; he positively enjoyed humiliating them. One sensed that having tormented an opponent to such an extent the poor blighter would not know which direction he was supposed to face. Waddle would then turn back and destroy the same defender all over again, just to delight the crowd. He protests, in Mel Stein's *Chris Waddle The Authorised Biography*, that humiliating his opponent was never his aim (although one suspects that a twinkle in his eye might have betrayed a lack of complete sincerity in this claim), but instead pleasing the fans was paramount: 'I never set out to make an opponent look foolish, but I do try to entertain. The crowd love it when you send a player this way and that, with the odd nutmeg thrown in for good measure, and it sticks in their minds.'

Capable of destroying a defender, on one famous occasion he so mercilessly and relentlessly beat an opponent he practically ended his career. The victim was Gus Caesar, at the time a full back with Arsenal of all clubs. As part of a marathon League Cup semi-final tie against their north London rivals, Spurs travelled to Highbury in February 1987 and won 1-0, a game Waddle remembers as one of his most memorable for the club, as he mercilessly tore apart the unfortunate Caesar. Waddle recalls, as quoted in his biography: 'On that day I had a good game and Gus had a bad one … I can't say I felt sorry for Gus at the time. If he'd have marked me out of the game he'd have been doing his job and I was just doing mine.'

Even die-hard Arsenal fan and author Nick Hornby looks back on the incident ruefully, writing in *Fever Pitch* that Caesar was 'painfully, obviously out of his depth' against Waddle that night, before detailing how his career went into freefall thereafter.

The following season was injury-hit for Waddle, and transitional for Spurs. Problems first with his ankle, and later a double hernia, meant he was frequently in and out of the team, notching up just two goals that season, as the club replaced manager David Pleat with Terry Venables, and playing personnel changed accordingly. However, 1988/89 saw Waddle's star shine brightly once again, and fans were treated to the very best of the winger. With Allen again missing much of the season through injury, Waddle often featured in attack and was in prominent goalscoring form, recording the club's first goal of the season away to former club Newcastle, and notching up 14 in total during an ever-present League campaign, to become Spurs' leading scorer.

After a faltering start, which saw the club slump to the bottom of the table before Christmas, Spurs picked up their form in the new year. A run of 9 wins in 13 League games followed in the spring months, with Waddle the driving force behind the run. In particular, three consecutive games beginning in late February – at home to Norwich, away to Southampton and, as detailed above, at home to Aston Villa – encapsulated the mercurial genius at his very best.

Against Norwich a trademark dribble on the right flank culminated in him scoring from an implausibly tight angle, virtually on the goal-line, in a 2-1 win. As reported by Clive White in *The Times*: 'There was no way that a low drive from Waddle in the 65th minute, from the finest of angles, should have beaten Gunn, Norwich's Scottish goalkeeper, at his near post … but it did.'

Four days later there came an extravagant first-time chip from 35 yards against Southampton at the Dell, in a 2-0 win. The sweetness of the strike was all the more impressive for the fact that the game was played on an absolute quagmire of a pitch, blades of grass so few they could be counted upon the thick muddy surface. As noted by Nicholas Harling of *The Times*: 'Waddle, who at the best of times, looks as though he is dragging his feet through treacle, continued to make light of the heavy going,' while fan David Durbridge recalls of the day:

"I was at The Dell for the Southampton game (my first professional League match). Terrible weather, the pitch was a mud bath. The Spurs away support was amazing though – a fantastic atmosphere. Chris was at his peak at the time and the media were all over him. It was a time when it seemed that people were going to watch Chris as much as to see Spurs! His goal was inspired – when it went in the fans all bundled forward (it was all-standing in the away end). Never been so happy and so cold and wet at the same time."

Inspired by Waddle, Spurs hauled themselves up to a respectable sixth-placed finish that season, but such imperious form had attracted the attention of foreign clubs, and when Marseille offered an outrageous sum of money in the summer of 1989, Spurs were obliged to alert the player. After protracted negotiations, Marseille got their man for what was at the time the third-largest sum in world football. One local newspaper in Haringey summed up the sense of incredulity at the mind-boggling sum with the headline: 'What Price? £4.25 Million?' With English clubs still banned from European competition, various top players had moved abroad in the 1980s, and the carrot of a move to France was too good an opportunity for Waddle to refuse.

It was a particularly heavy blow for Spurs fans. Tottenham's late-season form had given plenty of grounds for optimism, with Waddle having been the catalyst. Moreover, only days earlier the club had signed the most gifted English goalscorer of his generation, Gary Lineker. Following the success of Waddle as provider for Clive Allen two years previously, all associated with the club were positively drooling in anticipation at the prospect of Lineker and Waddle combining, particularly with a certain Paul Gascoigne having just enjoyed a successful debut season at the Lane. Lineker himself was spectacularly unimpressed by the sale of the winger, having cited the presence of Waddle in the Tottenham ranks as one of the key factors in his decision to move to Spurs, while a rueful Gary Mabbutt, by that time club captain, recalls, "It was a shame Waddle left when Lineker joined – virtually on the same day." As had happened so often in the history of Tottenham Hotspur, fans were left to wonder, *What if...?* However, despite the circumstances of his departure, Chris Waddle had already done more than enough to establish himself in Tottenham folklore.

PAUL GASCOIGNE

'GAZZA'

1988-1991

SPURS CAREER

Games	112
Goals	33
Caps	57

MAGIC MOMENT

Scoring the free kick against Arsenal at Wembley that set Spurs on the way to FA Cup semi-final victory

14 April 1991. Paul John Gascoigne places a football on the luxurious, hallowed Wembley turf, charges in off a short run-up and strikes it with power, dip and curl, over a ruck of players, past a flying goalkeeper and into the top corner of the net. It was the definitive goal of his Tottenham career, scored on football's grandest stage, in its most famous club competition, and against his club's biggest rivals. It is the goal that springs to mind first and lingers in the memory longest whenever his name is mentioned to any Tottenham fan. Gazza's free kick against Arsenal was a sensational moment, setting up the team for a famous victory, firmly imprinting the man's name in legend and ultimately proving the zenith of his Tottenham career.

Spurs' love affair with the FA Cup is long, and many of the club's greatest sons have inscribed their name in folklore through their contributions in the competition. In 1991 Tottenham Hotspur's was the name engraved on the Cup, but Gazza's was the name on everyone's lips on the road to Wembley, and it is by no means to the denigration of his team-mates that so many fans talk of him taking the club to Wembley that year 'single-handedly'. That sentiment was encapsulated in his goal against Arsenal – all his own work. Whereas later in the same game Gary Lineker's two goals owed much to the contribution of his team-mates – a cross of vicious curl from Paul Allen, an energetic decoy run from Vinny Samways – Gascoigne's was a moment entirely of individual genius, facilitated by his outrageous impudence in even attempting such a feat. In a single kick it summed up so much of his entire Tottenham career.

Gazza had joined Spurs three years earlier, in the summer of 1988. The move almost never was, and one wonders how different his career might have been under the watchful eye of one Alex Ferguson, had a mooted transfer to Manchester United instead transpired. Many an observer of English football has sagely pondered whether Ferguson – a man who has proved himself to have some competence when it comes to handling young talent – might have somehow cultivated Gascoigne's talent while minimising his penchant for self-destruction, a trait that was to feature so prominently at the end of his Tottenham career, and so desperately in the years since. Gazza had actually verbally agreed a move to Old Trafford, before Ferguson went on a summer holiday, and was also being courted by champions Liverpool, but then-Tottenham chairman Irving Scholar was not to be denied. He and manager Terry Venables had witnessed first hand the talents of the young midfielder when Spurs had travelled to Newcastle in January 1988 and been beaten 2-0, Gascoigne scoring both Newcastle goals.

Chris Waddle, a former team-mate of Gazza at Newcastle, and by that time plying his trade at Spurs, would later prove a key figure in selling the club to Gascoigne. Waddle's reward for his endeavours was to be paired with Gazza as room-mate, quite an honour given his new team-mate's insistence upon sleeping with lights and television switched on.

The pair had known each other at Newcastle, where a 16-year-old Gazza was made to clean Waddle's boots. On one occasion Gazza's attempts did not meet the required standard, but on being handed the boots back to clean again he advised Waddle to "F**k off and clean them yourself". Waddle responded by promptly bestowing upon him the gift of a dead leg, leaving Gazza not for the first or last time choking back the tears. Thus began a long-standing and close friendship.

Any worries Scholar and Venables may have harboured about their new protégé settling in to life in the capital were quickly addressed, as Gazza brought seemingly half the north-east down to London with him. Until he found his own home he was put up in the luxurious West Lodge Park Hotel. The club allowed him to have friends and family stay with him, to prevent any homesickness, and with guests in tow including the infamous Jimmy 'Five-Bellies' Gardner, the troupe drank their way through 38 bottles of *Dom Perignon* champagne in 3 days, before being kicked out of the hotel. A similar fate befell Gazza and his entourage at their next temporary home, the Hendon Hall Hotel, before he finally curbed his enthusiasm at the Swallow Hotel, and the club's top brass could breathe more easily.

The newly crowned Young Footballer of the Year made his Tottenham debut, almost inevitably, away to Newcastle, where the fans pelted him with Mars bars. It was a pointed reminder of his battles with his weight, which had been well-documented even during his time as a young player in the north-east, and would continue to follow him throughout his career. Naturally enough for one with his sweet tooth and sense of mischief, Gazza responded by picking up one of the chocolates and having a bite.

That game ended in a 2-2 draw, but if Newcastle fans were frustrated to see their hero departed, Spurs fans were given the perfect opportunity to welcome him, when he made his home debut against Arsenal on 10 September 1988. Receiving a pass from Waddle on the run into the penalty area, he actually lost his right boot in a collision with Paul Davis, en route to goal.

Gazza, one suspects, would happily have played a full game with just one boot if given the chance, and in this instance simply ploughed on undeterred. He had a shot from his stockinged foot shot saved by goalkeeper John Lukic before taking a second shot, again with his stockinged foot, and from a far tighter angle, this time finding the net. A typically low-key announcement of his arrival in lilywhite, it was the first of 6 goals he scored in 32 League games for Spurs that season, as the club recovered from a poor start to finish sixth.

Gazza simply did not seem able to abide the mundane and humdrum. Time and again he would bring the crowd to its feet with his ability to beat a line of players in almost cartoon fashion, through his combination of upper-body strength, balance, searing bursts of pace and control so exquisite the ball truly seemed tied to his feet. Within weeks of his Spurs debut he was in the England squad, making his bow as a late substitute against Denmark at Wembley on 14 September, in a 1-0 win. A maiden international goal came the following April in his third match, against Albania, when he dribbled at pace through a gaggle of defenders before slotting home, in a 5-0 win.

Such mesmeric, weaving runs, punctuated with outrageous dribbling skills, were his trademark, perhaps more than any other attribute marking him out as the outstanding player of his generation. It was a rare art-form, particularly in England in the 1980s, when Tottenham's style, with its emphasis on flowing, short-passing, was fairly unique in a League in which long-balls and hard workers were the rage. Spurs had lost one cult hero in 1987, with the departure of Glenn Hoddle, but the exciting young Geordie promised something just as wondrous, if different in style. While Hoddle's game had centred on his vision, passing range and spectacular long-range goals, Gazza was more the sort to run at opponents. He may have carried his fair share of puppy-fat, but hard hours in the gym turned it into a barrel chest rather than extra folds on his stomach, and with his immense upper-body strength he was even vaguely reminiscent of Diego Maradona on the run.

Gazza's antics were the stuff of legend during his time at Spurs. While fans were enthralled by his on-pitch performances, here was a player in whom genius and madness were inextricably linked, walking hand in hand before and after as well as during his time at Tottenham. He found willing allies at the Lane, notably in the mischievous, if typically more subtle Geordie soul-mate Chris Waddle, while Steve Sedgely was another partner-in-crime. When Gary Mabbutt, Gazza's captain during his Spurs career, is asked about the man's off-the-pitch antics, a weary, rueful smile speaks volumes, before he diplomatically states: "I don't think many of them would be suitable to tell. He certainly kept me on my toes as captain."

Some tales do emerge, however, like Gazza teaching English to new Moroccan team-mate Nayim, who dutifully reeled of the days of the week, "Monday, Tuesday, W*nkday ..." Poor Nayim was also on the receiving end when Gazza plied him with unrequested drinks at his welcome party, insisting that Long-Island Iced Teas were as non-alcoholic as their name suggested. Then there was the time he drove down from his Hertford home to the Lineker residence in London, parked his car in the Lineker driveway and went off into town, leaving his club-mate boxed in for the day; or the occasion he indulged in his love of air-guns by shooting out the rear windscreen of the new car bought by Steve Sedgely (he later paid for the damage). Mabbutt recalls one occasion in training when, having received some stick from his team-mates for his numerous, lucrative endorsement deals, Gazza emerged for training having stuck £50 notes all over himself, and proceeded to train in such attire – before dishing out the money to the club's youth players and apprentices.

Nor were his team-mates the only victims. Ball-boys were put in headlocks and swung over his shoulders; young mascots swept off their feet and carried onto the field; cameramen had their equipment doused in whatever liquid was at hand; while Gary Lineker's wife was once hauled overboard and into the water from a yacht in Italy. "He's loveable, even when he does something diabolical," Lineker is once reputed to have said of Gazza; whether the sentiment was the first to spring to mind on this occasion is debatable.

Supporters too were treated to the inimitable Gascoigne sense of humour, one fan, Darren Southcott, recalling, "My sister used to work in a hotel which Gazza stayed in over a few months in London. On a couple of occasions she drank with him at the bar and once she was telling him how her brother loved him more than any other player, but wishes he hadn't thrown his career away. It was my birthday and she passed him a card and asked him to sign it ... it says 'F*ck Off Darren Love Gazza' and it's my most treasured birthday card."

Team-mates, team-mates' wives, fans, ball-boys and countless hoteliers, camera-men and unfortunate law-abiding citizens in his vicinity at an inopportune moment may all have reason to disagree, but Gazza's madness was part of his charm, and one certainly suspects that on the football pitch he would have been nowhere near the player he was without his eccentricities.

While still the young starlet at Spurs he had the world at his feet, and duly conquered it with a stream of mazy dribbles and a burp at the nearest camera. A second successful season at White Hart Lane saw the club finish third in the League, even without the departed Waddle, and Gascoigne cemented his place in the England squad for the 1990 World Cup in Italy. Famously, he went to that tournament a Spurs player and came back a national icon. Impudence, outrageous ability and, of course, tears, were all exhibited on a global stage. The relentless barrage of practical jokes continued as well, inevitably, with Waddle finally gaining a measure of revenge for countless sleepless nights by slamming a chocolate birthday cake into Gazza's face.

Unprecedented media interest followed on his return to England. A slew of endorsements followed, naturally enough, and Gazza joined the list of White Hart Lane luminaries to enter the pop charts with a suitably dubious rendition of 'Fog on the Tyne', while accolades heaped upon him included BBC Sports Personality of the Year, and, more curiously, Best Dressed Man of the Year. Following Italia '90, the stage was set for Gazza to make a triumphant return to League football at Spurs in season 1990/91, and he, along with fellow Spurs and England hero Gary Lineker, duly obliged. Gazza scored one and Lineker two in Spurs' 3-1 win at home to Manchester City on the opening day of the season, a game played out to a television audience in over 60 countries. The following month this effort was surpassed with a sublime hat-trick at home to Derby County, including two long-range free kicks slammed past England's most capped player, goalkeeper Peter Shilton. It was the latest in a number of unfortunate contributions made to Tottenham folklore by Shilton, having previously been on the receiving end of a Jimmy Greaves wonder-goal in the '60s, and a first Spurs goal for Glenn Hoddle in the '70s.

After a roaring start to the campaign Spurs were in third place in Division One by autumn, but over 24 League games in 6 months from December onwards, they won just 3, sliding down to mid-table mediocrity, with a televised New Year's Day clash against Manchester United bringing Gascoigne a red card for dissent. Unfortunately, by this time, the consensus within the corridors of power at White Hart Lane was that Gazza's career would continue elsewhere. Venables had stated that while his phone had not stopped ringing after the World Cup his prized asset was not going anywhere, but by the turn of the year, momentum was building to reverse this stance. Gazza's heroics at Italia '90 had attracted the attention of the biggest and richest clubs in the world, and an £8 million transfer to Lazio was eventually pencilled in for the end of the season. Meanwhile there was further bad news at White Hart Lane, with rumblings emerging that Spurs were in dire financial straits, their debts so severe that the club's very existence was rumoured to be under threat. The club needed salvation off the pitch, and the fans needed silverware on it – the FA Cup was to prove the panacea.

After wining their first game in the competition that season, a Third Round tie against Blackpool, with a goal from Paul Stewart, Gazza grabbed the headlines in Spurs' Cup run, and would not relinquish his grip. Says Mabbutt looking back: "I'm not sure if it's possible for one player to single-handedly get you to a Cup final, but Paul seemed to do it. He played the best football of his career that season. He was a pleasure to play with. He could take a game by the scruff of its neck and turn it your way."

The Fourth Round saw lower-division Oxford United visit White Hart Lane, but their honest endeavour was no match for the audacity and talent of Gazza at his irresistible best. He was everywhere, demanding the ball all over the pitch, from deep in his own half to inside the opponents' penalty area. Chest puffed out, he dictated play with a confidence bordering on arrogance, picking short passes, pinging long cross-field balls and, most mesmerically, dribbling past what seemed like armies of opposition defenders – two, three, four at a time. Early in the first half he collected a short corner, and with a dip of his shoulder and burst of pace was bearing down on the Oxford goal. He played a slick one-two with Lineker, Oxford could not clear the danger, and Mabbutt scored for Spurs. Minutes later his header had set up Lineker for Spurs' second. Oxford rallied, but in the second half White Hart Lane was treated to vintage Gazza. Virtually shoving aside team-mate Terry Fenwick and taking the ball from his feet ("The crowd are pleased about that," noted BBC commentator John Motson at the time. "It was going nowhere that attack, it is now"), with a bustling dribble he jinked his way through half the Oxford team and homed directly in on goal, his electric burst of pace and upper body strength allowing him to decimate the opposition defence. "It really is going somewhere now," yelped Motson, beside himself with glee, as once inside the area Gascoigne played a one-two with Paul Walsh, and despite seemingly creating an impossibly acute angle, squeezed the ball into the net, with defenders lying strewn in his wake. Another Gascoigne goal was to follow, again evading the despairing, diving challenges of Oxford defenders, and Spurs triumphed 4-2.

Two further Gascoigne goals followed in the Fifth Round at Portsmouth, as Spurs came from behind. The first was something of a collector's item, a bullet header, after he had forced his way through a crowd of defenders. Later there was a more typical goal, collecting the ball on *terra firma*, dribbling into the area and finishing decisively. And so to the quarter-final against Notts County, and yet another virtuoso performance. Again, Spurs had to come from behind, but again Gazza grabbed the headlines, crowning another imperious midfield display with the winning goal, a gorgeous curling effort into the top corner.

By this time, however, Tottenham's off-the-pitch ills were mounting. Although few fans were aware of it at the time, the future of the club remained parlous, behind-the-scenes problems reaching critical levels. Gazza, already seemingly destined to depart, underwent a double hernia operation, and faced a race to be fit for the semi-final, while in his absence Spurs won only once. Just 4 days before the semi-final Gascoigne made his comeback, playing 60 minutes in a defeat to Norwich. It was all the match practice he would receive for the make-or-break semi-final, but one suspects that such was his talismanic presence he would have been thrust into the fray straight from the White Hart Lane treatment table if necessary. Inspirational throughout the Cup run, Spurs needed him more than ever as they prepared for their toughest challenge of the season. Against the backdrop of financial ruin, and a run of one win in six games since the quarter-final, Spurs were up against their bitterest rivals in the semi, an Arsenal side that had lost only once all season, and were marching towards the title and a possible Double. The venue, as for so many of Tottenham's finest moments and greatest heroes, was the old Wembley stadium, the FA Cup semi-final being played there for the first time in the history of the competition.

Hyperactive ordinarily, Gazza could barely be restrained before the game, having required sleeping pills the night before, and displaying his usual array of tics and twitches as the teams took to the Wembley turf. One month later, this barely containable energy would be unleashed in kamikaze fashion; but on this occasion he pitched it perfectly. After 5 minutes, a free kick was awarded to Spurs, in a central position a good 30 yards from goal. Cometh the hour, cometh the man.

"Is Gascoigne going to have a crack?" mused BBC commentator Barry Davies, more in curiosity than expectation, for it seemed unlikely to him, and to various others of the 78,000 at Wembley that day. Arsenal's goalkeeper, David Seaman, was similarly unconvinced that anything quite so audacious would be attempted, making only a perfunctory attempt to build a defensive wall. Who knew what was coming next? Perhaps manager Terry Venables suspected it, for the man who brought Gazza to White Hart Lane had unwavering faith in his ability. Team-mates such as Gary Lineker, Paul Stewart, David Howells and Gary Mabbutt jostled for position in the penalty area, in anticipation of a cross. The adoring Spurs fans were willing their hero to conjure up fresh magic, but again, they could hardly have expected quite what an explosive moment he was about to unleash.

If few knew what was coming next, nobody who witnessed it can possibly forget it, as Gascoigne produced one of the greatest moments in the history of the FA Cup, of Wembley stadium, of Tottenham Hotspur FC. In terms of its execution, context and author, for many Spurs fans Gazza's free kick flying into the top corner ranks amongst the greatest moments they can remember in their time supporting the club. It is right up there alongside Ricky Villa's goal ten years earlier, in terms of the club's greatest ever moments. Many consider the occasion of that semi-final versus Arsenal to have been greater even than the final itself, its date of 14 April 1991 having been christened in numerous Spurs-supporting quarters as 'St Hotspur's Day' in recognition of Gazza's wonderful feat.

Buoyed by the early goal, and inspired by a Gascoigne at his brazen, dominating best, Spurs took the game to their shell-shocked neighbours, and, with their talisman at their hub, they doubled their lead just five minutes later. Receiving the ball on the right of midfield Gazza orchestrated a slick one-touch move, receiving possession and exchanging short, flicked first-time passes with team-mates using the outside of his right foot. The passage of play was poetry in motion, the aesthetically pleasing football definitive of the club's philosophy. More pertinently, it cut to ribbons an Arsenal defence fabled for its miserly nature. From Gazza's flick Paul Allen whipped in a cross, Arsenal failed to clear and Lineker stabbed home. It was all too much for the dour Arsenal team, and they were unable to recover. Gazza exited to a rapturous ovation in the second half, Lineker scored again, and Spurs were on their way to Wembley. This time, the Chas'n'Dave anthem highlighted an astonishing quirk of Tottenham's history – 'It's Lucky for Spurs When The Year Ends in One'. Following FA Cup victories in 1901, 1921, 1961 and 1981 – not to mention the League title in 1951 and 1961, and a League Cup victory in 1971 – the irresistible manner of their semi-final victory strengthened the conviction of everyone associated with the club that further glory awaited in 1991.

At the final whistle an ecstatic Gazza led an impromptu half-lap of honour in front of the ecstatic Spurs fans, signalling to them that a celebratory beverage was in order. His brief but manic post-match interview broadcast live on the BBC immediately afterwards, in the Wembley tunnel, was almost as bewildering an assault upon the senses as his free kick had been 90 minutes earlier. Quite evidently still bristling with energy and euphoria, his words were punctuated with whoops and contorted grins, and delivered with all the excess energy of a hyperactive schoolchild. Little wonder that Arsenal had been unable to contain him on the pitch.

So, a month later Spurs were back at Wembley, for Gazza's final game in lilywhite, in the FA Cup final against Nottingham Forest. Once again Gazza was like a coiled spring before the match, although there were perhaps indicators that this time something was amiss. For a start, he took to the pitch for the pre-match inspection of the ground wearing slippers with his club shellsuit. It was, however, easy enough to dismiss that as a typical moment of impromptu Gazza madness. In the changing room prior to kick-off Gary Mabbutt recalls: "Before the game Paul was very tense, he was really up for it, couldn't wait for the game to start."

However, then-manager Terry Venables has written that all was not well, in *Venables The Autobiography*: 'It looked like his mind was somewhere else. He was not as hyped as normal, and certainly nothing like he had been before the semi-final.'

Ever the showman, Gazza was presented by Mabbutt to the late Lady Diana, Princess of Wales, as the teams lined up before kick-off, and marked the meeting of the two media darlings by kissing her hand. If the tabloid-writers were pleased with that, they were to be gorged just minutes later.

Nobody knew quite what to expect when Gazza took to the pitch and the whistle blew. So often his eccentric nature had manifested itself as genius in Tottenham's Cup run that season, but in the final he descended into madness. After just 90 seconds he executed a challenge on Forest's Garry Parker that had the watching millions rubbing their eyes in disbelief. He actually won the ball, but this is relegated to the status of mere footnote, for on his follow-through he swung his leg so wildly that his studs imprinted themselves upon Parker's upper chest. Football folk are rarely slow to criticise a referee, and to this day one wonders whether Gazza's whole career might have evolved differently, whether he would have become the world's greatest as he so regularly threatened during his time at Spurs, if referee Roger Milford had taken decisive action at that point. Milford however, adopted the alternative approach, and had a quick, smiling word with Gazza – which, history suggests, went in one ear and straight out the other. Mabbutt confesses: "I didn't actually see that Paul's foot had caught Garry Parker round about the neck area. If I'd have seen that I'd have been able to go over to Paul, to talk to him and try and calm him down."

However, a sadly convincing case can be made to suggest that Gazza's madness on Cup final day was no-one's fault but his own. A caution from the referee or a word from Mabbutt might well have proved ineffectual, for the self-destruct button already appeared to have been irreversibly thumped, and having escaped unharmed from that first challenge (as, miraculously, did Parker), he wasted little time in doing the job more effectively at the next opportunity. That opportunity came ten minutes later as Forest full back Gary Charles ran with the ball outside the Spurs penalty area, and Gazza, finding himself the last line of defence, aimed another reckless hack with his right leg. It almost chopped Charles in half, but again the referee took no action beyond the award of a free kick, and again, the Forest player was able to pick himself up, dust himself down and resume. This time, however, Gazza himself was not so lucky. Although he hobbled gingerly to his feet, long enough to see Stuart Pearce belt the resulting free-kick into the net, straight from kick-off he collapsed to the turf, and made his final exit as a Spurs player on a stretcher, in tears.

Gascoigne had begun the semi-final in similarly exuberant spirits, but on that occasion the opportunity to blast a long-range free kick in the opening minutes seemed to provide a positive release. Without such an opportunity in the final he had had another almighty swing of his right foot, on almost the exact same spot of Wembley turf, but into an opponent rather than the ball, shattering his own leg.

Until that point Gazza's fortunes in the Cup that season were inextricably linked to the club's. When he played well, they played well. And when his dream scenario turned into a nightmare, so Spurs' fortunes suffered horrendously. Following Pearce's goal – dubiously allowed, given that his shot had found a gap in the wall created by a rather unsubtle push on Mabbutt by Forest's Lee Glover – the only luck coming Tottenham's way was of the bad variety. Gazza was stretchered off, Lineker had a goal wrongly disallowed for offside, and then saw a penalty saved. Eventually however, the breaks came Spurs' way, Stewart equalising in the second half, before they benefited from an extra-time own-goal, to win 2-1.

Gazza for his part watched the finale from his hospital bed, having inflicted upon himself ligament damage that would keep him out of the game for a year, jeopardise his transfer to Lazio and, in the opinion of many, take away the edge that could have made him the best in the world. His Spurs colleagues were not about to forget his contribution, the first port of call for the victorious team coach on leaving Wembley being the Princess Grace Hospital, where he was given his winners' medal and presented with the trophy by his team-mates.

It was a desperately sad end to his time as a Tottenham player, but it would be wrong if that ill-fated Cup final day were to be the overriding memory of his Spurs career, because for three years he graced White Hart Lane with talent the like of which is unlikely ever to be seen again. Arguably the best years of his entire career were spent at Spurs, and while the demolition of Arsenal and passage to the 1991 FA Cup Final stands as a memorable *piéce de rèsistance*, his status as a Spurs cult hero is secured by a countless stream of magical moments.

JÜRGEN KLINSMANN

1994-95 & 1997-98

SPURS CAREER

Games	68
Goals	38
Caps	108

MAGIC MOMENT

Scoring four goals on penultimate day of 1997/98 season to help Spurs avoid relegation

'JÜRGEN THE GERMAN'

IT was one of the most iconic sights in the English game. Jürgen Klinsmann racing away in triumph before executing a full-length dive across the Hillsborough turf, followed in kind by several team-mates. As a parody of the accusations which had preceded his arrival it was impeccably-judged and executed; but perhaps more memorably it was the celebration that spawned a global movement, sparking a thousand and one imitations as players from professional to playground level scraped their knees in aping the Klinsmann-dive.

It was an aptly dramatic start to the fantasy adventure that was Klinsmann's sojourn in English football. His debut alone had prompted more column inches and media debate than most players do in their entire careers, the game against Sheffield Wednesday, the opening fixture of the 1994 season, unfolding as a madcap barrage of non-stop entertainment, in the finest tradition of Tottenham Hotspur. For a start there was the magnificent but utterly ridiculous teamsheet. Klinsmann made his league debut as one of five out-and-out attackers, alongside Teddy Sheringham, Darren Anderton, Nick Barmby and another new foreign recruit, Ilie Dumitrescu, a star of Romania's successful World Cup campaign that summer; while manager Ossie Ardiles picked only Colin Calderwood to protect an inexperienced back-four, and afforded the midfield no further consideration. One rather suspects that anyone politely clearing their throat in the Tottenham dressing room prior to kick-off, in order to offer a cautionary word about the potential flaws in this formation, would have been promptly marched off the premises and thrown out into the streets of Sheffield, while Ardiles dreamily espoused his romantic notion of the beautiful game, with Klinsmann as flag-bearer.

Pity Trevor Francis, manger of Sheffield Wednesday, whose awe on seeing the Tottenham teamsheet can only be imagined. "It is the most adventurous line-up I have seen in management," was his understated and most probably shell-shocked offering afterwards, a trenchant postscript to one of the most memorable matches in Tottenham's history. The gung-ho Spurs went two goals ahead, were pegged back and entered the final ten minutes with a 3-2 lead, in a breathtaking end-to-end game, before Klinsmann took centre-stage.

While he had seen little of the ball, his tireless performance that day had already done much to win over critics and counter accusations that he might be a work-shy *prima donna*. Ultimately, however, he will be remembered for the headline-grabbing finale he provided. First, displaying the instinctive movement typical of the very finest strikers, he worked himself a yard of space behind opposing centre-back Des Walker, enabling himself to climb and head into the net for a goal on debut – cue *that* celebration. More drama was to follow, however, as Wednesday pulled another goal back, and then moments later a clash of heads with Walker resulted in a bloodied and semi-conscious Klinsmann being stretchered off, to receive eight stitches to a mouth wound. The game finished 4-3 to Tottenham; breathless fans sat back to see what would could possibly come next.

Klinsmann had arrived at White Hart Lane three weeks earlier, on 29 July 1994, in one of the seminal moments in the history of Tottenham Hotspur, and indeed of the English game as a whole. Although the influx of foreigners into England was gathering momentum, this was still an era before the cream of world talent arrived in the country, and before English clubs dominated the latter stages of the Champions League. The most high-profile foreigners establishing themselves in England at the time included such luminaries as Anders Limpar and Stig Inge Bjørnebye. Suffice to say, a signing as audacious as that of Klinsmann was at that point still firmly wedged in the realms of fantasy.

And yet, completely and quite bewilderingly out of the blue, arriving at N17 was this undisputed global superstar, a veteran of Inter Milan and Monaco who had just ended Germany's World Cup campaign with five goals, having won the ultimate prize in football four years earlier. If this CV, amongst the very best on the planet, was unlike that of any player the club had ever seen, the man was just as unique off the pitch. Few footballers of any era have been fluent in four languages, steered clear of agents, championed numerous environmental causes, hitch-hiked across America in their spare-time and selected as their motor of choice a Volkswagen Beetle.

As heads were scratched across the country, the conclusion inevitably drawn in various quarters was that money talked, and the multi-lingual Klinsmann was a fluent conversant. However, it would be misguided to interpret the move to Tottenham as some lucrative pay-day to cushion imminent retirement, for as Klinsmann himself readily pointed out, he would have earned more money remaining in Monaco than moving to North London, while his three years in Italy had already guaranteed him financial security for life. Instead, he had turned down offers from Italy and Spain for the challenge of playing in the Premier League for Tottenham. The lure of life in London, as well as the prospect of performing in front of passionate English crowds each week in stadia full to capacity, were numbered by Klinsmann amongst the primary reasons for his move to Spurs.

Looking back fondly on Klinsmann's career in England, through spectacles with the rosiest tint, it is easy to forget that prior to and even upon his arrival in the country he was massively unpopular. Not only did a fierce footballing enmity exist between England and Germany, the product of the 1966 World Cup final and 1990 semi-final (in which Klinsmann played) as well as more obvious off-pitch reasons, but the striker also arrived in England as famous for what is officially known as 'simulation' as for his goalscoring. It ought to be noted that this reputation had been garnered, at least prior to his arrival in England, not without some justification. To describe as 'theatrical' his arched-back leaps of supposed agony in the previous years of his career would be to understate the case somewhat. As television pundit Ron Atkinson noted during the 1990 World Cup, "Terry Butcher's shaking Jürgen Klinsmann's hand … It's a wonder the German hasn't fallen over."

However, it was indicative of the German's modesty, humility and self-deprecatory charm that vitriolic accusations of gamesmanship were dissipating in the mouths of his detractors even as they took their seats for his first press conference in England. Before the sharpened knives could be thrust at him he opened up by asking the assembled media, with irresistible charm, "Is there a diving school in London?" The on-pitch dive soon followed, and would-be vultures were left wondering exactly what it was that they were meant to be preying upon. From villain to hero in the blink of an eye, Klinsmann displayed his intelligence both in the manner in which he handled the media, and also in the attitude he adopted on the pitch.

If Spurs fans were pinching themselves at Klinsmann's arrival – and they most certainly were – much-maligned chairman Alan Sugar was grinning like a Cheshire cat. Hounded by Spurs fans for the tempestuous manner in which he had severed Terry Venables' ties with the club, the chairman then saw Spurs given a six-point deduction, £1.5 million fine and season-long ban from the FA Cup, for financial irregularities, in the summer of 1994. Rather than walk away, as some had expected he might (and for which few would have blamed him), he instead pulled off the transfer coup of the decade, from aboard his luxury yacht *Louisiana*, in the suitably glamorous surroundings of Monaco.

Every lilywhite remembers where they were when the news broke of Klinsmann's signing, and his arrival instantly transformed the club. Share prices soared, ticket phone-lines were jammed and sales of 'Klinsmann 18' shirts in the club shop could barely match demand. For the time being at least, Spurs had become the most talked about club on the planet.

It was a transfer so sudden and unexpected that it was unknown even to manager Ardiles, until the final stages of negotiation. However, once the t's were crossed and umlauts dotted, the little Argentine was barely able to contain his delight. Ardiles was well aware of the role of exciting big-name signings to capture the imaginations of Tottenham fans. Such transfers were not just part of the club's history, they were – and still are – virtually demanded by fans. Said Ardiles at the time, as quoted in the *Independent*: 'It is a club that needs heroes, people who are a bit different, quality players with that touch of flamboyance.'

He spoke as one who knew better than most. Sixteen summers earlier the foreign superstar completing an extraordinary move to White Hart Lane had been Ardiles himself, arriving, to a reaction of utter incredulity, with compatriot Ricky Villa, the pair having just won the World Cup with Argentina. The similarities were not lost on Steve Perryman, team-mate of Ardiles in 1978 and assistant manager in 1994: "It is similar to 1978 in that the club I had joined … had had some barren years and Ossie and Ricky Villa put the style back into the club."

Klinsmann's new team-mates were as taken aback as the wider public ("It was a total shock," said Darren Anderton), but recall being pleasantly surprised and mightily impressed at how the superstar settled in.

A month after his arrival Teddy Sheringham was quoted in the *Independent* as saying:

'I have been very surprised how well he has fitted in. He's a World Cup winner, he could have come here and said "I'm a big star, England are crap, I'm going to do what I want", but he has become one of the boys and got involved. He is a workmanlike player with some unbelievable qualities.'

Steve Perryman recalls, in Jeremy Novick's *Winning Their Spurs*, 'The smallest of small little warm-up exercises with a ball, he was absolutely 100 per cent, whereas the normal superstar response would have been, "What are we doing this for?"'

Four days after his unforgettable League debut for Spurs at Hillsborough, Klinsmann made his White Hart Lane bow, to the suitably dramatic strains of Wagner's 'Ride of the

Valkyries' over the club Tannoy, in a Wednesday night game against Everton. While the protagonists can be forgiven for not quite matching the goal-count of the previous game, they nevertheless left another indelible imprint in the minds of Spurs supporters. Midway through the first half a loose, rising ball in the Everton penalty area sat up behind Klinsmann, who leapt and twisted in one movement to execute an acrobatic, volleyed scissor-kick, over his shoulder and into the net, sparking frenzied scenes in the Paxton Road crowd and the flashing sign of *'Wunderbar'* on the scoreboard.

It was not merely the goal that broke the deadlock, nor just the goal to mark his home debut. It was the sort of goal that elevates some players amongst their peers, the sort reserved for the greatest players of their era. It illustrated that for all his off-field charm and reputation, and on-field work-rate and positive attitude, Klinsmann's greatest, definitive talent was as a quite brilliant striker.

The quality of the goal, and unleashing of exuberance across White Hart Lane, prompted another celebratory dive – this time entered into by every single team-mate, including goalkeeper Ian Walker, the sight of whom running three-quarters of the length of the pitch was another unforgettable moment in the Klinsmann catalogue. Klinsmann scored again that night – celebrating in more restrained fashion, with handshakes and back-slaps – in a 2-1 Tottenham win. Within the first five days of the campaign the club's six-point pre-season deficit had been wiped out, and a cult hero had well and truly arrived – not just at Spurs, but amongst an awe-struck wider football public in the country.

Having announced his arrival in such style, Klinsmann simply did not let up throughout the course of the season, spectacular strike following spectacular strike in what amounted to a season-long highlights reel. While Spurs supporters idolised him, and fans across the country found themselves won over, the good folk of Sheffield Wednesday were likely to have been distinctly less enamoured of him, for, having scored against their club on the opening day of the season he proved their nemesis once more in December, at White Hart Lane. Chasing down the seeming lost cause of a long-ball, he muscled a defender out of his way, and before Wednesday keeper Kevin Pressman had time to set himself, from just outside the area he slammed a half-volley into the roof of the goal with such power it threatened to tear the net from its moorings. It was a goal that oozed confidence and class, Klinsmann celebrating by spinning off in little circles on his own, seemingly having surpassed even his own high standards.

Another of the striker's finest hours in a Spurs shirt came in a League Cup tie against Watford. Although the game had got off to the worst possible start, when Spurs conceded a goal within 26 seconds, Klinsmann racked up a sublime hat-trick before half-time in yet another absurd goal-fest, which eventually finished 6-3 in Tottenham's favour. As reported by Tim Collings of the *Independent*:

'For the neutrals among the lucky 13,659 this was a feast of flicks and one-touch show-play all inspired by the pace, power and athleticism of Klinsmann who struck three times in the first half … Klinsmann spun away from his marker, David Holdsworth, and then finished with all the elegance of a world-class predator, a flick sending the ball beyond [Watford goalkeeper Perry] Digweed. Dumitrescu kept buzzing, Popescu strolled and prompted, and Klinsmann struck again with a classic far-post header after 34 minutes before completing the beckoning hat-trick with another left-foot shot seconds before the interval.'

Ten days later Spurs notched up a 2-1 victory away to Wimbledon, in the Premier League. Klinsmann did not make the scoresheet on that occasion, but turned in a tireless display, capped by the assist for a late winner from Gica Popescu. The two performances – away to Watford on a chilly Wednesday night, and then away to the top-flight's infamous bully-boys – gave further indications of why he became quite so popular in his short time in N17. Many cynics had predicted that a player of his continental flair and repute would shirk the challenge of such unappealing fixtures; yet whatever the opposition, Klinsmann seemed to display an exemplary attitude. As Teddy Sheringham put it in an interview with *The Times*: 'When he came to England he was a World Cup-winner, but every time he played it was as if he was playing in his first game.'

However, while Klinsmann was proving a wildly popular success, Spurs' fortunes were decidedly less rosy. Following the burst of three victories in their opening four fixtures of the campaign, the club had begun to nose-dive as opponents grew wise to their recklessly offensive approach. The abundance of attacking flair barely masked an at times comically porous defence, and the following five League games included four increasingly heavy defeats. Klinsmann's rich scoring vein continued, but inevitably, time ran out for Ardiles. In November the Argentine was sacked, and former Tottenham striker Gerry Francis brought in to replace him. Initially it appeared that the bedlam of the Ardiles reign had remained, as Francis was christened as manager with a suitably manic 4-3 home defeat to Aston Villa. Spurs had trailed 3-0, before dragging themselves back onto level terms – Klinsmann, inevitably, amongst the scorers – only to concede a late fourth. Thereafter, however, the new managerial philosophy began to take effect, with the following game bringing Tottenham's first clean-sheet of the season as White Hart Lane witnessed that rarest of events, a goalless draw.

Fortunes also began to improve off-the-pitch, as that same month heralded a further feather in the cap of chairman Alan Sugar, with the revocation of the club's six-point deduction, followed two weeks later by the lifting of the FA Cup ban. Having initially been excluded from the competition in which they had such a proud history, the feeling swiftly began to grow, particularly amongst those of a superstitious bent, that Tottenham were now fated to win it. Such a sentiment was hardly dampened by the team's comeback from a two-goal deficit to record a scintillating 6-2 victory over Southampton in the Fifth-Round replay. The 'name on the Cup' mantra was being uttered even more fervently after the next round, a quarter-final victory away to Liverpool which ranks amongst the club's finest performances in its proud Cup history.

Liverpool were one ahead when, on the stroke of half-time, a slick touch from Klinsmann set up Sheringham to score the equaliser. The game appeared destined for a draw until the second minute of injury time at the end of the second-half, when Sheringham returned the compliment to his strike partner, providing the deftest of touches to release Klinsmann into the Liverpool area. Taking one touch to steady himself and draw goalkeeper David James, Klinsmann then finished clinically into the bottom corner. The goalscorer was mobbed by his team-mates; Francis and the coaching staff were besides themselves in the dugout; and the travelling support was in raptures. It was a magnificent team performance in what has gone down as one of the great modern FA Cup ties. Fittingly, at full-time Spurs were paid one of the ultimate compliments in the English game, applauded off the pitch by the home supporters in Anfield's famous Kop, while Klinsmann was almost in tears, celebrating with the Tottenham fans at the Anfield Road end.

The two goals also highlighted the mesmeric quality of the Sheringham-Klinsmann partnership, widely regarded as one of the greatest of the Premiership era. They amassed 52 goals between them in all competitions that season – each typically playing a crucial role in the build-up to the other's goals – but this statistic only tells part of the story, as the pair forged an uncanny understanding. Klinsmann has regularly described Sheringham as the most intelligent strike partner he has had in the game, while Sheringham is similarly fulsome in his praise for the German. As for supporters, they worshipped the pair of them. Where great striking combinations as Greaves and Gilzean, and Crooks and Archibald, had once enthralled Spurs fans and sliced opposition defences to ribbons, Klinsmann and Sheringham followed in 1994/95. To this day it is deeply lamented by Spurs fans that such an outstanding partnership was only to be seen for one season at White Hart Lane.

While momentum built in the FA Cup, Tottenham stuttered a little in the League, winning just two of eight games in the run-up to their FA Cup semi-final in early April. Qualification for Europe via the League had become increasingly unlikely, but Spurs fans seemed to develop an almost religious conviction that they would triumph in the competition from which they had initially been excluded. Perhaps such over-confidence also pervaded the minds of the playing and coaching staff, for the semi-final against Everton was to prove one of the most disappointing of Spurs' season. Under the stewardship of Joe Royle Everton had been nicknamed the 'Dogs of War', and they duly set about snapping and snarling at Spurs, preventing Tottenham from hitting their stride. Spurs conceded before and after half-time, but were thrown a lifeline after 55 minutes when a penalty was awarded. Although Klinsmann kept a cool head to convert, low and to the goalkeeper's right, Tottenham were unable to use this as a springboard, and were ultimately thrashed 4-1. The club's FA Cup adventure was over in hugely anti-climactic fashion, and having adhered to the dramatic script for so much of the season, Klinsmann's adventures at White Hart Lane were beginning to stray down an unforeseen route.

The Cup exit, and consequent end to European qualification ambitions, had lent a worrying degree of credence to rumours that Klinsmann might leave the club at the end of the season, his white-hot form having attracted continental interest, despite the widely held belief that he was contracted for a second year in N17. Gerry Francis moved swiftly to clarify the situation, asserting that he had been told by the player himself that he would remain for a second season, but in hindsight Klinsmann's own assessment of the situation, as quoted in the *Independent*, can be interpreted, to be a little less emphatic: 'I am here with Tottenham and all my concentration is with this club. We must concentrate on winning all our remaining games and make sure we qualify for the Uefa Cup next season'.

Back on the pitch Klinsmann's commitment to the Tottenham cause could not be questioned, and fittingly he was able to add a North London derby goal to his Tottenham scrapbook, his late header earning Spurs a draw at Highbury. By that time, however, late April 1995, Klinsmann had made up his mind, and announced that the game at home to Leeds, on 13 May, was to be his last for Tottenham – he was to move back home to Germany, with Bayern Munich, after just one season in north London.

Naturally, his decision to leave provoked weeping and gnashing of teeth amongst the White Hart Lane faithful, as distraught at news of his departure as they had been exultant at news of his arrival nine months earlier, even if, after weeks of speculation, the announcement had had an air of inevitability about it. Gary Mabbutt, room-mate of Klinsmann at the time, and still a close friend, recalls feeling desperately disappointed at the decision, but making no attempt to dissuade Klinsmann: "I didn't try to talk him out of it. Once Jürgen makes a decision, he's very focused."

However, chairman Alan Sugar, who less than a year earlier had basked in the glory of signing Klinsmann, was markedly less sanguine. Having been convinced that Klinsmann had signed for two years, Sugar was incensed when the German invoked a clause in his contract allowing him to leave after one. Sugar famously reacted in a television interview by hurling Klinsmann's fabled number 18 shirt to the floor and bellowing that he would not wash his car with it. While it was a crushingly disappointing end to his stay, and few fans wanted to see the relationship end with acrimony, many appreciated Sugar's point, for certainly in his early months at the club Klinsmann had given little indication throughout his stay that he had any intention, or contractual ability, to leave after just one season.

Klinsmann captained Spurs in the final game of the 1994/95 season, and although unable to add to his 29-goal tally, was given a sad but hugely appreciative ovation by over 33,000 fans at White Hart Lane that day. Whatever the disappointment at his decision to leave, the fans wished him well for the future, and were left to wonder what might have been. Would he have stayed if Spurs had won the Cup, or finished one place higher in the League – either of which would have ensured European qualification? And just how good a partnership might Klinsmann and Sheringham have become, given another season together?

While missing out on the FA Cup arguably proved the decisive factor in his decision to leave Spurs, Klinsmann did eventually collect some silverware that season – from, of all quarters, the very same English press who had been amongst his fiercest critics when he arrived in England (including *Guardian* columnist Andrew Anthony, who had penned an article facetiously entitled 'Why I Hate Jürgen Klinsmann' shortly before his arrival – later producing a follow-up entitled 'Why I Love Jürgen Klinsmann'!). Klinsmann became only the third foreigner to win the Football Writers' Association Player of the Year Award.

For all the incongruity, and indeed, even despite the most acrimonious and public divorce, Jürgen Klinsmann and Tottenham Hotspur had on many levels been a perfect marriage. Whether by accident or design, neither party could be kept out of the limelight for any length of time. Klinsmann was one of the world's most charismatic and skilful purveyors of his art; while Tottenham Hotspur were wonderful to watch, yet haunted by the constant threat of sudden and cataclysmic implosion. The eyes of the world, it seems, were glued to this pair, for like some high-octane celebrity couple transposed to the realm of football, it was impossible to tear oneself away. A pyrotechnic affair, the Klinsmann-Tottenham dream ticket was over seemingly before it had even begun.

Or so it seemed – for there was to be a stunning epilogue. Over two years later, on 28 December 1997, Jürgen Klinsmann and Alan Sugar sat side by side at a press conference at White Hart Lane, not to wash cars, but to announce that the German striker had re-signed for Spurs, for the essentially nominal fee of £175,00, until the end of the 1997/98 season.

On this occasion however, the circumstances were vastly changed from those heady summer days of 1994. Then a daring and sensational coup, this had to be viewed by all but that most blinkered romantics as a cold and pragmatic – if convenient – short-term fix. Spurs, by this time under the stewardship of the hapless Christian Gross, were flirting perilously with relegation, having become a little too familiar with the environs of the bottom three by the time Klinsmann signed. The German, for his part, while undoubtedly still retaining a fondness for the club, made little secret of the fact that the imminent World Cup, scheduled to begin six months hence, was a major motivating factor in his decision to return to White Hart Lane and its promise of first-team regularity. After the ill-fated whirlwind marriage of 1994, this seemed unashamedly more akin to a pecuniary arrangement for instant gratification. At the time however, the more diplomatic label 'mutually beneficial' was more commonly bandied about.

Klinsmann's Tottenham career had always had a sense of theatre about it, and the gods, it seems, could not resist decreeing that his second coming in lilywhite should be against the old enemy. As Spurs entertained Arsenal at White Hart Lane on 29 December 1997, the desperate throngs of Tottenham supporters were not the only ones praying for a glimpse of the old Klinsmann magic, for the assembled hordes of the media were gathered in similarly eager anticipation, anxious for the perfect headline.

Their wish was granted to an extent, because when Spurs took the lead it was through their blond-haired foreign import – but this was no fairytale return, for the scorer was Danish midfielder Allan Nielsen. The game ended 1-1, and Klinsmann had to wait two further games before returning to goalscoring ways, when he struck the winner against West Ham United.

Few would countenance the suggestion that Klinsmann's second spell was as spectacular or captured the imagination as had his first. The fact that second time around his shirt number bore his age – 33 – gave an obvious indication as to why former glories were not revisited with quite the same élan, while the surroundings had also altered somewhat, not only in personnel, but also in the conspicuous absence of confidence amongst the relegation-strugglers he had joined. Nevertheless, over the remainder of the season Klinsmann duly fulfilled his side of the bargain, and never more so than in the penultimate game of the season when he struck a blistering four-goal salvo in a 6-2 victory away to Wimbledon. Having dragged themselves out of the relegation zone without ever affording fans the luxury of mathematical safety, the team's win that day finally did ensure that a season of shredded nerves and decimated fingernails would at least end in survival. As fan Marlon Green recalls of the occasion: "More than just a game

– it represented our whole season in 90 minutes with victory guaranteeing our Premiership status. Selhurst Park resembled White Hart Lane for the day with three of the four stands filled up with Spurs fans. Klinsmann came alive in the second half, scoring a second-half hat-trick to go with his strike in the first half."

Thus, sighs of relief having been duly exhaled, the final day of the 1997/98 season was a vastly less fraught affair than had been threatened, and was marked by an appropriately memorable parting gift from Klinsmann, a first-time thunderbolt of a volley, struck from outside the 'D' and whistling into the top corner. His ninth goal in 15 games in his second spell, it was a valedictory gift marked with one final, celebratory dive.

No tenable argument could be made to suggest that Jürgen Klinsmann was a Tottenham man through and through, for while he did profess affection for the club and its fans, in deeds as much as words, the manner of his first departure, in 1995, confirmed that number 18 was number 1, while the Tottenham Hotspur was essentially another stop on his European journey. However, for one halcyon season he captured the imagination of Spurs fans like few others have done in the history of the club, arriving from international football aristocracy, and wowing all and sundry, both on and off the pitch. For that, as well as his vital contribution in the latter half of the 1997/98 season, a compelling case can be made for his inclusion on the list of Spurs' Cult Heroes.

DAVID GINOLA

1997-2000

SPURS CAREER

Games	126
Goals	22
Caps	17

MAGIC MOMENT

Scoring against Barnsley after a solo run past four defenders, in the 1998/99 FA Cup

'DAV-EEED'

SPURS fans love to be entertained, they demand it. It is famously written into the club's tradition, Danny Blanchflower's talk of winning in style rather than boring the opposition to death having become an unofficial club motto and prerequisite of generation after generation of players. In the dreary years at the end of the 20th century, as the club purveyed a brand of football that seemed almost deliberately to fly in the face of the Blanchflower mantra, one man proved himself an entertainer *par excellence*, one of those rare footballing beasts who threatened to create something every time he touched the ball, no matter what the situation. When David Ginola received the ball, 30,000-plus would rise from their seats as one, in anticipation of something happening. Rarely was this better exemplified than in his goal in the FA Cup quarter-final replay of 1999, away to Barnsley. Receiving possession at a standstill on the left-hand touchline, some 50 yards from goal, Ginola ignored all options, and began weaving his way forward. Past one challenge after another, gracefully sliding between players left and right like a slalom skier, never losing either his balance or control of the ball, he glided in and out of four players, inviting challenges and easing away from them with shoulder feints and body swerves, before advancing into the area to place the ball impudently into the bottom corner of the net. In the words of Martin Tyler, Sky commentator that night, "He's been moody ... but now he's simply magnificent", while as former team-mate and captain Gary Mabbutt rightly lauded it, "It was almost a replica of Ricky Villa's goal, in the 1981 FA Cup final."

Better goals may be scored – more crucial goals, or those scored against greater opponents – but few will look as aesthetically perfect as Ginola's against Barnsley. There was such a smoothness to his movement that it could have been choreographed – but then few players had quite the same sense of theatre as Ginola. Even the celebration worked perfectly for the cameras, as he found the time to whip off his shirt and run half the length of the pitch on his own, allowing him to milk the applause and bask in the limelight before his team-mates could eventually catch and mob him.

Perhaps most symbolic, and indicative of that particular era in the history of the club, was the fact that such a goal, from start to finish, was all Ginola. No-one provided a through-ball; there was no exchange of passes; he did not rely upon the decoy run of a team-mate. He had collected ball near halfway, alone on the left touch-line, beat half the Barnsley team on his own and then netted decisively. But then during his Tottenham career, from his arrival in 1997 to his departure in 2000, Ginola is often regarded as the only ray of light in an otherwise dull and often painfully underwhelming team, which failed to finish any higher than tenth in the League. Statistics may well show that in terms of, for example, ball retention or pass completion, he was actually less effective than his team-mates. Certainly, no particularly scientific analysis is necessary to conclude that tackling was never his forte. Indeed, Mabbutt's recollection that, "We worked a lot on him getting into defensive positions in training", is as likely to elicit an affectionate smile of ridicule as any commendation.

In the minds of the success-starved Tottenham fans, however, such misdeeds as these were eminently forgivable, for David Ginola was a release from the doldrums, and a reminder of the glorious, entertaining heritage of the club. Ginola seemed to represent the very essence of Tottenham's playing tradition, keeping its head above the waters of tedium and dross which threatened to drown the club. Moreover, as well as a style of play that had the regulars purring with pleasure, Ginola was frequently Tottenham's match-winner – or at least match-saver, for these were desperate times – typically scoring or creating the goals which earned the team its points of a Saturday afternoon. While his tendency to anonymity, or neglect of the less glamorous duties of the English game, ought not to be overlooked, just as often it seemed the decisive moments of a match would emanate from him.

As well as being two-footed, a mesmeric dribbler, an unerringly accurate crosser and capable of spectacular long-range shooting, Ginola also possessed the blistering confidence which allowed him to maximise his ability. Indeed, this rather understates the matter; it is not simply the case that Ginola was comfortable in the limelight, for he positively relished it.

One suspects he was uncomfortable to be out of it, for the long hair and repertoire of party tricks were hardly the traits of one anxious to keep a low profile. He loved the attention, and with his wonderful creative abilities and relish for showmanship he rarely disappointed. In an era in which Spurs had rather alarmingly honed mediocrity into an art-form, fans paid their money specifically to see him, and like some swashbuckling musketeer he duly entertained.

"He was the same off the field as he was on it," recalls Mabbutt. *Quelle surprise*. His performances in interviews virtually mirrored those he gave on the wing, as he offered an unpredictability that made him an infinitely more entertaining interviewee than many of his monosyllabic, cliché-happy peers. While his accent was unmistakeably French, his command of English was excellent; yet it is safe to assume that he was not familiar with such a phrase as 'shrinking violet'. And yet the man was anything but overbearing, the easy charm he presented to interviewers replicated amongst supporters. It is pleasing to note that, while appearing very much the *prima donna*, he cultivated a reputation for conducting himself impeccably amongst fans, tales abounding of him making time for requests and autographs. The public adored David Ginola, and the feeling appeared quite genuinely mutual.

Personable though he may be, his extra-curricular activities have always seemed closer to the realm of Hollywood than the Premiership. Player endorsements of products are nothing new – indeed, Danny Blanchflower himself was one of the pioneers in this arena, in the '50s and '60s – but only a handful of footballers would have had that confidence bordering on arrogance displayed by Ginola in becoming the face of shampoo manufacturer *L'Oréal*, shamelessly declaring himself, "Worth it" with a flick of his hair that was nigh on impossible to take seriously. While opposition fans and players, as well as pundits, hardly needed any further invitation to shower abuse upon him, to this day it remains something of which he claims to have no regrets, recalling in an interview with *Metro* newspaper:

'Oh my God, not at all. Every man washes their hair with shampoo, so why not use a footballer? A lot of fans took the mickey but the players didn't say a word as they'd never had so many bottles of shampoo in the shower room.'

Similarly, few other footballers would have been considered to follow in the footsteps of Princess Diana, yet Ginola was identified as a personality of comparable glamour and international repute, as he replaced the late royal as the face of the Red Cross anti-landmine campaign. Few will be surprised to know that he also has thespian leanings, having taken acting lessons at the Royal Academy of Dramatic Art and starred in the film *The Last Drop*.

For Ginola, it seemed that a job was not worth doing unless it could be done in style. Just as it is hard to imagine him ever rolling up his sleeves and sprinting back into defence to fly into a thunderous tackle, so there is an incongruity in the notion of him going down the road well-trod by many an honest British ex-pro, and buying a pub. Instead, on his retirement he grew his own wines – award-winning rosés which he described, inevitably, as "Sexy and tasteful to drink".

While such a lifestyle perfectly complemented his role as on-pitch entertainer, it would have counted for little – and indeed would have counted against him – had he not had the footballing talent to win over the fans. Fortunately, however, that talent was his trademark, and he effortlessly assumed his place on the pedestal of greats who have found Spurs the perfect club in which they can showcase their talents, its followers fully appreciative of the skills paraded.

Ginola was signed for Tottenham by Gerry Francis in the summer of 1997. Typically, modesty was conspicuous by its absence when he was unveiled to the press for his photoshoot. Not for him a staid pose holding aloft a Tottenham scarf. Instead, after donning his Tottenham shirt for the first time he whipped it off, and posed, bare-chested, holding alongside him the shirt bearing his name. It was a moment that was to illustrate another feature of the man, for he was to become one of the few footballers who transcended the sport, and achieved popularity on a completely different plane. While fully grown men openly proclaimed their adoration for him, in the manner peculiar to a football fan, Ginola attracted those women to whom sport was completely anathema. The ladies swooned over Dav-*eeed*, whether or not they were fans of Spurs, or even football, and that first photoshoot for Tottenham went some way to explaining why, as he happily paraded his movie-star looks. Carly Madden, a lifelong supporter of Arsenal rather than Tottenham, unhesitatingly crosses the North London divide when the subject turns to Ginola, seemingly speaking for legions of female fans when she says, "His sexy French accent, so very handsome … he always seems more sophisticated than the average footballer."

In inimitable style, tribute was duly paid to his popularity with the ladies by those in the White Hart Lane stands, with one terrace chant in particular speculating that in her more intimate marital moments Mrs Victoria Beckham would picture the face of the Tottenham number 14.

Ginola had arrived at Spurs with England striker Les Ferdinand, and at the time it was the signing of the latter – for a then club record £6 million – that attracted more headlines. Ferdinand's arrival was warmly welcomed, for he was widely acknowledged as one of the most complete English forwards of his time, and may well have become an England regular had he not been a contemporary of one Alan Shearer Esquire. Ginola's simultaneous arrival, for around £2 million, was greeted with nods of approval, but Ferdinand's with greater enthusiasm. Ultimately, Ferdinand was a success at Spurs, but although popular and boasting a healthy goalscoring record, his time at Tottenham was largely blighted by injuries.

Ginola himself made an unspectacular start to his White Hart Lane career, mirroring the fortunes of the club, which dismissed Gerry Francis within three months of the start of the season. Christian Gross was the new man at the helm as the principal excitement provided by the team was the unwelcome drama of a relegation battle. Spurs eventually finished just four points above the drop zone, in fourteenth. By that stage, however, salvation was beginning to emerge in long-haired Gallic form. Flamboyant and charismatic, Ginola regularly treated the Tottenham faithful to that attacking brio for which they had long yearned. Praise was duly lavished upon him, and such wild professions of adoration as that from fan David Durbridge were not entirely unusual: "I've always said I'd allow my wife to sleep with two other men, Gary Lineker and David Ginola. In David's case I'd thank him afterwards!"

Amongst his finest displays that season was the 3-3 draw at home to Liverpool in March, when he created two goals and himself scored spectacularly (not that he ever seemed to score any other type of goal) from 25 yards. As Norman Miller wrote in the *Independent* of his performance, 'Such moments of magic can be priceless.' When substituted in that game, he departed to a hero's ovation from the paying punters. However, it was noticeable that he received little more than a furrowed brow from his manager, for as Gary Mabbutt so diplomatically puts it, "David was not a natural defender".

The contrast between fans and manager in reaction to Ginola's contribution was to be repeated many a time and oft at White Hart Lane. As with a number of other geniuses who had pulled on the lilywhite shirt before him, managers saw in Ginola a liability, a man whose concessions of possession, eye for glory and disregard for the defensive side of the game failed to offset the creativity and flair he brought to the team. Glenn Hoddle, a man not wholly unfamiliar with such treatment, albeit more particularly at national level, has complained that since the work-horses in a team were not chastised for their failure to beat players and score goals, it was therefore unfair that he should be criticised for his low work-rate. A trenchant point perhaps, and one with which Ginola himself may well have concurred. Nevertheless, even though fans left the stadium each week agreeing that the only contribution of value had come from Ginola, it seemed that the frustration of the manager with his broader contribution to the team effort would be just as pronounced.

This situation was at its most critical when George Graham took over from Christian Gross as manager, early in the 1998/99 season. The debate about how – or indeed whether at all – flair players, with little regard for defensive responsibilities, could be accommodated within a team has rarely raged stronger than when Ginola wove his magic under the austere glare of Graham.

A fitting pantomime villain in the David Ginola Show, Graham had forged his reputation at Arsenal of all places, where his sides fostered the effective but unglamorous reputation of grinding out narrow wins upon the foundation of a water-tight defence. "One-nil to the

Arsenal" was a refrain sung with relish at Highbury, not only to the annoyance of Spurs fans, who throughout the decade (and beyond) had lived in the shadow of their North London rivals, but also to their utter bemusement. Anyone brought up in the stylish tradition of free-flowing, attacking football espoused at White Hart Lane will scratch their head in bewilderment as to how fans can celebrate and revel in the fact that their team specialises in one-nil wins. For one-nil will never be enough for Spurs fans – and this need not only to win, but to win in style, is what has made the Spurs job such a poisoned chalice for one manager after another.

A solid back four playing the offside trap to perfection hardly oozed the style that Spurs fans craved, but that was the promise brought by Graham, who saw a stable defensive basis as paramount in reviving the club's fortunes. A manager who would settle for one-nil if his life depended on two, Graham was determined to bring to an ailing, underachieving Tottenham an environment of consistency, discipline, organisation and effectiveness. Oh how Monsieur Ginola's heart must have leapt for joy when Graham's appointment was announced. Undeterred, Spurs fans adamantly demanded that such virtues were not to be introduced at the expense of entertainment, and that Ginola should retain a starring role. Combining flair with consistent results has been the bane of several Tottenham managers, who have either seen the team free-fall in entertaining fashion (à la Ossie Ardiles), or attempt to grind out results the ugly way, to the chagrin of the masses. To claim that Graham fell into the latter camp would be one of the less controversial assertions in the club's colourful history.

Unsurprisingly, it was to prove an uneasy marriage. Despite the sparkling array of attacking options he brought to the team, Ginola always faced an uphill battle winning round Graham. Ironically enough, Graham had himself had a reputation as a showman while a player, nicknamed 'Stroller' for his lackadaisical attitude to teamwork and general graft. While this may be greeted with downright incredulity by football supporters of a certain vintage, who have known him only as a dour manager managing dour teams, it did little to help Ginola's cause, and the feeling pervaded throughout Graham's tenure that Ginola constantly had to prove himself to his boss, who himself was just itching for an excuse to jettison the Frenchman.

However, whatever the nature of the stormy relationship between player and manager, the early signs were that the ambitions of both could be accommodated at White Hart Lane. Such was the Frenchman's level of performance that at the end of the season 1998/99 season, Graham's first in charge, at the age of 32 he achieved the astonishing feat of collecting both the Professional Footballers' Association (PFA) Player of the Year and Football Writers' Association (FWA) Footballer of the Year awards, despite the club finishing an unspectacular 11th in the League. To date he is the only player since the inception of the Premiership, in 1992, to have won both awards whilst playing for a club outside the top four. While this also serves as an indictment of the lack of competition within the division, it is nevertheless a testament to the man's panache and consistently high level of performance, particularly in a season in which the star-laden Manchester United team won the League, FA Cup and Champions League Treble. Meanwhile George Graham was able to offer a riposte to his critics, when his first season in charge ended in triumph at Wembley in the Worthington (League) Cup, the club's first silverware in almost a decade. In addition, Spurs had mounted a strong but ultimately unsuccessful FA Cup run, to the semi-final stage. Whatever their differences it appeared that Ginola and Graham may after all be able to help each other flourish at the Lane.

En route to the FA Cup semi-final was a Fifth Round replay at home to an impressive young Leeds team which had acquitted itself well in the Champions League. It proved a match of such rip-roaring entertainment that even such an arch-pragmatist as Graham was moved to describe it as, "a wonderful game, great entertainment". Indeed, at one point the manager found himself instinctively leaping to his feet and punching the air in reaction to more Ginola magic – a feat which some would suggest ranks just as highly as the Frenchman's Player of the Year awards.

Ironically, Graham's celebrations were, on that occasion, actually misguided – it transpired that the ex-Arsenal man was cheering a near-miss for Spurs. With the game goalless early in the second half, Ginola received possession on the right-hand touchline, some 35 yards from goal, and began cutting infield. Leeds defenders piled in and snapped away, but Ginola showed strength and control, to shrug off one challenge after another, retaining his balance and continuing to weave infield. By the time he was confronting his fifth opponent he had wandered all the way in from the right touchline to the left-hand corner of the area, where he let fly with his left foot. Goalkeeper Nigel Martyn got his fingertips to the ball at full stretch, deflecting it onto the inside of the post, the rebound agonisingly flying back across the goal-line and to safety.

It was inches away from being goal of the season, drawing comparisons to a similar solo effort from George Best against Sheffield United in 1971, a strike which flew in off the post and is commonly ranked as one of the greatest of all time. Instead, Ginola's shot left everybody in White Hart Lane holding their heads in agony – everybody, that is, apart from Graham. Television replays later showed the manager growing increasingly excitable and his eyes widening as Ginola's dribble unfolded, before he finally leapt to celebrate and punch the air in delight, thinking that the shot had gone in off the post, rather than out. It was left to a suitably embarrassed assistant, Chris Hughton, to extricate himself from the celebratory hug, and break the bad news.

Ginola's miss rather overshadowed the fine goal he did later score that night, a 25-yard first-time volley into the bottom corner. It followed a similarly astonishing long-distance effort from Darren Anderton, giving Spurs a 2-0 win and suggesting to fans that the years in the wilderness were drawing to an end. Nevertheless, these supporters still refused to sing the name of their ex-Arsenal manager, instead adopting the refrain: "Man in the raincoat's blue and white army".

The victory over Leeds granted Spurs safe passage into the quarter-final and that memorable night against Barnsley, when Ginola provided his personal, real-time demonstration of the phrase 'poetry in motion'. The FA Cup campaign would falter at the semi-final stage, but later that season Ginola was finally able to grace the hallowed turf of Wembley, as Spurs marched on to the League Cup final, their first major final since 1991. The road to Wembley had included a quarter-final victory against eventual Treble-winners

Manchester United, in which game Ginola had produced a goal from nothing – in possession, at a standstill, 25 yards from goal and offering no obvious threat, then suddenly accelerating several paces to the left and powerfully curling a sumptuous effort into the top corner. In conjuring something from nothing, and demonstrating the unique ability to execute such skills to perfection, it had provided yet another from the long list of examples of why Ginola was so adored at the Lane. While his inconsistency, and particularly his avoidance of defensive duties where possible, could lead managers to question his value in the team over the course of the season, his capacity for flashes of genius were proving particularly valuable in Cup competitions, where a single moment of magic could change a game and ensure progress in the competition. His contributions against Leeds and Barnsley were not swallowed up within the nine-month slog of a League campaign; they proved the decisive moments in one-off knock-out matches, moments from which the opponents were left too dazed to recover.

The stage was set for Ginola to deliver a typically virtuoso performance in the League Cup final at Wembley, but, to the credit of opponents Leicester City and their manager Martin O' Neill, the Frenchman's threat was largely nullified, as he was marked out of the game by Robert Ullathorne. With its star attraction given little opportunity to shine, the game as a spectacle was wanting. A goalless, and largely chanceless affair was rather turned on its head by the 63rd minute red card shown to Spurs defender Justin Edinburgh, for a flick at Robbie Savage, a man whose popularity (or lack thereof) at White Hart Lane rivalled that of George Graham. However, Leicester were unable to capitalise upon their numerical advantage, and in the dying seconds, a burst down the right by Spurs' Norwegian striker Steffen Iversen resulted in a cross-shot which Leicester goalkeeper Kasey Keller could only parry. Onrushing midfielder Allan Nielsen promptly wrote himself into Tottenham folklore, with a diving header to win the game. The final whistle signalled a trophy for Spurs at long last, and that summer, with his two personal accolades added to his winners' medal, Ginola signed a new, three-year contract with the club, which was to have kept him there until he was 35.

The League Cup triumph gave Spurs a European berth for the first time in eight years. It was hoped that the slower continental style of play would suit the club, and particularly Ginola, but rather than providing a platform for the revisiting of former European glories at White Hart Lane, the UEFA Cup journey was short-lived, and ultimately proved the beginning of the end of Ginola's Tottenham career. Following a comfortable 3-0 aggregate victory in the Qualifying Round, Spurs were knocked out in rather cruel fashion by Kaiserslautern, an occasion which proved particularly critical to the strained relationship between Ginola and his manager. Spurs had won the First Leg of the tie 1-0, at White Hart Lane, with Ginola featuring prominently, but the Frenchman was then controversially relegated to the substitutes' bench for the Second Leg. The move backfired, as in the final minute of the game Spurs conceded an own-goal and a penalty, resulting in a 2-1 aggregate defeat. Defeated and deflated, Tottenham's European campaign was over barely after it had begun. Graham's gamble had not only failed on the night, but had also given the clearest indication yet that as long as he was in charge, Ginola's days at the Lane were numbered.

After the success of the previous campaign, Spurs fared less well in the 1999/2000 season, and the relationship between Ginola and Graham became ever more fractious. The player was repeatedly substituted, to his often ill-disguised disgust, and was eventually told that he was no longer guaranteed a place in the starting line-up. In July 2000 the club agreed to sell him to Aston Villa, for a fee eventually settled at £3 million. The man himself endeared himself to Tottenham folk one final time with his valedictory comments on his website:

'It totally ruined my summer. I never asked to leave, I was happy at White Hart Lane and my family were settled in North London. But it was quite clear that Spurs – and I am not quite clear whether Alan Sugar or George Graham – didn't want me around any more and so were prepared to let me leave. Once I got over the shock I was very disappointed to learn that the club had put a £3m price-tag on my head. I am 33 and, although I feel I have still got at least two years left in me, playing at the highest level, I felt I should have been rewarded for my time at Spurs with a free transfer. That would have given me far more freedom in choosing which club to join.'

Whether Villa fans were quite as enamoured of such quotes is debatable, but this last pledge of loyalty was warmly-received – even if, in truth, many fans considered the sum good business for a player well into his 30s, and with his best days behind him.

It was perhaps to Ginola's credit that he remained in Graham's favour for as long as he did – for the Scot's managerial reputation and history militated firmly against such flair from the moment of his arrival. However, while Ginola's popularity in the eyes of the manager plummeted, it remained at astronomical levels amongst supporters, even beyond his departure. The feeling it seemed was mutual – witness the opening line in his autobiography, the typically modestly entitled, *Le Magnifique*: 'I never wanted to leave Tottenham'. Having been a figurehead for the club's fine tradition during a period of underachievement, Ginola's popularity at Spurs was recognised when he was inducted into the Tottenham Hotspur Hall of Fame in December 2008, and to this day he remains one of the club's most popular players of the modern era.

Bibliography

Newspapers:
The Times
Sunday Times
Independent
Guardian
Observer
Daily Mail
Daily Express
Tottenham and Edmonton Weekly Herald
New Statesman

Websites:
Allactionnoplot.com
Channelbee.com
Statto.com
Topspurs.com
Tottenhamhotspur.com
Fourfourtwo.com
Nationalfootballmuseum.com
Spurshistory.com
Sportsillustrated.cnn.com

Videos/DVDs/Television Production
Nice One Cyril
The Greatest Ever Spurs Team
Tottenham Hotspur 101 Great Goals
Big Pat (BBC)

Books
'Chris Waddle: The Authorised Biography' by Mel Stein (Pocket Books, 1998)
'Venables: The Autobiography' by Terry Venables and Neil Hanson (Penguin, 1995)
'Match of my Life' by Matt Allen and Louis Massarella (Know The Score, 2007)
'Tottenham Hotspur: The Official Illustrated History 1882 – 1997' by Phil Soar (Hamlyn, 1997)
T'ottenham Hotspur: Player By Player' by Ivan Ponting (Know The Score Books, 2008)
'David Ginola: Le Magnifique' by David Ginola with Neil Silver (HarperCollins, 2000)
'Fever Pitch' by Nick Hornby (Penguin, 1992)
'The Boys From White Hart Lane' by Martin Cloake and Adam Powley (Vision Sports Publishing, 2008)
'Ossie's Dream' by Ossie Ardiles with Marcela Mora y Araujo (Bantam Press, 2009)

'Hard as Nails: The Graham Roberts Story' by Graham Roberts with Colin Duncan (Black & White Publishing, 2008)

'The Spurs Miscellany' by Adam Powley and Martin Cloake (Vision Sports Publishing, 2008)

'The White Hart Lane Encyclopaedia' by Dean Hayes (Mainstream Publishing, 1996)

'Winning Their Spurs' by Jeremy Novick (Mainstream Publishing, 1996)

'The Lane of Dreams' by Norman Giller (NMG Enterprises, 2009)

T'he Glory Game' by Hunter Davies (Mainstream Publishing, 2007)

'The Double' by Ken Ferris (Mainstream Publishing, 1999)

'Big Chiv' by Martin Chivers and Paolo Hewitt (Vision Sports Publishing, 2009)

'Down Memory Lane' by Harry Harris (Green Umbrella Publishing, 2009)

'Spurred to Success' by Glenn Hoddle (Queen Anne Press, 1987)

'Greavsie' by Jimmy Greaves (Time Warner Books, 2003)

'Gazza: My Story' by Paul Gascoigne with Hunter Davies (Headline Book Publishing, 2004)

'Against All Odds' by Gary Mabbutt with Harry Harris (Cockerel Books, 1989)

'Danny Blanchflower: A Biography Of A Visionary' by (Dave Bowler, Vista, 1997)

'Newcastle's Cult Heroes' by Dylan Younger (Know The Score Books, 2006)

'West Brom's Cult Heroes' by Simon Wright (Know The Score Books, 2006)

'Spurs: Day To Day Life At White Hart Lane' by Graham Betts (Mainstream, 1998)

'The Little Book of Spurs' by Edited by Louis Massarella (Carlton, 2006)